YOUR
CAT

YOUR CAT

Simple New Secrets
to a Longer, Stronger Life

ELIZABETH M. HODGKINS, D.V.M., Esq.

THOMAS DUNNE BOOKS
St. Martin's Press
New York

Remember, never start or continue any veterinary medical treatment program for your pet without the supervision of your pet's veterinarian. Information available in this book is for general information purposes only and is intended to supplement, but not replace the advice of your pet's health care provider.

THOMAS DUNNE BOOKS.
An imprint of St. Martin's Press.

www.thomasdunnebooks.com
www.stmartins.com

Design by Kathryn Parise
Illustrations by Nicole Brune

ISBN-13: 978-0-312-35801-3
ISBN-10: 0-312-35801-6

No two medical conditions are the same. Moreover, we cannot be responsible for unsupervised treatments administered at home. Therefore, we urge you to seek out the best medical resources available to help you make informed decisions on pet care. Mention of specific companies, organizations, or authorities in this book does not imply endorsement by the publisher, nor does mention of specific companies, organizations, or authorities imply that they endorse this book. Internet addresses and telephone numbers given in this book were accurate at the time it went to press.

First Edition: June 2007

10 9 8 7 6 5 4 3 2 1

This book is dedicated to Punkin, my much loved diabetic kitty whose suffering and recovery started this book over a decade ago. Without this wonderful cat in my life, I might never have begun to ask the questions that finally revealed the important truths I now hold. It is also dedicated to my wonderful son Matt who insisted we adopt Punkin from his hopeless, homeless life at a campground in Kansas. Matt's act of compassion for a defenseless kitten made all the difference.

CONTENTS

PART 3

The Glorious Years of Young Adulthood

PART 4

The Truly Golden Senior Years

PART 5
Ten Myths of Cat Care

FOREWORD

Today, cats outnumber dogs as the most popular pet in our modern society. At the same time, Americans will spend 62 percent more time on the planet, due to increases in life expectancy compared to earlier times. City dwellers and aging baby boomers, growing families, and those who live alone can all have the joys and companionship of cats because they are quiet, easy to care for, and adapt to virtually all types of living quarters. Cats are now often accepted even in senior citizen accommodations.

In the recent past, society has discovered, documented, and increasingly recognized the human-animal bond as a necessary part of healthy human interactions. This unique bond has healing powers and health benefits directly related to the companionship, pleasure, sport, recreation, and service provided to humankind by companion animals. Pets provide people in diverse life situations with opportunities for nurturing and feeling connected and loved.

While the attachment between women and felines is well known, the man-cat bond is also out in the open now. Men of all ages have always loved their cats, but in the past, this particular relationship was overshadowed by the relationships men seemed to share with dogs. In today's society, men can openly profess without embarrassment their interest and love for cats. In fact, in my work to advance the human-animal bond, I've coined this particularly deep relationship the "CAT-MAN-DO" bond.

Philosophically, we owe our feline friends and ourselves the favor of reading this book from cover to cover. Within its pages, Dr. Elizabeth Hodgkins opens up her treasure chest of firsthand and scientific knowledge as a veterinarian, cat breeder, nutritionist, immunologist, and internist giving many precious pearls of wisdom to cat lovers. As head of legal and claims division in the pet health insurance industry for a part of her professional career, Dr. Hodgkins was privy to the actuarial data of illness and death in the nation's private pet population. She saw the disease trends that twenty years of modern data collection accumulated.

With the clarity and the skill of an excellent courtroom attorney, Dr. Hodgkins provides the scientific rationale for her viewpoints on feline health, nutrition, behavior, vaccines, illness, and longevity. Her illuminations make sense and shed light in the gray zone of established habits and accepted tradition which all of us have accepted as "the way" for the past twenty to forty years. Dr. Hodgkins's discussions are provocative and disturbing, and the problems they identify will not be easy to rectify quickly. Nonetheless, they are long overdue.

Dr. Hodgkins's understandable book is intended to educate caregivers and spare pet felines from preventable illness. If cat lovers become informed and follow Dr. Hodgkins's proposed feeding and management guidelines, they will bypass the heartbreak and expense of many common illnesses, including cancer, seen in today's typical household cats. Caregivers may also enjoy extra years of companionship with their feline friends as they attain a longer life span.

Dr. Hodgkins writes on behalf of cats on a global basis. In her exclusively feline practice, she has observed, diagnosed, and treated a set of basic feline diseases (inflammatory bowel disease, skin disease, diabetes, hyperthyroidism, feline triad disease, fatty liver, cancer). These feline diseases routinely fester in the backdrop of chronic illness related to obesity, malnutrition, and management issues. She truly hopes that feline fanciers everywhere will be motivated to change what is accepted as the status quo of convenience feeding with dry food and over vaccination. Anyone who loves cats will want to improve the management and feeding of their feline best friends along the parameters of Dr. Hodgkins's insightful, scholarly, and practical suggestions. What better time than now for all mankind to refresh and recommit to its stewardship role for all the animals in the environment. As ethical animal caretakers, we must strive to do what is best, and correct what is not best.

Today, my husband and I live with two beautiful Ocicats reared by Dr. Hodgkins. They enrich our lives every day with their beauty, intelligence, and willingness to forgive our human failings. Following the advice in this book, we know we will continue to enjoy them to the fullest for decades to come.

—ALICE VILLALOBOS, D.V.M.
American Association of Human-Animal Bond
Veterinarians President, 2005–2006;
Animal Oncology Consultation Service,
Woodland Hills, Torrance, California, and
Pawspice Care Clinic, Norwalk, California

ACKNOWLEDGMENTS

In any project as ambitious as a book, there are always many individuals whose contributions have been as invaluable as the author's to the success of the effort. This book is no different. I must first thank my husband, Richard, who was the first to suggest that I stop muttering under my breath and put my experiences down on paper. His support and encouragement made completion of this "labor of love" possible. I must also acknowledge all of the many others, such as Dr. Lisa Pierson, Lynette Ackman, Anne Jablonski, Shelby Gomas, Doug Cohn, Kristi Martin, and the many other knowledgeable individuals who have assisted and encouraged me. They are as commited as I to making life better for cats everywhere by raising the awareness of pet owners about the mistakes we are making in caring for our beloved felines. Their collaboration and support was indispensable. My deep gratitude goes to Punkin, my first diabetic cat, who gave me the opportunity to learn so many important things about the harm we have done to our cats over the past several decades. Finally, a very sincere thank you to Marcia Markland, Diana Szu, and everyone at Thomas Dunne Books and St. Martin's Press who believed in this project and helped to make it happen.

PREFACE

As anyone who has ever been around a cat for any length of
time well knows, cats have enormous patience with the limitations of the human mind.

—CLEVELAND AMORY

Today, the cat is *the* favorite house pet in the United States, outnumbering the
dog, the previous favorite, for a decade or more. Sources estimate there are between 60 and 70 million "kept" cats living in about 35 million homes in this country at
the present time, and this growth trend shows absolutely no signs of slowing or reversing itself anytime soon. Veterinarians are seeing unprecedented numbers of well-cared-
for felines, belonging to individuals and families that are intensely attached to their kitty
family members. Men as well as women, in all walks of life, are bonded with their pet
cats in a way that I could never have anticipated in 1977 when I graduated from veterinary school. In short, the cat has become not only legitimate as a pet underfoot in our
home, but also as a focus of attachment and affection for humans who are often willing
to do anything and everything necessary to provide their felines with long, healthy, and
happy lives.

This desire to care for a pet cat's every need has resulted in some significant im-
provements in health and longevity for today's felines. For example, the increasingly
common indoor existence cats enjoy has reduced the incidence of most infectious dis-

eases within cat populations, and has curtailed death and injury to cats from automobile accidents, attacks from dogs or wildlife, or other sources of trauma. More routine spaying and neutering of household pet cats has positively affected the number of abandoned and neglected cats put to sleep in shelters.

Unfortunately, while so much is better for cats today, they have paid a high price for the heightened level of care they receive from the millions of devoted cat owners in this country. That price is loss of health associated with such harmful influences as poor nutrition in the form of commercial dry cat food diets, potentially excessive vaccination practices, and a general failure to understand the cat's unique needs and behavior as distinctive from those of any other pet species.

Virtually all of the major lethal diseases of cats—obesity, diabetes, bladder problems including inflammatory cystitis, kidney failure, hyperthyroidism, inflammatory bowel disease, and even some forms of cancer—are directly related to mistakes loving humans make in caring for their felines. Decades ago, cats were not pets; they were workers around the property, in charge of controlling the vermin population in a ranch, farm, or neighborhood setting. We humans provided certain protection to the local cats, in exchange for the service of ridding our homes and towns of disease-carrying and grain-consuming rodents. In this particular symbiotic relationship, it was not necessary, and not even particularly desirable, that the cat become a true pet. Because its work required that it retain all of its keen, wild hunting instincts and hunger, the cat was left outdoors, seldom fed from the family's table, and generally encouraged to remain feral in all aspects. To be of service to humans, it was necessary that the cat remain just as it had been before its relationship with humankind began.

Contrast this with the domestication of the dog by humans in earliest times. In that relationship, the services the family dog provided included safeguarding the family and home, herding livestock under direction of the master, and assisting humans in the hunt for game that would be food for the householder and other members of the community. These kinds of services required a very close working relationship between man and dog, with a substantial alteration of the dog's temperament, anatomy, and even dietary needs. To work together constructively with humans, the wild, primitive dog needed to change to match its master's household environment. Thus, differences in dogs and cats that already existed when both species were essentially undomesticated became even more pronounced once the process of integrating these animals into human civilization was underway.

Because it ate from the master's table, the dog became an increasingly successful omnivore, like its master. This adaptation was accelerated by selective breeding practices. Thriving on a wide variety of animal and vegetable source dietary substances, the dog retained and expanded its nutritional flexibility. The cat living with humans was not influenced in this way. A true carnivore from the outset, it did not experience any evolutionary pressures, or breeding selection, from humans or its environment to become more omnivorous. Indeed, had the cat acquired a taste for grain or other vegetable crops as the dog began to do, the species might well have been driven from the presence of humans altogether. The cat's sole value in its relationship with people was to eliminate the creatures that robbed the community of its harvest and, in the process, assist in the management of vermin-facilitated disease, such as the black plague.

It is true that in a few ancient societies, the cat was revered, even deified, as in the Egypt of approximately 2000 BC. Some historians even suggest that the cat was domesticated at this time, but it is entirely unclear how far this process of integration of cats into human life actually progressed and whether there would have been any useful reason to try to modify the felines' natural behaviors or nutritional predilections. There certainly is no historical evidence that deification altered in any way the cat's basic nature and metabolism during this period.

Some evidence from the ancient Middle East shows cats seeming to live in the homes of the Egyptians and even to assist in the hunting and killing of small game and fish. Tombs of cats from the Egypt of four thousand years ago, however, show such funerary offerings as milk, dead rodents, and other animal-source nutrition were provided to accompany the mummified felines into the afterlife. Those entombments lacked the much wider assortment of food types provided to mummified humans, suggesting that the Egyptians understood the natural inclinations of the cat.

Cats kept by the Egyptians, like the house cats of today, probably had relatively docile temperaments compared with those of feral cats of the past or present time. This shift in personality was, and still is, largely a matter of socialization (taming via deliberate training), or a natural selection process called neotenization, rather than true domestication as occurred with dogs, cattle, and the like. A socialized house cat that is released outside the home to shift for itself will revert to a genuinely wild, self-sufficient set of behaviors in a short period of time. Conversely, kittens from feral colonies, and even some adult ferals, adapt very well to life in close contact with humans, with adequate careful socializing.

The cat's unique, primitive metabolic and nutritional needs have not been changed through this simple process of socialization. The workings of the cat's mind and body remain intensely prehistoric, molded through thousands of years of selective environmental pressures into the perfect carnivore, the top predator of its environment. Nothing that humankind has done to harness the useful qualities of this predatory mammal has changed that in any way.

It is these special and ancient characteristics that distinguish the cat, past and present, from all other animals in our lives. In our failure to understand these characteristics as we bring the cat into our homes and hearts, however, we have begun a process of un-witting harm. Today, we rush to live our lives at breakneck speed, placing trust in the tidal wave of consumer advertising that inundates us hourly from all corners. This mis-placed trust has led us to inflict a poisonous lifestyle upon our felines, even as we be-lieve that we are doing everything possible to keep them healthy and happy.

This book will change that. In the following pages, we will explore all of the major health problems of today's pet cat and come to understand how we humans are causing some of these problems; and how we, and only we, can make things right again.

PART

 # 1

A Twenty-first-Century
View of the Cat

1

The Predator Among Us

Most pet lovers are familiar with the idea that dogs and cats are carnivores. That is, both animals can and do derive valuable nutrition from the voluntary consumption of meat. In this regard, many mammals, including people, pigs, bears, raccoons, and myriad others have seemingly similar carnivorous tendencies. When meat is available, such animals will take advantage of the situation and eat it. There is a significant difference between cats and all of these other mammals, however. Dogs, people, pigs, bears, and raccoons, etc., are all omnivores that eat meat when it is available. Cats, big and small, are *obligatory* carnivores. The omnivore does not eat meat as a mandatory requirement for life; vegetable food sources can make up a very large part of their diet, and may even be properly balanced to provide all needed nutrients for health. For the cat, however, meat, and the nutrients found only in meat, are essential for survival.

The Cat Is Not a Small Dog

Critical differences between dogs and cats, the most popular of all household pet animals, are clearly illustrated in the genetic, anatomic, and metabolic differences between the two. Scientists who have studied the dietary habits of carnivores, omnivores, and herbivores tell us that these "rungs" on the food-chain were established and reinforced during the evolutionary histories of each type of animal (see www.catinfo.org/zorans_article.pdf). The work of these experts suggests that the members of the superfamily *Feloidea*, including today's cat, evolved rapidly in distant prehistoric times, but then stopped abruptly in that progression. Carnivorous animals belonging to other families of animals, including the *Canoidea*, to which the dog belongs, seem to have progressed beyond this point to meet changing evolutionary needs.

Good evidence for the cat's relatively ancient nature can be found in the lower number of chromosomes in its genetic makeup, compared with a much larger number for the group that includes modern dogs. The cat's cells carry thirty-eight chromosomes, while the dog's cells carry seventy-eight. This does not mean that the cat lacks physical and genetic sophistication equal to the dog. It means that it made a perfect and permanent fit within its spot in the environment early on and experienced little additional pressure to change its genes.

Dogs and cats also have remarkably different, but highly specialized, anatomy. Dogs have forty-two permanent teeth, whereas cats have only thirty. Dogs have more molars than do cats, with a specialized shape for crushing, associated with their intake of plant material. In contrast, the shape of feline teeth is specialized for grasping and tearing flesh. By its structure, the cat's jaw has far more restricted side-to-side and front-to-back mobility than does the dog's, limiting its ability to grind a varied vegetation-containing diet as the dog can do. The cat's eyes and ears are positioned forward on the head to provide exquisite acuity of vision and hearing when tracking prey, particularly at night. Retractable claws, seen on cats but not dogs, are another specialized feature of an animal that must chase, catch, and bring down all of its food in the form of wild prey.

The gastrointestinal tracts of the two species are also quite different. Those differences emphasize the differences in the natural diets of each. Science tells us that modifications in the basic structure of this important organ system from species to species are closely connected to diet. The cat's stomach, caecum (appendix), and colon, segments of the gastrointestinal tract most associated with digestion of vegetable matter, are smaller than those segments in the dog. The length of the feline intestine in proportion to its body length is short compared with that of the dog, indicating that the cat's evolutionary diet was highly digestible (protein and fat), whereas the dog consumes far more vegetable matter. The inner lining of the cat's stomach has significantly greater surface area than does the same part of the dog's stomach. Anatomists believe that increases in the relative size of this stomach area are an adaptation to the digestion of higher-meat, more calorie-dense diets. The caecum in the cat is very primitive, whereas it is much better developed in the dog. Once again, this portion of the gastrointestinal tract assists in the processing of fibrous, nonmeat dietary constituents.

Equally telling of the cat's strictly carnivorous origins are its nutrient requirements, especially its requirements for protein. Research done on the 1970s and '80s showed conclusively that protein requirements in kittens and cats far exceed those of puppies or dogs. The cat, unlike omnivores such as the dog, "burns" protein to make energy for its everyday use, under all circumstances. Most other animals burn large amounts of protein for energy only when protein is plentiful in the diet.

In contrast, the cat has an ongoing high requirement for protein to turn into energy, even when dietary protein intake is very limited. During starvation or excessive protein-restriction, the cat is forced to disassemble its body's own constituent proteins (enzymes, antibodies, organ tissues, and so on) to produce fuel for energy to keep the cells alive and functioning. Thus, in the most fundamental way, the health and tissue integrity of the cat is dependent upon the continual intake of highly digestible protein, especially protein from meat.

Another of the cat's claims to the top-predator spot in the food chain is the absolute requirement for an essential fatty acid, arachidonic acid, found only in meat. Also, cats must consume preformed vitamin A from animal-source foods because they are unable to make this essential vitamin from the beta carotene found in plants. The list of the specializations of the cat's internal machinery that reflect its evolutionary adaptations to a life as an obligatory carnivore goes on and on.

Not All Livers Are Alike

By far, the most fascinating characteristic of the cat compared to omnivores like the dog is the manner in which its liver functions. The cat's very high protein and amino acid requirements arise from the constantly high activity of certain enzymes in the feline liver. These enzymes disassemble the amino acids in protein to make them available for production of energy in a process called *gluconeogenesis*. Essentially, the liver is the organ that is responsible for the high and constant burn rate of protein in the cat's body. Omnivores such as the dog have a liver that is also capable of this function, but omnivores turn the rate of this function up or down depending on how much dietary protein is available. In contrast, the cat's liver protein "burn rate" is set high at all times, even when dietary protein is scarce or entirely absent. Death from protein starvation can be very rapid in this species.

In the liver, protein amino acids are processed into glucose (sugar) and sent into the bloodstream to supply the body's need for this energy nutrient. In a meat-eating species like the cat, accustomed to little dietary carbohydrate in its evolutionary environment, the liver will manufacture the great majority of the animal's needed glucose, which is the primary energy supply for the animal's brain. Because there is little glucose in a high-meat diet, this is an essential task for an obligatory carnivore. The liver of omnivores, including people and dogs, have multiple enzyme systems for handling dietary carbohydrate; the cat has only one such enzyme system, with limited capacity to deal with high carbohydrate consumption.

Such specializations make the cat fit its niche perfectly; indeed, the fittest animal in a niche will be the one with the fewest and simplest systems to meet its survival needs. The cat's ancestors did not need the ability to turn their liver's protein burn rate up and down. Similarly, they did not require significant carbohydrate-handling capabilities. The specialized glucose-from-protein systems that have been genetically retained by the modern cat are always active at a high rate, obligating felines to eat more protein than their omnivorous counterparts. Because of this, unfortunately, the cat will suffer far more harm than will omnivores in situations where protein is insufficient or absent. We will see how important this requirement is when we discuss many of the common diseases of our pet cats.

Out of Africa

The present-day house cat (*Felis domesticus*) is generally thought to have descended thousands of years ago from a small wild cat (*Felis lybica*) native to the deserts of North Africa. Such a dry climate heritage would explain many distinct characteristics of this species. Cats are capable of surviving for long periods without water, and will naturally consume very little free water when they are feeding on canned cat food or fresh meat.

Cats can produce urine that is highly concentrated compared to that of the dog and other animals that evolved in more water-rich environments. The cat's natural tendency to produce urine with a great deal of metabolic waste in a highly concentrated form can be dangerous if a cat feeds on a diet that is low in water, because this desert animal has a naturally low thirst drive. The cat that is consuming dry cat food seldom drinks enough additional free water to balance the dry state of the food. This results in especially concentrated urine with attendant medical problems, including certain kinds of bladder disease. Dry food also contains ingredients that interfere with the natural acidity of the cat's urine. Highly concentrated, alkaline urine from dry food consumption is associated with serious, even fatal urinary tract problems.

The Predator Lifestyle

The cat's ancient predator–behaviors are very much a part of its present-day life. Some wild cat species live solitary lives, associating closely with other adults of their species only during mating season. The most familiar of such solitary wild cats is the mountain lion, or cougar (*Felis concolor*). Other species, such as the African lion (*Panthera leo*), live relatively sedentary lives in small groups of animals, hunting and caring for the young in a collective manner, with a very defined geography that belongs to each group and which is protected by the group from outsiders that might take resources from that territory. Our pet cats are still very influenced by the primal behavioral instincts of their wild ancestors.

The domestic cat is like the lion in its social orientation. Despite the common belief that house cats are aloof and solitary, most naturally prefer to have companionship with a few members of their species. In such groups, which claim set territory with well understood boundaries, there is a clear pecking order, with the leader, or "alpha cat," often a female, living communally with its associates that have decreasing amounts of influence within the group. As long as the range of this group is large enough for the group size, there is general harmony, with only minor dominance "debates" between the alpha and associates.

From time to time, however, there may be individuals that do not fit with the group as a whole. For reasons that are not often clear, a young adult may become a pariah, or outcast. Such pariahs are individuals that cannot find friendship with the other cats in the community; rather, they will be chased and sometimes attacked by even other low-level members of the group. In the wild setting, such cats would either leave the colony and seek other outcasts with which to start a new colony, or would live at the edge of the group, finding food and shelter as best they could without interacting with the others. Sometimes a youngster, often a male, will suddenly begin to demonstrate inappropriate and persistent dominance behaviors relative to others with high and low positions within the hierarchy. Dominant behaviors from a nonalpha cat are very disruptive of the welfare of the group and such a cat would also be driven from the colony, unless it can win the battles with older, more established members of the group and take their place in the hierarchy.

Feral cat colonies typically have clusters of same-sex cats that associate most closely. Females of reproductive age spend time together, and naturally their young kittens stay close to this female grouping until some time after they are weaned. Young adult males associate with one another in a sort of "bachelor band," but this group does not intermingle much with the females because one or a few older, more dominant males do the breeding that takes place within the colony. Dominant males live more solitary lives, except during the breeding season. Breeding males are highly competitive with one another, and each maintains a subterritory that is his own within the colony. Serious fights occur when a young male or another breeding male invades the well-marked subterritory of an established male. If there is insufficient space within the colony's total territory to allow for each assertive male to have breeding space, someone has to leave. Assertive males that cannot successfully challenge the dominant breeding male will be driven from the group and will seek to establish their own new groups.

Understanding these natural group relationships and interactions, and the possibilities for disruption of those dynamics, has great importance for understanding the behavior of pet cats, especially when they are kept in groups indoors.

Living with a Predator

The lesson in taking time to understand the cat's natural physiology and lifestyle is that altering that lifestyle will result in disease and behavioral disability. For all of their advanced intelligence, house cats cannot adjust to highly unnatural living circumstances any better than their much larger wild cousins on the African savannahs or the rainforests of Asia could. *The domestic cat is not domestic.* It is a small, essentially feral species that has made only modest accommodations to living intimately with humans.

I find the attraction some people feel for keeping wild species of felines as pets ironic. The seemingly less-exotic domestic cat is as wild in its mind, heart, and soul as the grand, fierce, big cats could ever be. Today, knowledgeable animal lovers understand that keeping a big cat requires great attention to such a cat's urgent needs for the right food, the right environment, and the right handling. We assume, however, that our house cats are so much different in their requirements for health and well-being. This is a mistaken belief.

True, our familiar house cat is not, generally speaking, a dangerous creature capable of killing or injuring us the way big cats are. Its size and deceptive amiability makes it a delightful and easy-to-keep pet. The differences between house cats and the lions, tigers, leopards, and innumerable other wild felines of movies and wildlife documentaries stop there, however. The predator that greets us at the door at the end of a busy workday, that shares our bed on a cold rainy night, and that slumbers in utter contentment on the top of our computer as we work in our office is an ancient, instinctive, hunting machine. I believe that the dreams of our beloved feline pets are filled with the thrill of the chase after prey, the comfort of napping in the incandescent equatorial sun, and the smell of monsoon rains beating relentlessly down on the towering shelter of jungle canopy. This is the smallest, gentlest cat's heritage and the core of its physical and psychological being.

If we would keep our cats healthy and happy throughout their naturally long lives, we cannot forget this truth.

2

The Life of Today's Cats

The Indoor Life: Benefits and Risks

Decades ago, pet cats lived almost entirely outdoors. Their lives were not much different from those of their earliest feline ancestors. They hunted for much of their own food. Their humans occasionally provided scraps of food from the family table, but most cats were expected to fend for themselves. In fact, cats in those days were often kept not so much as pets, but as useful workers around the ranch, farm, or home. Cats were expected to control vermin, such as mice, rats, and gophers. This they did, and did well, and not because they wanted to be helpful, but because they had to hunt to survive. Living outdoors, cats associated with other animals, including other cats, according to age-old hierarchical rules. There was generally plenty of space for outdoor cats to spread out, associate with their natural social groups, and avoid others at will.

This outdoor life could be very dangerous. Unprotected from larger predators and other sources of accidental trauma, cats living outdoors often died relatively young. This danger increased as automobile use increased. Nothing in a cat's evolution could have prepared it to deal with four thousand pounds of metal bearing down upon it at high speed. As farms, dairies, and ranches gave way to subdivisions in the 1960s and after, many pets died sudden violent deaths on streets and roads. As human and animal population density increased with urbanization, the cat also faced increased dangers from infectious disease. Epidemics of viral, bacterial, and parasitic diseases could decimate outdoor feline populations. Veterinary care for outdoor cats was relatively uncommon. Even spaying and neutering of pet cats was rare, and unwanted kittens appeared at astonishing rates. These unprotected youngsters were exposed in turn to all of these dangers.

The cat living on its own outside the house maintained an independent demeanor, and many owners believed that the cat was not really an affectionate, companionable part of the family. Many people believed the cat had a naturally unfriendly, human-avoiding personality. The cat of the mid-twentieth century would wait for decades to become the adored close member of the family that we know today.

During the 1980s and '90s, cultural changes in society had a profound effect on the lifestyle of the pet cat. The living space of the family, including the outdoor space, became smaller or disappeared altogether. The pace of life for most people became much faster. Many households had two or more working adults, instead of one adult who stayed home. Homes were deserted during the day as all members of the family left for work or school. People found it harder to keep dogs, especially large dogs, as pets, and looked increasingly to the cat as the animal companion of choice. The cat's small size and relatively self-sufficient nature became attractive to people who wanted an animal companion that could live closely with them without demanding constant attention and care.

In the past two decades, the cat has become the most popular pet in the United States. Today, most pet cats spend the majority or all of their lives indoors, where they are protected from many of the dangers of the outdoor life. Death and injury from accidents are far less common now that cats are protected within the home. Infectious diseases spread less quickly and widely because cats associate less with large numbers of strays and also because felines enjoy much better veterinary care today. Indoor pet cats are routinely spayed or neutered, and unwanted litters of kittens among this group are now a rarity.

All of this improved safety has come at a price, however. Now that indoor cats are dependent upon their human families for food and shelter and living arrangements, new problems have sprung up. Cats today are plagued with serious medical conditions, often at youthful ages, which seem new and associated with this new lifestyle. Obesity, diabetes mellitus, bladder and kidney problems, hyperthyroidism, and allergies are just a few of the more common of these problems. In addition, indoor felines experience a variety of behavioral problems, such as poor litter-box habits and aggression toward feline housemates, that perplex and frustrate their owners. Unfortunately, these problems can become so serious that a much-loved pet cat may die or be put to sleep because of them. This is especially sad because all of these seemingly new problems are the result of man-made influences on the cat through its new indoor lifestyle. All can be reduced or prevented through understanding of those unnatural influences and how to correct them.

Feline Nutrition: A Cat Is What It Eats

For more than two decades now, conscientious cat owners have been unwittingly treating their cats as though they were small dogs. This was an easy mistake. The cat followed the dog into favor as an "underfoot" pet in the home, thereby inheriting many of the pet-care habits owners had established already for their canine family members. Adding to the problem, veterinarians and major pet-care product companies entirely failed to recognize the implications of carnivore/omnivore distinctions as they encouraged and supported the cat's newfound status as a kept pet.

Most particularly, the foods that had been developed already for dogs in the second half of the twentieth century seemed easily adapted for the cat. Even though good research done decades earlier proved the very special nutritional needs and limitations of the cat compared to the dog, the companies that geared up to make cat foods did not understand how profound these differences really were. They believed that these differences could be addressed with minor changes to vitamin/mineral supplements added to the same basic dry canine diet. Pet nutrition scientists ignored the very different ways in which the cat processed and used energy nutrients (protein, fat, and carbohydrate) compared with the omnivorous dog. For a few years, this disregard seemed harmless.

Cats did not find most dog foods very palatable at first. Ingenious inventors devised additives for pet foods that would make them tasty for almost any cat, much as the breakfast cereal companies had done when they sugarcoated their products to make children clamor for them in the grocery store aisles. Cats came to accept these makeshift diets, and their convenience and short-term adequacy "proven" in limited, six-month feeding trials seemed to satisfy owners and veterinarians. Everyone seemed happy with this new arrangement in which the carnivorous cat gobbled down the foods originally designed for the omnivorous dog.

Slowly but surely, problems began to arise. Veterinarians began to recognize cases of a mysterious and frighteningly common bladder disease, especially in neutered male cats. Scientists studied this problem and declared it to be the result of an unfortunate narrowing of the urethra in these altered male cats. These experts also blamed the sedentary lifestyle and inadequate water consumption of the increasingly indoor pet cat. Some nutritionists insisted that this problem was also related to minerals in the diet of these cats and a strange shift in the urine acid levels of affected cats. Even though this theory pointed to the truth that the food was at fault, not the cat, still no one thought to stop feeding cereal to cats. Instead, the industry devised yet more additives for the existing flawed diets to try to correct the problem with these cats.

Unfortunately, bladder disease in many cats was not controlled with these dietary additives, and a large number of pets either died of the disease or were subjected to a very mutilating and painful surgery to save their lives. During this frustrating period of research and new product development, no one came forward with the now-obvious solution to the problem.

Some years after the first observations of the urinary tract problem in commercial-food-fed cats, veterinarians started noticing that more and more of their feline patients were obese, and an alarming number were becoming uncontrollably diabetic. The blame was placed on the new sedentary couch-potato lifestyle of the cat. According to the popular theory of that time, house cats didn't exercise, were bored with indoor life, had nothing to do but eat all day, became lazy and unmotivated, and obesity naturally resulted. It was the cat's fault, again.

In an effort to save the cat from itself, pet food company nutritionists once again modified the formulas of their diets, took fat out, added cellulose (indigestible, completely non-nutritious fiber) to diets designed for an omnivore or herbivore rather than a carnivore, and insisted that owners feed smaller portions to their already nutrient-starved cats. Despite the superficial logic of such an approach, it failed to work to reduce the incidence of obesity or diabetes. The cats got fatter, they developed diabetes in increasing numbers, and their diabetes proved far more difficult to control than the similar type of adult-onset diabetes seen in humans or dogs.

Bladder problems, obesity, and diabetes are not the only chronic diseases that have become epidemic among cats. Today, veterinarians are presented with more and more cats with symptoms of allergic disease than ever before. Skin rashes and self-mutilation from intensely itchy skin, chronic ear infections, asthma, and inflammatory bowel disease are on the rise. These are all signs of an immune system out of control, which has turned on itself. Unfortunately, the widespread use of steroid medications, prescribed to quiet these signs of allergic distress, can cause disease in the cat that is as severe as the original allergy.

Once again, pet food companies have came up with newer, much more expensive cereal-based diets with "designer" ingredients to solve the problem. Nonetheless, the problems persist, few cats improve, and the cat's "faulty" immune system gets the blame. Each time a new disease syndrome is recognized, the pet-care industry's response is the same.

Despite the dramatic increases in diagnosed chronic disease in cats, few individuals have stepped back and asked the obvious questions: "Why is a healthy, previously well-adapted species developing these problems now? Is it possible there is something fundamentally flawed with our basic care of these cats? Are we making things worse by adding more and more unnatural substances to the cat's diet to patch problems of our own making? Is it the cat's fault, or ours?" The answer to all of these questions is clear. In attempting to make life more healthful for our pet cats, we have been putting the wrong fuel into their internal engines, with disastrous results.

While our cats may be protected better from early death due to trauma and infectious disease in the comfort of their new home-based lifestyle, they are now suffering from often lethal dietary diseases. Making matters worse, those diseases have always been treated by mainstream veterinary medicine with even more inappropriate dietary "solutions" that lead to even more disease and suffering. For the cat, this has become the ultimate vicious cycle.

The cat's natural diet is high in protein and low in carbohydrate, with moderate amounts of animal fat. Today's dry cat foods have high levels of processed carbohydrate, low levels of fat, and modest levels of often low-quality protein, much of which may come from vegetable matter like gluten and soy. The damage caused by such an upside-down diet for such a specialized animal cannot be overstated. Such an obvious mistake has created nearly all of the important medical conditions of cats today. (See D. Zoran, "The Carnivore Connection to Nutrition in Cats," www.catinfo.org/zorans_article.pdf.)

The diet of the feral top predator will contain almost no carbohydrate, usually less than 2 percent by weight. This small amount of carbohydrate will come from seeds and grasses, plus a small amount of muscle glucose consumed with the prey. On the other hand, dry cat foods contain between 25 and 50 percent carbohydrates from cereal grains like corn, rice, or starchy vegetables like potatoes. These types of ingredients are very high in carbohydrate to begin with, and they break down into sugar during the process of turning them into kibble. The cat consuming dry cat food is eating the kitty equivalent of sugarcoated breakfast cereal.

Dry cat foods are harmful for another reason. Cats are descended from desert predators, and they drink little free water naturally. Most of their water for survival comes from the foods they eat. When we feed dry, starchy kibble to a cat, we promote a constant state of subclinical dehydration, because the cat's thirst drive does not compensate for the low water content of the diet. This dehydration contributes to bladder disease and kidney disease, at the very least. Certainly, constant dehydration is an unnatural physical stress on our cats. Most important, it is an *unnecessary* stress.

We all know that a steady diet of such junk food would be harmful to humans. For an obligatory carnivore like the cat, the result is disastrous. Fortunately, the solution is clear and easy. We need simply stop feeding our cats unnatural foods meant more for fattening cattle than nourishing a top predator. Many canned pet foods, although flawed in some ways, still provide far superior nutrition compared to dry foods, even the so-called premium brands. Another alternative that appeals to many pet owners today is a raw meat–based diet. Raw meat is the natural food of the cat, and is really the "gold standard" of diets for any obligatory carnivore. We will discuss in the succeeding chapters how to choose the best canned cat foods, and how to safely feed raw meat to your cat.

By doing something this simple and obvious, we can cause changes in the health of our cats that are nothing short of miraculous.

Bad Cat? How Living Indoors Affects Feline Behavior

Because the so-called domestic cat is still very wild in its interactions with other cats, harmony between larger groups of even well-cared-for house cats is not assured. One of the most common complaints of my clients is aggressive behaviors between their pets. Such behavior may arise without warning, involving individuals that have previously been compatible. Such irritable or aggressive interactions can occur between same-sex cats or opposite-sex cats, even if they are all spayed or neutered.

While the exact inciting cause of such sudden changes in intercat relationships is often unknown, there are usually some key factors that contribute to trouble. The single most important factor is the number of cats in the "territory." In the home, the territory is the space within the house itself. If we consider the size of the range of feral communities of cats, it is easy to understand that even sizable homes of 2,000 to 3,000 square feet are not adequate for more than a small number of animals to live in peace. When sizable numbers of cats are confined in a static amount of space and are unable to expand their territory by moving further away from other cats in the group, friction and aggressive behaviors may result. My experience suggests that keeping more than one cat per 500 to 750 square feet of living space will create a kind of territory stress that can cause disharmony among pet cats.

Male and female cats do not live in constant close proximity to each other within the group's territory in the wild, and forcing them to do so in the limited space of the home environment can create stress. Sometimes, alpha-type females will become aggressive against other younger or less-dominant individuals. Although females do live relatively closely together in the wild, their companionship in that situation revolves around bearing and caring for kittens. When spayed females do not share this common focus, the potential for unpredictable irritable interactions between them is very real. Neutered males seem to make the most continuously harmonious companions with one another within the home environment. Nevertheless, even they can become socially aggressive if their environment is too small, they must share the home with too many others, or if the environment is chaotic.

All cats, whether living feral or within the home, are stressed by large-scale changes in their lifestyle. Moving from one home to another, home remodeling that is long term and extensive, sudden introduction of new animal or human family members, and similar disruptions to the status quo can ignite considerable disharmony among pet cats that have previously established good living relationships with one another. In the wild setting, a cat colony will naturally maintain as much lifestyle stability as possible, removing any disruptive influences quickly, reestablishing the group's routine with minimal long-term disruption. In the home environment, cats experiencing chaos do not have this ability to control their own situation. With significant and continued upset to their customary routine, otherwise peaceful cats may respond with intercat aggression, and a breakdown of previously perfect litter-box habits.

I am often asked to explain and treat house soiling misbehaviors in my client's pets. We sometimes find an organic explanation for such a breakdown, that is, a disease process involving the kidneys, bladder, or gastrointestinal tract. All too often, however, the problem stems entirely from an overcrowded and unstable living environment that causes the patient to feel anxious and threatened by the uncertainty of the changed routine. Highly stressed cats will "act out" in such circumstances, attempting to dominate others with whom they may previously have been equals, or establishing control over territory within the house.

Acting-out behaviors often take the form of territory-marking with urine or feces, as a cat attempts to regain some control and safety in its life. Owners may see this behavior as spiteful. Certainly it is controlling and manipulative, in some sense. The underlying cause, however, is not mean-spiritedness on the part of the cat, but merely an instinctive reaction to the helplessness the animal is experiencing when the environment seems persistently threatening. The cat is simply doing what its wild ancestors have learned to do in such frightening conditions: reasserting its dominance and staking out some space for itself.

When we understand the underlying cause for such bad behaviors, we can understand that the best way to reverse them is to restore the pet's sense of security and stability. Punishment will not help, it simply makes the cat feel even more insecure. Antidepressant drugs such as Prozac or Buspar may help, but they merely mask the problem, they do not resolve it. Most owners do not want their cats on such medicines for the long term, and rightly so.

Be Proactive!

The very best way to deal with these problems is to prevent them in the first place. When you first plan to become a cat owner, be realistic about the number you can bring into the same home. Even cats that are raised together or that have a parent-offspring relationship can become hateful toward each other in crowded, stressful situations. A small apartment cannot accommodate more than two or three cats comfortably. Even a sizable house has its limits, yet I have seen a dozen cats in such a home. Inevitably there are many disputes in such a large group. If you already have an overcrowded cat population, you may have to consider reducing the size of this group or at least segregating friendly cats from aggressive ones. Most of us know other cat lovers who could give loving new homes to cats that are stressed and need more space and attention. This is not to suggest that your present cat family should be disbanded to a shelter or rescue group, only that finding a new, "forever" home for a cat that is unhappy in any group may be an alternative to consider if providing separate territories within the home is not feasible.

Beyond keeping the size of the group small, cat owners must understand the effect that sudden continuous changes in the cat's environment will have. Stress is cumulative, no matter what the cause. Pets that are unhappy with their available space or living companions will tolerate much less upheaval in their routine than those that feel they have room to escape the threat of a changing home life. When changes are inevitable, limiting the time the disruption will continue is important. If big changes will be permanent, there will be a period of adjustment as pets learn to accept and become accustomed to the new order. Owners can anticipate this adjustment period and work to reassure pets and restore an environment that is safe and comforting. If aggression and marking behaviors become a problem, there are methods for reducing and eventually reversing these behaviors. We will discuss these as we explore the care of cats in the chapters ahead.

In short, to keep our cats healthy and happy for the two decades or more of their expected life span, we must never forget that we live with wild, exotic creatures. Like any other tamed but wild-hearted animal, the cat has its own special needs for health and well-being. We know what those needs are, and providing for those needs is easy. Read on to find out just how easy that is.

3

The *Real* Problem with Commercial Pet Foods

In the past decade, many books have been written about the evils of commercial pet foods (for example, *Food Pets Die For: Shocking Facts About Pet Food* by Ann Martin; also, *Dr. Pitcairn's New Complete Guide to Natural Health for Dogs and Cats* by Richard Pitcairn). These books describe many different kinds of additives, contaminants, and unsavory ingredients in the foods that line the shelves of grocery stores and pet stores offered as "complete and balanced, high-quality nutrition" for your furry family members. Undoubtedly, there is some truth to these claims of undesirable, even toxic components used in pet foods. To be fair, however, I can draw on my own past experience as an executive of one of the leading pet food manufacturers to say that not all pet foods contain these harmful ingredients.

Some commercial dog and cat foods actually contain pretty good-quality ingredients.

Let's face it; a pet owner would be foolish to believe that canned tuna-flavor cat food, as an example, has the same amount or quality of human-grade tuna that a can of tuna for human consumption has. The product intended for people will typically cost several times as much as the cat food. Clearly there is a big difference between the tuna quality and quantity of two such differently priced products. That is just common sense.

The can of human-grade tuna is pure tuna, usually from the fillet of the fish, and processed under USDA inspection to be fit for human consumption. On the other hand, tuna cat food may have heads, tails, and other non-human-grade parts of the fish, and usually there will be substantial amounts of nontuna ingredients as well. If this were not the case, cat food (and dog food as well) would be far most costly than it presently is. While many pet owners would bear such a huge increase in cost for feeding their pets, many others would be unable to. Certainly, the pet food companies would have a harder time marketing such costly products.

The big differences between pet foods and human foods do not *always* mean that any particular cat food is bad for your cat. The truth is, however, labels on pet foods can be very misleading, so it can be difficult for owners to choose these products wisely. Sometimes ingredients in the food may not even be listed on the label. The amounts, as well as the quality of the various ingredients in pet foods, can vary widely between two seemingly similar products manufactured by different companies. The quality control and commitment to a set ingredient formula by different companies varies as much as the ingredients. This is true even though virtually all pet food packages today contain claims that they "meet or exceed AAFCO [American Association of Feed Control Officials] requirements" of some sort.

A Cat Is Not a Small Dog

Things are even more complicated when we focus on commercial foods specifically for cats. Here, the varying *combinations* of meat and vegetable ingredients in commercial foods is as important as ingredient quality and wholesomeness. This will surprise many readers, but is absolutely true. As I will discuss at length in succeeding chapters, the ratio of the three energy macronutrients (carbohydrate, fat, and protein) in a food, as well as the amount of indigestible fiber, will affect the long-term health of the cat, as much as the purity of the various ingredients. These long-term effects start with the food the kitten consumes.

It is just as dangerous for cats to eat imbalanced combinations of high carbohydrate, high non-nutritive fiber, or low protein, as it would be for a cat to eat foods with inferior-quality ingredients. This is because of the very specific dietary requirements of the obligatory carnivore that we discussed in chapter 1. Such dangerous nutrient imbalances are commonplace in cat foods even in the scientifically enlightened time in which we live. All of them run counter to the documented scientific understanding of the needs of the cat, yet they are responsible for many of the medical problems we veterinarians see in our feline patients.

Pet Food Is an Unregulated Industry

(see www.leda.law.harvard.edu/leda/data/784/Patrick06.pdf)

The pet food industry in the United States and the rest of the world is essentially unregulated by any third-party regulatory body. Even though the Food and Drug Administration (the federal regulatory agency known as the FDA) has legal authority over the labeling and claims for pet foods, the FDA does not exercise this authority in any meaningful way. There are three important reasons for this unfortunate state of affairs:

1. The FDA is also responsible for making sure that the massive U.S. pharmaceutical industry is supervised for the safety of human prescription and over-the-counter medication users. At times when the federal budget is squeezed (nearly always), this agency has few resources available for exercising stringent oversight on the safety of pet food.

2. Another governmental regulator, the AAFCO, is the organization through which the fifty state governments try to work together to establish and enforce animal feed requirements. AAFCO's primary responsibility is ensuring the safety of feed for human-food-producing livestock. Like the FDA, AAFCO must commit the lion's share of its limited resources to human health safety concerns, not companion animal health concerns. AAFCO requires essentially no *meaningful* testing of foods before companies may use its broad endorsement language on pet food labels.

3. The Pet Food Institute (PFI) is the lobbying group in Washington DC that watches out for the pet food manufacturing industry's interests at the governmental level. This group is exceedingly well funded and can outspend FDA's

and AAFCO's budgets for pet food–related regulatory activities at all times. PFI makes sure that federal and state legislation that would impose more supervision and stronger regulatory oversight on pet food companies does not pass.

Pet Food Is So Very Profitable

Today's pet owners spend many billions of dollars on the commercial foods they purchase and feed to their dogs and cats. The cost of producing these foods is low because the ingredients are inexpensive compared to human food ingredients. Further, there is little *genuine* scientific testing of any kind done on the nutritional suitability and safety of pet food, and virtually *no* long-term adequacy testing (the most costly of all tests). To make long-term feeding claims, pet food companies only have to meet basic minimum nutrient-content requirements without any testing at all, or may use small, six-month acute toxicity testing to earn the government's quality certification. These tests typically are conducted by the companies themselves, and the results are not closely monitored by the government. These extremely lax validation requirements help to keep the profit margins for pet foods extremely high.

I have no quibble with corporations' making a profit. Without a profit motive, no company would ever bother to produce a particular product. Excessive profits are intolerable, however, when they come at the expense of genuine science in the development and production of a product so that it is safe and meets its label's claims.

Most of the pet foods now available in groceries and pet stores claim to be "complete and balanced" as a sole food for the entire life of a pet. This claim cannot possibly be valid unless the food has been tested scientifically for the life of at least a large enough number of animals to be statistically believable. To be convincing, such studies would have to show that the food does not cause acute or chronic nutritional diseases when compared to other, species-appropriate foods. No such scientifically valid long-term testing has ever been done on any of these products.

As of the time of the writing of this book, no fewer than two large-scale pet food recalls have been issued by two major pet food companies in the past year. One of these recalls occurred because the food carried lethal amounts of aflatoxin (a poison from fungus) in some of the batches of food. Many dogs and cats became ill and some even died of this poisoning before the problem was discovered and the company had to recall the foods involved. Another recall occurred in several "prescribed" foods for pets made by one company. These foods had very high levels of vitamin D, which caused high calcium levels in a number of the pets fed the food.

Once this was discovered, the foods were recalled. In the latter incident, a company spokesman was quoted as saying that as a result of reports of affected pets "we started an exhaustive nutrient analysis of our canned products." In other words, the company felt compelled to conduct their rigorous nutrient analyses *after* the problem was discovered, but not before the foods were available for feeding to pets! This seems a backward approach to quality assurance in foods labeled as safe for lifetime feeding to cats and dogs.

These two most recent problems of untested foods are not isolated events. Such acute problems happen with some frequency, but do not always cause enough disease and death to create a national or international uproar. Both illustrate perfectly how pet foods truly are inadequately tested for safety and efficacy by the self-regulated pet food industry.

If the testing needed to properly validate even short-term safety of pet foods isn't being done, imagine how much more unjustified are the lifetime safety claims on pet foods, considering that such tests are even more expensive than short-term tests. Further, long-term safety studies would delay the marketing of pet foods, increasing their cost. The pet food companies are simply not willing to make this investment in science, and the FDA and AAFCO do not require such testing before they allow broad claims. *In reality, the only long-term tests of pet foods that ever occur are the tests that owners themselves conduct when they feed these foods to their own pets.*

Your Cat Is an "Experimental Animal"

If a food is marketed as "complete and balanced for the life of a pet" with the AAFCO statement on the label assuring this completeness, pet food purchasers have no reason to doubt the safety of that food. This assurance is unfounded, however. Because of the strong profit-motive of the pet food companies to rush products to market, and the lack of governmental regulation controlling this rush to market, pet owners are themselves providing the experimental animals for testing the actual truth of adequacy claims. It is hard to imagine a more unfair, and unsafe, situation. Having pet food purchasers test the foods on their own pets is only half of the problem, however.

Not only are pet owners unaware of the untested nature of the claims on pet foods, the veterinary profession is equally unaware of it. Veterinarians are familiar with the rigorous safety testing imposed on pharmaceuticals they use for their patients. They receive assurances from the pet food companies that products with AAFCO label assurances undergo similar kinds of testing to validate the claims on those labels. Naturally, veterinarians assume that a government statement of adequacy deserves their trust and endorsement. Most veterinarians today make commercial pet food recommendations to their clients. Few, if any, would provide those endorsements if they understood how little meaningful testing those recommended foods actually undergo. This point has been amply illustrated by recalls of dry food for alflatoxin contamination in 2006 and a massive recall for kidney toxins in canned cat foods in 2007. In both situations, the packaging of all contaminated foods carried AAFCO nutritional safety and efficacy guarantee statements, despite not being uniformly safe at all.

Without their knowledge, veterinarians have been assigned the role of professional evaluators of the results of long-term pet food feeding trials in which their patients are experimental animals. But if veterinarians don't understand that they are unwittingly cast in the role of pet food researchers, how can they possibly know to watch out for negative effects of these untested foods? If veterinarians believe the foods they are recommending have already been proven safe in real tests, why would they become alarmed or even suspicious of nutritional disease when large numbers of their feline patients develop chronic degenerative problems like obesity, diabetes, bladder problems, inflammatory bowel disease, kidney problems, and many others?

This is exactly the situation in which we all find ourselves. The short-term and long-term feeding tests needed to earn the label claims on pet foods have not been done in the manufacturer's laboratory. Instead, they are being done in the general pet population, with millions of test subjects. This is certainly enough test animals to satisfy any statistician, but the veterinarians who are monitoring the results of this huge test don't know what to watch for in this experiment. In fact, these medical professionals have no reason to believe they are to watch for anything at all.

These testing inadequacies apply not only to the "well-pet" cat foods, but also to the so-called prescribed foods that are commonly used to manage disease in cats. Although these special foods often claim to have been validated in scientific studies conducted at veterinary schools, these claims are also misleading. The third-party research these foods undergo is actually quite limited. Not only are the numbers of diseased cats involved small, by scientific standards, the studies themselves are very narrowly designed and funded by the various producing companies. Usually the purpose of such studies is to prove the food does what the manufacturer already claims that it does.

Because these studies are specific-results-oriented and funded by an interested party, there is too little objectivity in their design and implementation. Further, if a study fails to provide a positive result for the company's marketing purposes, the company will not publish that information. Veterinarians do not get to see research results that reflect negatively on the manufacturer's claims. Unfortunately, without pet food company funding for research, academic veterinarians do not have the resources to conduct genuinely objective, thorough evaluations of these disease-managing diets.

In the next sections of this book, we will see over and over again how pet foods are not safe for the lifetime feeding of pet cats. We will see how these foods cause many life-threatening diseases without veterinarians or pet owners suspecting the link between a cat's diet and its disease. We will also see how the very "prescribed" foods that are marketed to solve these already diet-caused problems ignore the true causative factors and create more problems.

Think About It

To bring a new drug to market and make legal claims for the safety and effectiveness of that drug, pharmaceutical companies must spend hundreds of millions of dollars and work a decade or more testing that product. All claims for an available drug's safe use have been verified, and possible negative side effects identified, before it is available to the public. We have nothing even remotely close to this kind of rigorous safety testing in pet foods. Now, to be fair, it is unthinkable that any company would spend the kind of time or money to assure the safety of a pet food comparable to what pharmaceutical companies must spend to bring a drug to market. Yet, the fact remains that the kinds of claims that pet food companies are allowed to make on their product labels are emphatic and bold, but simply not tested as true. Pet owners and veterinarians are misled to believe that the foods labeled with health claims are backed by scientific tests proving those claims are valid. This mistaken belief causes nearly every veterinarian to endorse pet foods with such claims.

PART

2

Starting Over in the

Twenty-first Century:

A Kitten's Story

4

A New Cat in the House!

Before You Bring Your New Pet Home

The excitement of bringing your new kitten home is hard to describe. There is nothing cuter than a baby cat and nothing more loving and playful, either. Whether your new one has come from a breeder of pedigreed cats, the local humane shelter, or from a friend whose family pet has delivered an unexpected litter, you will want to provide your new little family member the best possible start in life. Ideally, you should plan to pick up your new pet when you can be at home during the kitten's first days in its new environment. The necessary bonding between the baby and its new family will happen swiftly if everyone is available to spend lots of quality time with the new kitten.

The first stop after you've selected your new pet is your veterinarian's office. If possible, make an appointment even before the day of the kitten's arrival, and make sure your veterinarian knows your appointment is for a new pet's examination and consultation. You will want the little one to receive any needed preventive or therapeutic care before you head home. Your kitten may need vaccinations at this initial medical exam. If you have documents from the breeder or shelter where the kitten grew up, those will probably show what vaccines and deworming treatments the kitten has already received. With this information, your veterinarian can advise you about any further preventive care that is needed and when. Today, vaccines are only given to cats after careful consideration of their risk factors for exposure to the diseases the vaccines protect against. Not all cats should receive all available vaccines every year. There are a great variety of vaccination programs and schedules that are appropriate under differing circumstances and kitty lifestyles. This process of risk-factor-focused vaccine protocol development is discussed at length in chapter 10.

During the first veterinary visit, be sure that you ask *all* of the questions you will undoubtedly have about the newest member of your family. If you don't already have a strong working relationship with a veterinarian you trust to care for your cat and to answer all of your questions, find such a person even before you get your new kitty. Your relationship with your cat's veterinarian will be one of the most important tools you possess for keeping your cat well for the next twenty-plus years.

Having said that your new cat must have a thorough medical exam at the very beginning of your relationship together, I remind the reader that some veterinarians do not have up-to-the-minute information about cats. Beyond their skill in performing a good physical exam on your new cat, many veterinarians in general practice have much greater expertise with puppies and dogs than with cats. This is because canines are by far the most common patient in most practices. If you don't already have a regular veterinarian for all of your pets, try to find a doctor who really enjoys cats and works with them frequently. A referral from another cat owner may be helpful, or you may seek a cat specialist in your area (see www.aafponline.org). Cat-only practices are growing in number all over the United States.

To be the best possible partners with their veterinarians, cat owners themselves should have a thorough understanding of a number of basic cat care subjects, including cat-specific diseases, cat nutrition, vaccines, socializing training, and the like. A good veterinarian will answer all of your questions fully and patiently. There are a number of good reference books about cats, including this one, to give you the information you need. You may even learn things that your chosen veterinarian is unaware of. None of us knows everything. Do not hesitate to discuss cat care subjects with your veterinarian. Sometimes learning can be a two-way street!

The Baby's Room

Right away, your new kitten will need a space that he or she can claim as "safe territory." As soon as the youngster arrives home, I suggest introducing it to a spacious litter box near a soft bed in a warm corner or room in the house. Cats need to know that their immediate living area is safe from danger, and they spend plenty of time inspecting every square inch of new surroundings to make sure there is nothing to fear. Do not interrupt this inspection process. Once it is completed, the kitten will turn its attention to other important activities like eating, playing, and using the litter box.

Most kittens are perfectly litter-box-trained by the time they are five to six weeks old. This training is a natural process, essentially instinctive, and will take place even if the mother-cat is not around. I have observed many orphaned litters teach themselves to use available litter for bathroom needs as long as a box is available. This happens because cats are hardwired for a high level of cleanliness; they naturally detest soiling their living areas. Many different types of litter are acceptable and safe for your new baby. Make sure the kitten can get into the box and that the box is always clean (see chapter 11).

In the rare event that your kitten fails to use the accessible, clean litter box you provide, this may mean there is some illness present, especially if you see loose stool at the same time. Be sure to check with your veterinarian if this happens. Also, make sure the box is placed in a quiet, foot-traffic-free spot. If the box occupies a busy area in the home, the kitten may be fearful of using it. While cats are using litter facilities, they are temporarily quite vulnerable to surprise events in the immediate area. Noisy distractions near the box will discourage the use of the box.

It is fine to allow your kitten to sleep with family members, but it is also quite all right to insist the baby learn to sleep in a warm secure kitty bed in the safe area you have set aside as the kitten's home base. In either case, be sure your kitten is free of fleas and other ectoparasites (mites, ticks, and the like) before you bring him or her home. Your veterinarian can advise you about this during that initial exam. We will discuss parasite control in depth in chapter 7.

Taming the Shy or Aggressive Kitten

Young kittens may have shy or fearful personalities, especially if they have not experienced a lot of gentle affectionate handling before they are adopted. As a breeder, I seldom allow one of my kittens to leave my home before it is fourteen to sixteen weeks of age. It takes this long, with the youngster living in a secure environment with lots of handling and confidence-building experiences with humans and other cats, for my kittens to have the self-assurance and outgoing personalities that their new families want them to have. A kitten adopted at six to eight weeks of age from a shelter or home where little deliberate socialization has taken place is certain to be skittish or, worse, aggressive. Such babies are merely acting defensively because they have an inborn mistrust of human beings and their noisy home environments. Overcoming this natural mistrust, which allows survival in the wild, takes time and plenty of careful, gentle handling.

If you adopt a kitten that is not outgoing but rather defensive and fearful, you will need to commit the time in the first weeks after adoption to socializing your new family member. This *can* be done with enough time and patience, and will reward that effort with a gentle, confident, friendly cat in the end. Remember to start slowly. The fearful kitten must become convinced that the world is a loving, caring place, not a dangerous one. This change of attitude does not happen in a day or two.

It is a good idea to keep a shy or aggressive kitten in a small area with no furniture at first. This will prevent the kitten from hiding under couches and beds where it becomes difficult to provide positive experiences that will convince the baby that its new home is a safe one. A small room, such as a bathroom or utility room, can be made into the kitten's safe space for the first weeks in its new home. Place the litter box; porcelain, metal, or glass dishes for food and water; and a nice bed in this area. The kitten will spend the first few minutes in this new territory investigating every nook and cranny, to make sure that there are no unseen dangers. It is a good idea not to interrupt this investigation or interfere with it in any way. This is typical behavior for any cat in a new environment. Once the kitten knows the room is a safe place, it will turn its attention to settling in, and the owner can sit quietly in the area, allowing the kitten to approach at its own pace.

Offering food or perhaps a toy to play with is a good first step toward winning the kitten's trust. Do not attempt to pick up the kitten if it resists this by struggling or hissing. Unless a kitten has been picked up and held safely already, and learned to expect good care from someone who lifts it, it will fear being dropped or otherwise mishandled when held above the ground in human hands. It may be best just to allow the kitten to approach slowly. Make no sudden moves that will seem threatening. After a period of time of quiet companionship with the baby, you will notice the kitten relaxing, at least a bit. This kind of socialization, with the human present but with no forced contact, can work wonders with any kitten that has the ability to adapt to human presence.

Hand-feeding foods that are especially appetizing, like meat baby food or canned cat food that the kitten likes, can break down trust barriers rapidly. The key to success with a fearful kitten is not to rush the process, but to make the times together very pleasurable for the baby. If the kitten is so terrified that it will not approach the owner at all, it may be necessary to take the affection to the kitten. Petting a young cat that is cowering in a corner, as long as it is not rushed or rough, will usually cause a kitten to relax and begin to open up. Take as much time as necessary, in as many sessions a few hours apart as is necessary, to start bringing the kitten's defenses down.

Don't persist in sessions that fail to cause the kitten to relax. Sometimes, certain family members will have greater success in creating a calm atmosphere for the kitten than others. Some kittens will prefer the company of children or teenagers during this socialization period, others will be more open and accepting around adults. Experiment with different family members to find the "kitten whisperer" among the group. This person will have the best success in bringing the kitten to a greater level of trust and security in the new home.

Over time, you will see the kitten become more confident in its own territory. The kitten will begin to be pleased when humans come to visit and play. As soon as this starts to occur, enlarge the kitten's territory by allowing it to have free roam in other parts of the house. Place litter boxes and beds in these other areas. Bring the kitten back to home base after periods of time exploring other environments. Soon the kitten will be able to enjoy the entire house. It will display outgoing and confident behavior during these adventures outside its first room.

Never chase the kitten and never discipline it physically as this will undo your progress. If the kitten misbehaves in some way, give it a time-out in its room. The best way to deal with misbehavior is to avoid providing opportunity for that misbehavior. For example, if the kitten relieves itself in inappropriate places when outside its room, make sure there are plenty of boxes available throughout the house. Alternatively, supervise its exploring time so that if it begins to look for a spot to relieve itself, you can take it back to its room immediately. Kittens and cats remember physical abuse for their lifetime. It can become impossible to overcome the fearfulness or aggressive behavior of a cat that has been physically abused. Corporal punishment or any retaliation that frightens (like shouting at the kitten) are never constructive approaches to socializing a shy young cat.

Adopting a new cat, whether it is very young or already adult, is a significant commitment that can span decades. If you follow through on that commitment with love, care, and attention to the needs of your new pet, you will experience a relationship that will fill your own life with the deep satisfaction that animal companionship can bring.

5

What to Feed, What to Feed?

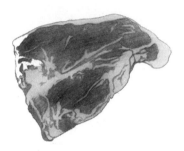

A Dizzying Array

Today, grocery store isles and pet food warehouses are literally packed with cat foods of every flavor and shape, in canned, semimoist, dehydrated powder, and dry kibble forms. How may the cat owner choose the food that is best for the kitten, and later, the grown adult cat? At first view of the thousands of possible choices, it seems an impossible task. In truth, however, all we need do is remember the basics about the cat's true nature, and the best choices become obvious.

The cat is an obligatory carnivore, which means it *must* eat meat to survive. Finding the best food for your kitten means finding the food with the most meat.

The reader may be surprised to know that we can eliminate all dry cat foods from consideration right away. Dry cat foods, even the high-priced premium brands with their high starch and overprocessed nutrients, are the equivalent of junk food for pets.

It is true that kittens may have a certain tolerance for junk food, as human youngsters do. Ideally, however, we want to prevent our pets from becoming addicted to unhealthy foods, just as we want that for our children. Feeding carbohydrate-loaded junk food to cats leads to several devastating diseases later in life. When a kitten becomes accustomed to nutritious foods during its youth, it will prefer and seek that same level of nutrition throughout its life, leading to better health and longer life span.

Another reason not to feed dry foods to cats and kittens is the very low moisture content of those foods. When we feed our cats foods with little or no water, we cause them to begin to dehydrate. Even though cats eating dry foods drink more water than do cats eating canned, they struggle to maintain normal water balance. This constant low-level dehydration has long-term health consequences for the cat, as we will discuss in later chapters about bladder problems and kidney disease.

If Not Dry Food, Then What?

Semimoist cat foods have been around a long time. Of all of the three forms of pet food, semimoist is the most artificial and least nutritious of all. Because of the tendency of early formulations of this form to cause serious anemia in cats, most veterinarians, including the author, strongly discourage their use. Semimoist foods can be very palatable for cats because of their high sugar content and added flavorings. This taste appeal for cats should not be confused with nutrient content. Semimoist foods are expensive as well as nutritionally empty, making them a very poor choice for feeding cats of any age. For our choice of foods, then, we are left with two good options: various canned foods on the store shelves, and homemade diets. Let's discuss both of these options.

Fortunately, there are a number of commercially available canned cat foods that can be nutritious for the kitten. The key to choosing the right canned food is knowing how to read the labels on the cans (see appendix I). We want plenty of meat in a kitten's diet, and very little or no cereal grains, fruits, and vegetables. Grains, fruits, and vegetables are inexpensive filler ingredients added to cat foods because they appeal to the pet food purchaser. Some manufacturers even add cranberries with the promise that cranberries are good for feline bladder health. This is absurd. In fact, the sugar from cranberries can increase the cat's urine pH, actually contributing to bladder problems. Cats do not need fruit or vegetable matter in their diet; they consume little or no plant material in the wild, and get no benefit from having plant ingredients added to their diets at home.

A typical label on a reasonably healthful canned food will contain meat, meat broth, meat by-products, and a vitamin/mineral supplement for balance. Additional ingredients that are less desirable but usually added in small amounts will include wheat gluten, corn gluten, or soy flour to increase the protein content of the food. Good-quality canned foods will always have higher protein content, from meat, than either dry foods or semimoist foods, and this is a crucially important factor.

Much has been said about the evils of meat by-products in pet foods. Pet food buyers must realize, however, that not all by-products are equal in value as food for cats. For example, beef spleen and lung tissue are considered by-products, and can be an excellent source of nutrition for the obligatory carnivore. Less desirable by-products include meats that are not passed by inspectors as fit for human consumption. Yet, surprisingly, even poor-quality meat by-products can be superior foods for cats compared to cereal grains, because cats living the feral life will inevitably eat plenty of these kinds of by-products as part of their prey captures. No feral cat seeks to add corn, cereal, or vegetable matter, including fruits, to its diet.

To make sure that the meat ingredients in the canned food you select for your kitten are high quality, expect to pay more for the better brands, but avoid even the more expensive products if they contain fruits, vegetables, or grains. They do not contribute essential nutrients for the feline diet. Rather, they are designed to "extend" the product, make it cost-effective to the manufacturer, and appeal to the pet food buyer.

Should You Prepare "Homemade" Meals for Your Kitten?

Contrary to common belief, food from our own tables is not taboo for our kittens and cats. As long as the foods we select to feed are not high in carbohydrate, these additions to the pet's routine diet can be nutritious and enjoyable for your cat. Some experts worry that a kitten or cat eating table food will develop nutritional deficiencies. Certainly, if you feed your cat exclusively from your table, you must have a considerable understanding of how to balance that diet to avoid such problems. Usually an owner just wants to provide the occasional piece of meat from the kitchen, and this is absolutely fine nutritionally.

I personally feed ground meat and bone mixtures with a single vitamin/mineral/

essential fatty acid supplement to my kittens as soon as they are weaned. I have a number of clients who do the same. Our results are uniformly excellent (see appendix II for information about such a diet). Although many kitten owners do not want to feed a homemade diet, those that wish to should merely be careful to address all of their pet's needs as they provide this extra measure of care. It can be done quite successfully and easily.

6

Indoors or Out?
Where Should Your Cat Live?

Aren't Cats Naturally Outdoor Animals?

The cat has become the most numerous and arguably the most popular pet in the United States over the past twenty years. Along with this growing popularity, cats are increasingly kept indoors at least part of the day, and many live entirely indoors all of their lives. Despite this trend, some cat lovers still wonder if the indoor life is really best. Clearly, the cat evolved in the outdoors and, under the best of circumstances, can take very good care of itself there. Once weaned, even fairly young feral kittens are quite successful in finding food and companionship with other cats. Together, colonies of cats find ways to protect themselves from the lethal dangers of most environments, or at least most members of the group manage to do so.

Anyone who owns an indoor cat has seen the fascination the cat has with the goings-on outside the screen doors or windows of the house. The sights and sounds of birds, squirrels, insects, and the like are endlessly entertaining, even mesmerizing for the "captive." In fact, cat-entertainment videos with hours of tape designed to bring the outdoor world inside to the housebound feline are widely available and sell well. It seems inescapable that the cat is in its element outdoors, and longs to be there as much as possible. Without a doubt, the little wild cat in even the tiniest kitten seeks the natural life of the outdoors. This is the reason many cat owners feel conflicted about the almost unanimous advice of cat care specialists to keep pet cats indoors exclusively.

In an age when it is unusual for large special-interest groups to agree on anything, there seems to be one thing upon which all mainstream animal-welfare organizations can agree these days. Pet cats should not roam free outdoors. Groups such as the Humane Society of the United States, the Animal Humane Association, the American Veterinary Medical Association, and the American Association of Feline Practitioners all advise strongly that cats be cared for and enjoyed within the safety of the home. The advantages to this lifestyle are obvious and very compelling.

How Can an "Unnatural" Lifestyle Be Best?

Up to this point, I have argued that to care for cats best, we must understand their wild natures and provide for those natural needs as much as possible. Unfortunately, we humans choose to live today in environments that are almost always exceedingly dangerous places for an outdoor cat. In the past, when automobiles were many fewer in number and many people lived in greater isolation from neighbors and urban centers, cats could live outdoors in relative safety. The dangers from predators of the cat, such as roaming packs of dogs and wildlife species like coyotes, were far less intense. Even the dangers of contracting diseases such as infection with the feline leukemia virus and the feline immunodeficiency virus were less because of the lower population concentration of free-roaming cats and less chance of contact between cats.

Today, most of us live in congested, high-density human populations, with their corresponding concentrations of dogs, wildlife, feline disease organisms, and fast-moving automobiles. Even the wiliest, most sharp-clawed, speedy cat is no match for these new "natural enemies." In my neighborhood in Yorba Linda, large numbers of coyotes live and even occasionally lope down the streets of a town placed squarely in the middle of their ancient range in Southern California. It is not the coyotes' fault that we have taken over hunting grounds that this species has used successfully for thousands of years, but doing so has made life outdoors even in town a death sentence for any cat residing there.

Even when predatory wild species are not a problem for outdoor cats, death from automobile accidents is a huge problem in all suburban and urban areas of this country. As intelligent as cats are, they cannot safely navigate even residential streets, much less high-traffic city thoroughfares. Nothing is more heartbreaking than discovering a beloved kitty lifeless at the side of the road, a victim of a very unequal confrontation between a small animal and a very large machine.

Diseases which can be spread from cat to cat, or even from another species to cats (most notably, but not limited to rabies), lurk unseen in the outdoor world. While we do have effective vaccines for some of these diseases, we cannot provide protection from many others. Cats that roam free to come in direct contact with other cats, dogs, skunks, raccoons, bats, and the like risk immediate injury from fights during these encounters as well as later development of serious, even fatal diseases. Even bite wounds from fights with other cats, while seldom serious or fatal in themselves, can cause infections called abscesses which require veterinary care and can be expensive to treat.

The feline equivalent of AIDS, known as FIV (feline immunodeficiency disease), is most often transmitted through the bite of one cat by another during combat. The feline leukemia virus, FELV, is transmitted from one cat to another through friendly behaviors such as mutual grooming and close association over extended time periods. Once infected, a cat will usually carry either or both of these viruses for life and can infect other cats through contact. The infected cat may develop many serious or fatal consequences of these lingering viral infections later in life.

Today, responsible cat ownership starts with adapting the kitten to life inside the home. Cats raised indoors enjoy the pleasures of that lifestyle. What cat does not enjoy an afternoon nap on a family member's bed or comfy family room sofa? Where else but in the house can the cat keep track of all the goings-on of the family? What thinking feline doesn't love the computer, with its warmth and soft hum, as a fabulous place to lounge and supervise the mysterious work that humans do there? Cats, like people, are creatures of habit. If their habit is living indoors, they will be comfortable, secure, and happy there.

When Can I Take My Cat Outdoors?

Even though I have argued for the necessity of keeping cats and kittens indoors as a routine, there are circumstances where a cat can safely spend time outside the home. Getting out can be fun for everyone, especially if the kitten takes trips on a regular basis and becomes comfortable with strange sights, sounds, and people. Almost every kitten can be harness- and leash-trained at eight to twelve weeks of age (or even older), and will walk on a leash attached to the harness much as a dog would. Cats should not be walked on a leash attached to a collar (rather than a harness) because of the possibility of choking, harm to the trachea at the front of the neck, or escape when the collar slips off the cat's neck during any struggle.

With your kitten safely attached to you, you can walk outside in areas where other animals are not likely to visit. Cats on a leash are in danger, just as small dogs are, when they encounter big dogs or other cats during the walk. When strange cats and dogs meet each other face to face, aggressive behavior may ignite between them without warning.

In my opinion, there is no harm in allowing your leashed cat to spend time in the grass and smelling the flowers in your garden, or to explore safe areas around the neighborhood. Many of my clients will even take their cats, on harness and leash, to pet stores that allow pets inside.

My clients often ask whether these trips to the outdoors will make the indoor cat long to roam free outdoors. Some worry that the ordinarily happy house cat will develop the desire to dash through an open door the first chance that presents itself. I have never heard of such a change in a cat's previous contentment with the indoor life. I believe this is because trips outdoors in the security of the owner's presence are perceived very differently in the cat's mind than the insecurity of being outdoors alone. As long as the indoor cat does not spend time outside by itself, it is quite unlikely to become comfortable with being outdoors without having its favorite people nearby.

A note of caution: If you like to have a collar on your kitten's neck to carry identification tags in the case of accidental escape from the house, be sure to use a "breakaway" or "safety-type" collar. This kind of collar is specially designed so that it will give way and allow the cat to free itself if the collar becomes hooked or tangled in a fence or other object while on the cat. This will prevent the tragedy of finding a cat strangled by its collar. When purchasing such a collar, test it to see whether it opens easily, but not so easily that your pet will pop it open in everyday wear.

The idea is to have fun and enjoy your new kitten. Once your kitten has been weaned and taken from the security of living with its mom, you become the sole source of protection for the little one. By all means, allow your kitten to grow emotionally and become well socialized through a wide variety of encounters with the world, inside and outside the home. Never forget, though, that you and you alone are responsible for your kitten's physical safety.

The Microchip: A Better Way to Safeguard Your Cat

Better than a collar and ID tag for identifying your cat should it become lost outside the house is the microchip. Microchips are tiny electronic devices that carry an identification number unique to the cat in which they are implanted. Special scanners can read this number, and locate the cat's owners through registration of this number.

When a lost cat is brought to my clinic, I always scan the area of the animal over the shoulders and along the backbone. This is the area where chips are placed using a hypodermic needle. If I find a chip is present, and the cat does not belong to one of our own clients, we contact the registry to learn the owner's name and contact information. Many a lost cat has found its way home by means of its microchip. Unlike tags on collars, a microchip cannot be lost during the cat's travels, ensuring that the cat *and* its identification will arrive together at a site where the chip can be scanned. Almost all veterinarians and shelters have microchip scanners. I strongly recommend that my clients consider this very effective form of identifying their cats and getting them home if they are lost. Be sure to provide the registration company with up-to-date contact information if you move or the cat obtains a new owner.

7

Does Your Kitten Have Parasites?

What Are Parasites?

All animals, including humans, are susceptible to infestation with certain species of parasitic organisms. Parasites invade the organs of the host animal and live off the nutrition that the host takes in. They are capable of depriving the host of needed nutrients and can even interfere with important organ function. We see this when intestinal worms block the gastrointestinal tract, blood parasites cause red blood cells to be destroyed, or heartworms cause the lungs or heart to become diseased. All kittens are susceptible to a wide variety of parasites, and it is important to work with your veterinarian to make sure that your kitten gets the right dewormers to keep it free of parasite-caused disease.

How Do I Know If My Kitten Has Parasites?

We can assume that all young kittens will have at least some parasites living inside or on the outside of their bodies. Roundworms are an extremely common internal parasite in kittens as young as four to six weeks of age. Other types, such as coccidia (a type of very small, one-cell parasite called a protozoan) also occur frequently in young cats. Some kittens that have parasites show signs of infestation, such as diarrhea, vomiting, weight loss, weakness, or dull, scruffy coat. Others do not show these signs, even though they have small numbers of parasites living within their bodies.

Your veterinarian may want to perform a test known as a *fecal exam* on the stool that your kitten produces to see if there are eggs or other stages of internal parasites being eliminated from the kitten's body. With information from a fecal exam, your veterinarian can decide what kinds of dewormers to use to rid your kitten of these parasites. Even if the fecal exam does not show the direct evidence of parasites, your veterinarian will probably prescribe a broad-spectrum dewormer just to make sure that parasites aren't a problem for your growing baby. External parasites are usually more easily identified by visual inspection and good drugs are available for eliminating them. Let's discuss the more common parasites your kitten may have:

Internal Parasites (Endoparasites)

ROUNDWORMS

(see www.marvistavet.com/html/body_roundworms_in_cats___kittens.html)

Roundworms are the most common type of parasite that affects kittens. This is because kittens can become infested with the larvae (young stage) of this parasite when they nurse from their mother. The female cat (called a *queen*) will often have these larval stages of the roundworm within her body tissues as a result of infestation when she herself was a kitten. When she gives birth to her litter, these young roundworms leave her tissues and travel into the milk she produces. When the kittens nurse, the roundworm larvae pass to the kittens.

From the gastrointestinal tract of the kitten, the roundworm larvae burrow into the lining of the intestines and migrate to many different tissues of the infant's body. Some of these larvae will go to the kitten's lungs and be coughed up into the youngster's throat and swallowed. Once again in the gastrointestinal tract, these larvae will mature to adults where they can cause serious disease. They reproduce and shed eggs into the kitten's feces. When the feces pass to the outside, the worm larvae will develop further and can infest other cats after a period of additional development.

Cats can also develop roundworm infestations if they eat meat from another animal, such as a squirrel or mouse, that has roundworm larvae in its tissues. Fortunately, there are a number of very effective dewormers that will rid your kitten of this parasite. Your veterinarian may suggest more than one treatment with a dewormer, spaced a few weeks apart, to make sure that all of the larvae that are traveling within your kitten's body are killed.

There is another reason to keep your kitten free of roundworms. Roundworms from both dogs and cats can cause a type of human disease, particularly in children, called *visceral larval migrans* (see www.emedicine.com/ped/topic2407.htm). This happens when children contact canine or feline feces that have infective roundworm larvae. Keeping children out of sandboxes and gardens where pets may use these areas as litter boxes is an important part of preventing this disease. Keeping your kitten free of parasites and indoors are important measures as well.

TAPEWORMS
(see www.marvistavet.com/html/body_tapeworm.html)

Cats of almost all ages can have tapeworms residing in their intestines. The cat becomes infested when it inadvertently eats a flea containing the infective larvae of the worm. Cats that do not have fleas cannot become hosts for tapeworms, so good flea control of the kitten and its environment is the best way to control this kind of parasite. You will know your kitten has tapeworms when you see small, ricelike white flecks in the kitten's stool. Sometimes the "grain" of rice will even move as it leaves the cat's body during a bowel movement.

After a short time outside the cat's body, the tapeworm segment dries out and becomes immobile, but it still looks much like a grain of rice. It is really a single segment of the much longer tapeworm that remains inside the cat. The segment contains many tapeworm eggs that will break free of the segment coating and begin to mature in the environment. When a flea ingests the egg, the larvae continue to develop. When the cat eats the flea containing the maturing tapeworm, the life cycle continues inside the kitten's intestines.

Tapewom infestation seldom causes the same kind or seriousness of disease in the kitten or cat that the other internal parasites do. Still, it is important to keep your kitten parasite free. Start by making sure your little one is protected from fleas at all times (see below). If you do see the characteristic tapeworm segments around the kitten's rectum or in its stool, check with your veterinarian for an effective tapeworm dewormer, and ask for advice about a good flea-control medication at the same time.

COCCIDIA

(see www.marvistavet.com/html/body_coccidia.html)

Coccidia are tiny, one-celled parasites of the gastrointestinal tract of dogs and cats. The kitten picks up this disease from oral contact with coccidia-containing feces deposited by another infected dog or cat. Once in the gastrointestinal tract, the coccidia multiply rapidly and begin to cause inflammation in the intestinal tissues. Serious, even bloody diarrhea is typical of heavy coccidia infestations in a young cat. Young cats become rapidly ill when they lose fluids and electrolytes during this disease process. It is even possible for a kitten to die from severe coccidian parasitism.

A fecal exam will usually show your veterinarian if coccidia are present in your kitten. Drugs for this disease stop the reproduction of the organism and allow the kitten's immune system to overthrow the infestation. If your kitten is debilitated from this disease, other types of supportive care may be needed, as advised by your veterinarian.

GIARDIA

(see www.sniksnak.com/cathealth/giardiasis.html)

Like coccidia, giardia is a one-celled parasite that lives in the gastrointestinal tract of many different hosts. In kittens and some cats, this parasite can cause serious diarrhea. The organism can pass from one infected cat to another very quickly, usually through drinking water contaminated by an already-infected animal (dogs and humans can get this parasite, too) or from contact with contaminated feces. If a fecal exam shows the organism in your kitten's stool, or if the signs of disease suggest this organism is present even if a fecal exam is negative for giardia, your veterinarian will prescribe an effective drug to rid your kitten of these disease-causing microorganisms. There is a vaccine available against this parasite but it is not widely used because of the ease of treating this parasitic condition compared to the risks of overvaccination of cats (see chapter 10 for more information on this).

HEARTWORMS

(see www.sniksnak.com/cathealth/heartworms.html)

Most cat owners would be surprised to learn that cats, like dogs, *can* get heartworms and the secondary disease in the heart and lungs that they cause. Just as in dogs, cats can develop an infestation with heartworms when a mosquito carrying the infective stage of the heartworm larvae injects those larvae into the cat during a bite. Unlike the dog, the cat is not a good host for the heartworm, so only a small percentage of cats that receive larvae will actually get adult worms in their hearts and lungs.

Even though feline heartworm infestation is rare in most parts of the world, this disease can be very serious in cats. Fortunately, even when it does occur, full-blown heartworm disease does not occur in kittens. This is because the life cycle of the worm in the cat takes several months from the time of injection by the mosquito until the mature worms appear in the heart and lungs. At diagnosis, most cats are fully adult.

Feline heartworm disease is most common in areas like the southeastern United States, where heartworm disease is common in dogs. Heartworm disease occurs in cats at about 10 percent of the rate it occurs in the dogs in the same area. Because of this lower rate, most veterinarians do not recommend dosing cats with daily heartworm preventive medication in areas where heartworms are not a significant problem in dogs. Be sure to check with your cat's own veterinarian to find out if you should consider using such a preventive for your particular cat.

The symptoms of heartworms in cats are somewhat similar to the symptoms in dogs, but not identical. Also, there is no good treatment for ridding the cat of heartworms once they are present. Fortunately, this disease is self-limiting in the cat because it is a poor host for the parasite. That is, heartworms will generally die off in about two years in most infected cats. Before this happens, veterinarians treat the affected cat with anti-inflammatory medications to minimize the allergic reactions the worms can cause. Heartworm disease in the cat causes lung disease as a primary problem. A cat with chronic cough should be tested for heartworms, even in geographic areas where the disease is not common in dogs.

External Parasites (Ectoparasites)

EAR MITES
(see www.cah.com/library/earmite.html)

Feline ear mites are tiny, crablike insects, related to spiders, which thrive in the ears of cats. Over time, these parasites cause serious inflammation in affected ears, resulting in a dark, powdery discharge. Often, a kitten with ear mites will shake its ears vigorously or rub and scratch at its ears. Clearly, these parasites cause lots of discomfort. They can spread rapidly from one cat to another, and even to dogs in the household. Left untreated, ear mites can cause serious damage to the fragile structures within the ear, and can even cause the eardrum to rupture. Mite infestation can also make it easier for bacteria and fungus to infect the ear, causing even more damage and discomfort.

Your veterinarian can easily diagnose this problem by taking a swab from your kitten's ears and examining the discharge under a microscope. If possible, ask to see the mites under the scope yourself. It is an astonishing sight to see these little bugs up close. Once it is certain that the problem is ear mites, your veterinarian will want to thoroughly clean the infested ears and apply or inject a medication to kill the remaining mites. Be sure to follow the protocol your veterinarian prescribes.

MANGE MITES
(see www.marvistavet.com/html/body_sarcoptic_mange.html)

The parasitic mites that cause the skin disease known as mange are related to the spiderlike creatures that infect the ears of cats (see Ear Mites). Like ear mites, they cause intense itchy discomfort for the kitten or cat. Mange mites burrow into the layers of the cat's or kitten's skin, causing obvious scaly, crusty areas, usually on the head of the cat. Your veterinarian will diagnose this disease by scraping an affected area and looking for the mite under the microscope. Sometimes it can be very difficult to find the mites if they have burrowed very deeply into the cat's skin. In such a case, a skin biopsy may be necessary for diagnosis. There are different types of treatment for mange, from injections to dips, but all are effective in dealing with this group of parasites.

Even though mange can be self-limiting over a long enough period of time, it is extremely uncomfortable for the affected cat, and can even spread to other animals and even humans. Prompt diagnosis and treatment is an absolute must. Mange can mimic several other parasitic skin diseases and even some nonparasitic conditions. See your veterinarian to sort these conditions out at the first sign of nonhealing skin rash on your kitten or cat.

FLEAS
(see www.fabcats.org/fleacontrol.html)

Everyone knows what fleas are. They are a problem parasite for virtually all mammals, and were responsible for the deaths of millions of humans during the Middle Ages when the black plague spread throughout Europe. In those unenlightened times, almost all homes were overrun with flea-ridden rats. The fleas carried the plague bacterium and readily transmitted that bacterium to humans.

Today, fleas are much less likely to carry lethal disease, but controlling them is extremely important to the health of kittens and cats. Not only do fleas cause serious skin irritation and allergic reactions in cats, they can cause significant loss of red blood cells leading to anemia in kittens if there are enough fleas on one youngster. Fleas also carry the larvae of the tapeworm, which can mature into an adult worm in the cat if the infected flea is inadvertently eaten by the cat or kitten.

In recent years, the pharmaceutical industry has introduced several excellent flea control products for use on cats and dogs. Even in areas where fleas flourish through all seasons, such as the southern and western parts of the United States, it is now possible to protect kittens and cats from flea infestation virtually year-round. These products are generally applied topically to the cat's skin, providing weeks of flea-free living for pets and their humans. Be sure to ask your veterinarian for advice about what product to use and the frequency of use for your kitten or cat.

RINGWORM
(see www.fabcats.org/ringworm.html)

Ringworm is not really a type of worm, it is a fungus (called a *dermatophyte*) that infects the skin of many animals, cats and humans included. Areas of fungal growth on the cat often appear to be crusty rings, or circular bald spots, at least at first. The spores of the fungus spread to the cat from other animals or the ground or other contaminated surfaces. Ringworm spores are very resistant to environmental conditions, and can live dormant for very long periods in the home or outdoors. Infected cats or dogs readily spread this parasite to other animals, even people.

Typically, kittens are more susceptible to developing ringworm disease than are adult cats. This is most likely because the immune system of the kitten is less well developed and vigilant than that of older cats. Even so, when adult cats contact a large number of ringworm organisms, they, too, can show the classic circular, scaly areas of hair loss so typical of this infection.

Ironically, ringworm is a self-limiting disease in all but the most immune-depressed animals. Left untreated, this disease will spread over a large area of the cat or kitten's ears, head, body, and feet before the immune system begins to fight back, killing the fungal organisms and self-curing the condition. Even so, because the cat can become very uncomfortable and serve as a source of infection for other animals and humans, this parasite should be treated immediately when it is detected.

There are a number of orally taken drugs that are effective against ringworm. There are also a number of antifungal creams that can be used on the affected areas of the cat's skin to stop the spread of the fungus on the kitten or cat. Perhaps the best method of treatment, however, is the oldest method. Lime sulphur dip is an extremely effective, inexpensive, and nontoxic treatment for ringworm in cats.

Generally, I recommend dipping the affected cat or kitten in a dilute solution (1 part dip to 15 parts water) of lime sulphur every other day for four dips in total. Be sure to protect the cat's eyes from the dip. Although the dip has a strong smell of rotten eggs (sulphur is the molecule that causes rotting eggs to smell as they do), the speed with which this treatment works and the lack of adverse effects in the treated cats makes it my favorite treatment for ringworm in cats of all ages. I have even used this method in kittens as young as six weeks.

TICKS
(see www.thepetprofessor.com/articles/article.aspx?id=363)

Ticks are parasites that are related to spiders. Like fleas, they feed on the blood of mammals but, unlike fleas that hop on and off the host animal, ticks attach permanently to the host for long periods. Cats that live entirely indoors have no exposure to the wooded outdoor habitat of the tick, so they rarely acquire these parasites.

Ticks can transmit serious bacterial diseases such as Lyme disease and Rocky Mountain spotted fever. They can also cause uncomfortable skin irritation and inflammation in the infested cat. Once an attached tick begins to suck blood from a cat, it will appear to be a dark, blisterlike bump on the skin. If you are inexperienced in safely removing ticks from a pet, see your veterinarian for this. It is important to avoid leaving the mouth parts of the tick in the cat's skin when it is removed, as these pieces of tick will continue to irritate and can become infected.

Some of the newer topical flea-preventive products also protect against the attachment of ticks to a pet's skin. If you live in an area where ticks are plentiful in the outdoors, and you allow your kitten or cat to spend time outside the house, check with your veterinarian about how to protect your pet from this parasite.

We have discussed the most common parasites of the cat. Kittens are the most likely hosts for most of these, because they have reduced immune defenses in their young growing bodies. Careful watchfulness of your kitten's skin and hair coat health, as well as its body weight, appetite, and general activity level, will allow you to notice changes that may signal infestation by parasites. Kittens are so much fun to observe and play with, this will be easy!

8

Can My Kitten Get a Cold or the Flu?

Everyone knows how often human infants and young children become ill with virus-caused diseases. Ask any day-care center worker or kindergarten teacher about this, and you will learn that epidemics of colds and flu sweep through such groups of youngsters regularly. Even children who do not attend school or day care get their share of such troubling illnesses. Kittens are much like human children in this respect.

Young animals have immature immune systems with limited preexisting defenses against the viruses that are everywhere in the environment. Diseases that are caused by bacteria can also create serious problems for youngsters of all species. Viral and bacterial infections may even spread to adult cats in the household from the infected kitten. Let's discuss the most important of these infectious diseases.

Feline Herpesvirus (Rhinotracheitis)

(see www.animalhealthchannel.com/rhinotracheitis/)

Sometimes called "feline flu," herpesvirus infection is the most common of the several types of upper respiratory infections (URI) affecting cats. Although this virus can cause disease in cats of all ages, we see herpesvirus most often in kittens. The herpesvirus that cats get cannot infect humans, but it is highly transmissible to other susceptible cats. Secretions from the infected cat's mouth, eyes, or nose carry live virus to other animals, and the virus also spreads readily from kitten to kitten on contaminated clothing, toys, or other inanimate objects.

The kitten with herpesvirus infection appears to have a bad head cold. Sneezing, nasal discharge, red watery eyes, and loss of appetite are all classic signs of this infection. In some kittens, the virus will infect the deep tissues of the eyes and cause serious damage to the cornea, the clear part at the front of the eyeball. Also, left untreated, herpesvirus infection can become chronic (long-lasting) in a kitten, persisting into adulthood and even the entire life span of the cat. If your kitten shows signs of this kind of disease, it is important to seek a veterinarian's care right away to avoid serious complications.

Although antibiotics aren't thought to be effective against viruses, they are quite helpful in cats with herpesvirus disease. This is probably because most cats with virus-caused conditions also contract secondary bacterial infections, and the antibiotics help to fight these bacterial complications. Also, antibiotics may have anti-inflammatory effects in addition to their antibacterial effects, and they may assist in relieving the discomfort of the kitten's "cold." *Nebulizing* (sometimes called *vaporizing*) an infected kitten is extremely helpful when the signs of disease are severe and the kitten is having difficulty breathing.

Nebulizing consists of placing the kitten in the presence of warm steam that helps to relieve the congested nasal passages and lungs. I have my clients nebulize their kittens at home, just as they might nebulize a child with a very stuffed-up nose, several times per day until the congestion is relieved (human nebulizers can be easily adapted for the kitten or cat). This usually takes two to three days. It is well worth the time and effort. I usually add an antibiotic to the nebulization fluid to assist the fight against the secondary bacterial complications we see.

Sometimes the kitten with URI will stop eating because it cannot smell its food when its sense of smell is reduced by congestion. Kittens should not be allowed to go without food for more than a day at a time. If your kitten won't eat for longer than this, you will need to hand-feed it some easy-to-eat foods until its appetite returns. I have found that meat baby foods are excellent for this purpose. They are very tasty to cats (lamb baby food has the strongest smell and taste), and caretakers can place the soft meat into the kitten's mouth with a spoon, tongue depressor, or syringe, usually without difficulty. By themselves, meat baby foods are not complete and balanced, but for short periods of time (a few days), there is no harm in feeding them to keep the kitten from losing weight and body condition. As the congestion in its nose resolves with treatment, the kitten will start eating on its own again.

If your veterinarian believes that a herpesvirus is causing your kitten's upper respiratory infection, he or she may also prescribe L-lysine powder to add to your little one's food regularly. L-lysine is an amino acid that has virus-suppressing activity against herpes and can help to control the spread of the virus in the cat's body. Most kittens treated early in the course of this infection can recover completely, but a percentage will carry the virus for long periods, even for a lifetime. Such chronic "carriers" are able to shed the virus and infect other cats, even when the carrier is not acting ill at all.

Herpesvirus is one of the viral diseases that we can vaccinate against. The core vaccine known as the "three-way" contains components that protect against most herpesvirus infections, as well as calicivirus and panleukopenia (feline distemper) virus. It is very important that the young kitten begin to receive vaccination with the "three-way" vaccine at about eight weeks of age, and then receive boosters every three weeks or so thereafter for a total of about three vaccinations. Talk with your veterinarian about the schedule of vaccinations that is right for your kitten.

Feline Calicivirus

(see www.animalhealthchannel.com/calicivirus/)

Calicivirus is the second most common cause of upper respiratory infection in young cats. It causes disease that appears to be very much like herpesvirus infection and it is spread in the same way. Your veterinarian can take a swab from inside of your kitten's eyelids to test for the specific virus that is causing your cat's "cold" symptoms. This is usually done, however, only if your veterinarian wishes to discern between herpes and calicivirus to decide whether to add special treatment against herpes.

Usually, kittens with calicivirus infection should be treated much the same as those with any of the other URI-causing agents. This will consist of antibiotics and TLC such as nebulization and hand-feeding if necessary (see page 59). Like herpesvirus infections, calicivirus can cause ulcers in the mouth and nose of the kitten, with additional discomfort. Calicivirus is less likely to cause serious damage to the globe of the eye, and less likely to become a chronic infection than herpesvirus. Even so, you must seek veterinary help whenever your kitten develops even early signs of a cold.

Most calicivirus, like herpesvirus, can be prevented by vaccination of your young healthy kitten with a series of three-way vaccinations followed by annual boosters. Ask your veterinarian about this protection as soon as you get your new kitten.

Chlamydia

(see www.animalhealthchannel.com/felinechlamydiosis/diagnosis.shtml#treatment and www.users.bigpond.com/drdavid/zithromax.htm)

Unlike the other two common causes of URI, herpesvirus and calicivirus, chlamydia is a bacterium that can infect animals besides cats. This bacteria causes inflammation of the soft tissues of the eye, called the *conjunctiva*. Kittens with chalmydia infection typically have puffy, red eyes with a watery discharge. Sneezing and other signs of upper respiratory infection are less common, unless the kitten contracts both chlamydia and one of the other URI agents at the same time. Chlamydia is transmitted from one cat to another through eye or nasal discharges from the infected cat.

Because it is a bacterium, chlamydia is very susceptible to treatment with certain antibiotics. Antibiotic eyedrops are effective in controlling the inflammation in the kitten's eyes, but many veterinarians also recommend additional antibiotics by mouth. Doxycycline or azithromycin are good choices for systemic administration in kittens with chlamydia. Although there is a vaccine for protecting cats against chlamydia infection, it is not universally recommended the way herpesvirus and calicivirus vaccination is. This is because of questions about the effectiveness of the vaccine, the low virulence of this disease, and the relatively low incidence rate of chlamydia in the cat population compared to other diseases. Your veterinarian can discuss with you whether to vaccinate your kitten or not against chlamydia. As we will discuss in chapter 10, more is not necessarily better when it comes to vaccines for cats. Every cat deserves its own customized vaccination protocol based on consideration of many risk factors.

Feline Bordatella

(see www.felinebb.info/index.asp?content=http://www.felinebb.info/main.html)

Bordatella infection in cats is caused by a bacterium identical to or related to the organism that causes kennel cough in dogs. As is true in dogs, the characteristic feature of this infection in cats is a recurrent, deep, throaty cough. No other upper respiratory illness of cats causes this unmistakable sign. Very young kittens that contract bordatella may sicken very quickly and die, almost without warning. Older cats are better able to survive this disease but will need antibiotics to help fight off the infection before they will recover. Fortunately, a wide range of commonly available drugs are effective against the bordatella organism.

Some experts believe that both chlamydia and bordatella are diseases that accompany or take advantage of kittens with a preexisting infection with herpesvirus or calicivirus organisms. This may well be true, but it is clear that bordatella can also cause upper airway disease and pneumonia in cats without other preexisting infections.

Recently, a U.S. biologicals manufacturer introduced a vaccine against the feline bordatella organism, for inoculation of cats and kittens in areas where this infection is common. Although this disease is still uncommon in many parts of the United States and the world, it appears to be spreading. In Southern California, I personally saw very few clear cases of bordatella in cats prior to a year ago. In 2005, however, I am certain I treated several such cases. I do not at present recommend vaccinating for this condition because of my own personal aversion to overvaccination of cats (see chapter 10 for an in-depth discussion of the pros and cons of feline vaccination strategies).

Although I have too little experience with the newly available feline bordatella vaccine to have strong confidence in its safety and effectiveness, I have no reason to doubt it either. I would certainly revise my thinking about routine use of this vaccine if I were to see more cases, especially in young kittens. Ask your veterinarian about the advisability of vaccinating your kitten against feline bordatella.

Feline Panleukopenia

(see www.avma.org/communications/brochures/panleukopenia/panleukopenia_faq.asp)

Panleukopenia (FP), also called *feline distemper,* is a virus in the parvo family (related to the parvo virus that affects puppies and dogs) that causes gastrointestinal diseases in cats. Kittens that are unvaccinated or have had only a partial series of three-way vaccine shots are especially susceptible to infection with this virus. This is because they have poor immune defenses, and panleukopenia virus is a very aggressive, devastating infection for the very young cat. The virus is transmitted from sick cats to healthy ones through contact with any secretions from the sick animal. The virus is very hardy and can remain alive in the environment outside the infected cat for long periods.

The cat with FP seems to have a very bad case of intestinal flu. Vomiting, lack of appetite, diarrhea (often bloody), and listlessness can set in rapidly in a kitten with this disease. Unfortunately, FP can be rapidly fatal, especially if the kitten is only a few weeks old or if supportive treatment is delayed for even a short period. The FP virus depresses the normal white blood cells that fight all kinds of infection and the blood loss from the gastrointestinal tract can cause severe anemia because of low red cell count.

Veterinarians do not see many cases of FP these days. This is because almost all pet cats are vaccinated regularly and the available vaccine is very effective at protecting against this terrible disease. When faced with a kitten suspected of having FP, your veterinarian will recommend intensive supportive care. Such care will consist of antibiotics to deal with secondary bacterial infections, intravenous or subcutaneous fluids to deal with dehydration, and nutritional support until the kitten is well enough to eat on its own. Even with such intensive care, the fatality rate among very young cats with this disease is very high.

The key to dealing with FP successfully is to avoid it altogether by having your new baby vaccinated at regular intervals according to your veterinarian's recommendations. Until your kitten has had at least two vaccines, it is best to isolate the baby from contact with any cats whose vaccination history is unknown.

Feline Leukemia Virus (FeLV)

(see www.vet.cornell.edu/fhc/resources/brochure/felv.html)

FeLV is a very special disease-causing pathogen. It causes not only the suppression of the infected kitten's immune system, but can also actually cause a type of cancer to arise. FeLV is most likely to cause these problems in young cats, although older cats can also become infected and suffer disease as a result. Kittens become infected through contact with other, FeLV-positive cats, including their own mothers. An FeLV-infected female can pass the virus to her kittens prior to their birth, or during the nursing period.

The signs of FeLV disease vary widely from kitten to kitten, and cat to cat. We see the most severe and rapidly fatal disease in youngsters. If a kitten becomes infected early enough in life, it may become seriously depressed and die within days or weeks after infection. Infected kittens may show elevated or depressed white blood cells, anemia, fever, lack of appetite, and similar signs. Older kittens and cats may simply seem mildly ill for long periods before the virus overwhelms the immune system, causing fatal secondary infections with other viruses or bacteria. Some infected cats develop cancers such as leukemia or lymphoma before they become deathly ill. All kittens with vague illness should be tested for FeLV as part of the diagnostic workup of their disease. Similarly, older cats with nonspecific signs of illness and unknown FeLV status should also be tested for this virus.

Because FeLV-infected cats may carry the virus for long periods, even years, without showing significant signs of the virus's presence, it is possible to have infected cats living with susceptible uninfected cats and kittens, without the owner or veterinarian realizing it. Fortunately, FeLV infection is no longer as commonplace as in decades past, perhaps due to the availability of good tests for the virus and a reasonably good vaccine against the virus. Even so, FeLV testing of cats living in groups is a good idea, especially if one or more of the individuals in the group have unknown exposure histories.

Cats that live exclusively indoors alone or among other cats that are not carrying the FeLV virus have no risk of infection. Cats that live outdoors, or spend at least some time outdoors, always risk exposure to the virus carried by strange cats they may contact there. Cats that spend time outdoors unsupervised should be tested for FeLV to be certain they are FeLV-negative and then vaccinated against this infection according to the recommendations of the cat's veterinarian. FeLV vaccination is not without risk (see chapter 10). If at all possible, the best way to prevent infection and illness from FeLV is to keep your FeLV-negative cat or cats indoors and away from potential exposure to FeLV-positive cats outside.

Feline Immunodeficiency Virus (FIV)

(see www.vet.cornell.edu/fhc/resources/brochure/fiv.html)

FIV, also known as feline AIDS, is related to the FeLV virus but is very different from FeLV in many ways. FeLV is transmitted from cat to cat through close contact, usually prolonged close contact. FIV is transmitted usually through a bite from an infected cat through virus-containing saliva. Thus, FeLV is known as "a disease of *friendly* cats," whereas FIV is "a disease of *unfriendly* cats." Typically, the FIV-infected cat is an older adult, not a youngster, usually a male that spends considerable time outdoors. There have been cases of kittens born to FIV-infected females and infected during the birth process or during nursing, but such cases are rare compared to the much more common scenario of the older cat infected through bite wounds during fights with other cats.

Like FeLV infection, FIV infection can remain dormant for long periods without causing disease in the infected cat. In some cases, the first signs of FIV may be a severe inflammation of the gums. Feline immunodeficiency virus, as the name suggests, causes depression of the infected cat's own immune system, with other secondary infections taking hold much more easily in the cat carrying the virus. Once a cat begins to be affected by this virus, a lingering ill health results. As in the case of FeLV, cats that seem to be ill without obvious cause and opportunity for exposure should be tested for this infection. Supportive care may help the FIV-positive cat to regain some quality of life, but death from some overwhelming viral or bacterial secondary infection is likely, unfortunately. FIV has also been associated with a form of often-severe gum disease, stomatitis. FIV-associated stomatitis is treated with antibiotics and by keeping the mouth as clean and pain free as possible. Removal of inflammatory tissue in the mouth with a laser may be helpful in some cases. (See chapter 19 for more about gum disease.) Steroids and other immune-system-suppressing drugs are not used to manage this aspect of FIV infection.

An FIV vaccine is now available to prevent this infection. Its use is, however, somewhat controversial because a vaccinated cat will always test positive for FIV after it has been vaccinated. Some veterinarians fear that this false-positive state caused by the vaccine will confuse any attempt to determine a cat's true FIV status later in its life. This would certainly be a problem if a vaccinated cat changes homes without its vaccination record, becomes ill, and is then tested for FIV as part of a diagnostic workup. Still, vaccination provides a way to protect the outdoor cat from contracting this virus. As with FeLV, the best way to protect your kitten or cat from the diseases caused by FIV is to keep it indoors throughout its life. Discuss with your veterinarian whether your pet's risk factors justify vaccinating with the FIV vaccine.

Rabies

(see www.peteducation.com/article.cfm?cls=1&cat=1316&articleid=346)

Rabies is a viral disease that can infect a very wide range of animals, including cats, dogs, people, and many wildlife species. In all areas of the world, wild animals provide the reservoir that harbors and perpetuates the existence of the virus, while livestock, pets, and humans are incidental hosts for this deadly pathogen. Fortunately, due to widespread use of highly effective dog and cat vaccines against rabies, this disease is exceeding rare in pets in the United States and most parts of Europe, even in countries where wild animals are known to be infected.

Rabies is a uniformly fatal infection for pets and humans once invasion by the virus has progressed within the animal body much beyond the initial exposure through saliva containing the virus. A bite from an infected animal is the most common route of exposure. Obviously, indoor cats have a very low likelihood of being bitten by a carrier species such as a rabid bat, skunk, raccoon, or fox. Fortunately, squirrels and rabbits are not susceptible so are not a threat for infecting even the outdoor cat.

Several very effective rabies vaccines are available today, and your veterinarian is your best source of information about which of these is the best choice for your kitten or cat, and how often this vaccination is needed given your pet's particular risk factors.

9

FIP—An Enigma Wrapped in a Riddle

Feline Infectious Peritonitis

(see www.sniksnak.com/cathealth/fip.html and
www.winnfelinehealth.org/health/FIP.html)

Feline infectious peritonitis, also known as FIP, is perhaps the most frustrating and devastating of all feline diseases. Although we have known of its existence and its viral cause for decades, there seems so much that we still do not know about this elusive killer of cats. FIP is caused by a pathogenic virus in the coronavirus family. Ironically, the FIP disease-causing organism is a mutant of a very common, relatively non-pathogenic coronavirus that inhabits the gastrointestinal tract of many cats.

At present, we do not understand the sequence of events that causes or allows the transformation of the "benign" gastrointestinal virus to the very virulent pathogen that manifests as fatal FIP. Although the majority of all pet cats will carry the benign coronavirus as kittens after exposure from their mother or other cats, most of these exposed cats will never develop FIP. Usually, the cat's immune system will defeat the gastrointestinal infection by the nonpathogenic coronavirus in a matter of weeks.

In some of these coronavirus-infected cats, however, the virus mutates and enters the body to create a derangement within the kitten or cat's own immune system. The animal's immune defenses literally go wild, causing severe damage and inflammation within some of the vital organ systems. Thus, even though FIP is initiated by a virus, the ultimate body system damage is due to the cat's own immune reaction. That is, FIP is a disease in which the cat's own body becomes "highjacked" by the virus and unwittingly participates in its own destruction.

We see two different types of feline infectious peritonitis: "wet" FIP and "dry" FIP. Cats with wet FIP typically have fluid accumulation in their abdomens or chests, or sometimes in both areas of the body. Fluid accumulation in the chest causes breathing difficulty and accumulation in the abdomen causes a very potbellied appearance. This fluid is evidence of the severe inflammation that is occurring when the virus excites the cat's immune defenses. Unfortunately, this extreme excitation of the immune system is ineffective in eliminating the virus from the cat's body. Rather than being helpful in controlling and eliminating this virus, the immune system's response becomes the fatal aspect of this disease.

So-called dry FIP is different from the wet form in that we do not see fluids accumulating in the chest or abdomen of kittens and cats with this form of the disease. Even so, dry FIP is a disease of immune system overreaction, just as wet FIP is. The lymph tissues, bone marrow, kidneys, eyes, and liver are the organs most directly affected by both forms of FIP, but the central nervous system may also become involved, especially in the dry form of the disease.

What Are the Signs of FIP?

The cat with FIP is usually a young cat under three years of age, although the disease has been seen in much older cats on rare occasions. Young kittens seem especially predisposed to this disease. Early signs of FIP may be quite subtle. An affected cat may simply lose its appetite over a period of days, or may become lethargic and quiet. As the disease progresses, the tissues of the skin may become a yellow color (jaundice) as liver involvement increases. In the wet form, the affected cat will begin to breathe very deeply and rapidly, or gasp for air. The abdomen will become visibly distended with fluid. Kittens that reach this point will die very quickly, but older cats may linger for weeks or more, especially with intensive care treatment.

How Do We Diagnose FIP?

Diagnosing FIP in a sick cat can be difficult. This is because the early signs of illness in the cat are quite nonspecific and we lack a good test for FIP that can be used when a kitten or cat first begins to act sick. The cat with early FIP is usually just a little bit "off," maybe not eating well or starting to be a little lethargic. Perhaps it is running a fever, perhaps not. At this stage, FIP mimics so many other infectious diseases that it is virtually impossible to distinguish between them all without a reliable, specific laboratory test.

One of the best tests available today for the diagnosis of FIP is the FIP PCR (polymerase chain reaction) test. There are other tests available as diagnostic for FIP infection in the cat, but some are, in fact, unreliable and even misleading. The most familiar of these nonspecific tests is the FeCoV (feline coronavirus) test. This assay "looks" for antibody in the cat's system against the gastrointestinal (GI) coronavirus, not the mutated FIP virus. Results of the FeCoV report the relative amount of GI coronavirus antibody that exists in the cat's bloodstream when the sample was drawn. Because so many kittens and cats in the general population have been exposed to and transiently infected with the coronavirus, a great many of them will have positive FeCoV antibody levels with no disease at all.

Information from the FeCoV is of little diagnostic help except in those cats with a number of other key clinical and laboratory red flags signaling FIP. These include chronic poor appetite, lethargy, and weight loss in the face of aggressive supportive care, combined with recurring fever that is not controlled with antibiotics. The astute clinician also looks for an elevated white blood cell count, low red blood cell count (anemia), high liver enzyme levels, elevated total protein due to elevated globulin fraction of the serum proteins, and, of course, development of abdominal and/or chest fluid, in the case of wet FIP.

If the FeCoV is high in the presence of several or all of these other signs, then a presumptive diagnosis of FIP is possible. Unfortunately, veterinarians who are not familiar with the limitations of the FeCoV in diagnosing FIP may jump to the conclusion of FIP in a kitten or cat that has a positive FeCoV titer but is suffering from some other, much more treatable disease. In this way, the FeCoV may be more of a hindrance to diagnosis than a genuine help.

Another test that is available for the diagnosis of FIP is the B7 antibody test. Less commonly used than the FeCoV test, the B7 antibody assay has been criticized by experts who study FIP. These experts believe that the test does not accurately target and identify antibodies to a portion of the mutated FIP virus and fails to provide any genuinely helpful information about the presence of this pathogen in the cat's system. Although the B7 antibody test has been commercially available for decades, its advocates have been unable to dispel the experts' misgivings about it.

As I mentioned above, the FIP PCR test does provide reliable information about the presence of the FIP virus (not just the GI coronavirus) in a sick kitten or cat. This test uses abdominal fluid, chest fluid, or a sample of infected tissue to isolate and replicate a millionfold the DNA of the FIP virus. The greatest limitation of this test is that it cannot be performed on a blood sample from a cat. Thus, the patient with no available fluids or infected tissue samples (that is, the cat with early FIP) cannot be PCR-tested for FIP. The clinician who must diagnose a feline patient with the early general signs of FIP and countless other diseases of young cats faces a significant challenge. It is the responsibility of veterinarians who deal with feline patients to have an up-to-date understanding of the scientific information about FIP, its diagnosis, and helpful treatment strategies.

Is There a Treatment?

Unfortunately, there is at present no curative treatment for FIP. Supportive treatment in the form of fluid therapy, forced nutrition, antibiotics to stave off secondary bacterial infections, and immune suppressive drugs such as glucocorticoids (steroids) may reduce an affected cat's discomfort and improve the overall quality and length of its life. Some experts recommend the use of drugs such as interferon, with mixed results. The sad reality is that FIP is still nearly 100 percent fatal, even in cats that receive the most aggressive treatment. Until we know more about how and why the mild-mannered GI coronavirus mutates in some cats into a devastating pathogen, and why the cat's immune system subsequently becomes an out-of-control killing machine, we are unlikely to find the cure for this mysterious disease.

How Do We Prevent FIP?

A vaccine is commercially available for vaccinating healthy cats against FIP. Mired in controversy since its introduction a decade ago, this vaccine was considered ineffective at best and potentially disease-causing at worst. Recent studies suggest that the FIP vaccine does not, in fact, cause illness in cats, but experts still debate its effectiveness in preventing disease. Because FIP is not a purely infectious disease in the strict sense, understanding it and preventing it presents complex problems not seen with diseases like herpesvirus infection and panleukopenia. I am strongly against overvaccination of my patients, and I require very convincing evidence of a vaccine's safety and effectiveness before I will use it in my feline practice. I do not routinely recommend vaccination of kittens and cats with the currently available vaccine.

Recently, scientists at the University of California–Davis have shown that there is a probable genetic component to feline infectious peritonitis. That is, a cat's genes may well make it more or less likely to contract this disease. This finding is an important one, but not at all surprising. We know that most cats that become infected with the GI coronavirus do not ultimately develop FIP. We also know that it does not spread "horizontally" to any great degree. That is, it is not transmitted from sick cats to healthy cats the way most other infectious diseases are. While the GI coronavirus does pass from cat to cat, usually via contact with virus-contaminated feces, the fatal FIP virus does not appear to do this to any extent. Instead, some as yet unknown trigger in only some cats allows or causes the GI coronavirus to transform into the pathogenic FIP virus, invade the cat, and wreak havoc.

For many observers of this enigmatic disease, including myself, it has seemed clear for some time that an individual cat's unique genetic makeup must play an important role in this uncertain and unpredictable outcome. Further, we know that the cat's own immune surveillance and attack system is a crucial element in the damage done during the course of this disease. The reactivity of this system is genetically programmed, like all other aspects of the body's function. It should come as no surprise, then, that certain cats would have innate susceptibility or resistance to this terrible feline plague.

If this is the case, then, scientists may be able to study families of highly susceptible cats in an attempt to better understand the nature of FIP. Perhaps such studies will yield answers about how to design good early diagnostic tests, maybe even DNA tests, that would allow veterinarians to check young kittens for susceptibility long before they become ill. Research with genetically susceptible families of cats could even yield clues about effective treatments, and better preventive tools. Like all feline disease research, studies into the nature of FIP are seriously underfunded because there are no government subsidies for this work. However, a number of organizations currently solicit public donations to provide research grants to scientists who study FIP.

These organizations include the Winn Foundation (www.winnfelinefoundation.com) and the Orion Foundation (www.orionfoundation.com). I encourage readers to contact these organizations for information about how to contribute to this very worthwhile effort to help us better understand and eradicate this horrible disease.

10

Which Vaccines, and When?

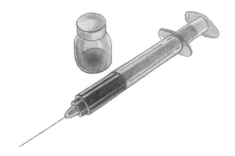

The Benefits of Vaccinating Your Cat

Today, vaccines are familiar weapons against many viral and nonviral diseases. Thanks to the invention of vaccine technology decades ago, millions of people and animals today enjoy nearly complete protection from debilitating and fatal diseases that have taken countless lives over the centuries. Over the last two decades, scientists have developed excellent vaccines for immunizing kittens and cats against previously devastating diseases such as panleukopenia, feline leukemia virus, and feline herpesvirus infection. Without question, cats today enjoy better health and longevity as a direct result of this miraculous medical technology.

All veterinarians recommend that kittens begin a series of vaccines against three of the more common contagious diseases, panleukopenia, herpesvirus, and calicivirus, at about eight weeks of age. Typically, such a series consists of two to four vaccines given a few weeks apart. This series should be followed with an annual booster. Experts also recommend that all kittens be vaccinated against rabies at about four to six months of age, with boosters at one- or three-year intervals depending on the rabies vaccine used. Beyond this, recommendations for vaccination of any individual kitten or cat vary depending on the lifestyle of the cat, and the prevalence of other diseases in the area in which the kitten lives.

Vaccination Is *Not* Without Risk

In the past, most veterinarians, like most physicians, believed that vaccination was an entirely safe procedure. We knew that the administration of effective vaccines prevented disease, but we did not suspect that they could actually cause disease as well. Veterinarians learned over a period of time, however, that some of the available vaccines are capable of causing reactions as immediate and severe as anaphylactic shock, as intermediate as injection-site reactions, and as long-term as the delayed development of cancers related to the vaccine components themselves.

The cat seems to have a highly reactive immune system. It is one of the only species in which we see eosinophils, white blood cells that participate in the inflammatory process, normally circulating in the bloodstream. Although routine annual vaccination of cats for many different diseases has been considered a prudent preventive measure for decades, we know now that this is not necessarily so. A few years ago, veterinarians started noticing that a particular type of very deadly cancer known as *fibrosarcoma* would start growing at the site of vaccination injections in some cats (see www .marvistavet.com/html/body_vaccine_associated_fibrosarcom.html). It took several years for the veterinarians who first noticed this association between vaccine injection sites and the site of fibrosarcoma development to convince their colleagues and the vaccine manufacturers that this association was real and an important source of cancer for cats. Finally, thorough studies showed that, in fact, multiple repeated vaccination injections could lead to the development of cancer in some cats.

Vaccine manufacturers continued these studies to try to understand what factors in these vaccines were most important. Some studies suggested that the FeLV and rabies vaccines were most responsible for causing fibrosarcoma, but other studies suggested that a larger number of products could lead to disease as well. Some studies seemed to show that adjuvants, "immune-booster" substances added to certain types of vaccines, were the problem, but experts are not unanimous in agreement about this. Because of all of this research, the American Association of Feline Practitioners developed recommendations for the vaccination of cats to minimize the risk of not only the most serious vaccine-associated complication, fibrosarcoma, but also lesser complications (see www .winnfelinehealth.org/health/vaccination-guidelines.html).

All veterinarians should be following these guidelines when recommending a vaccination program for their feline patients. All cat and kitten owners must have a thoughtful discussion with their veterinarian of their particular pets' risk factors before vaccines are administered. Not all kittens and cats should receive all vaccines every year. As a matter of fact, most cats should not be vaccinated yearly at all, especially after the kitten series and the first few annual boosters. Some experts argue that the actual risk of vaccine-associated reactions are small in a large population of cats. Although this may be true, it is equally true that the risk of contracting many diseases is even smaller for some cats than is the risk of serious vaccine reactions, especially for cats kept indoors. It is this comparison of one kind of risk versus another kind of risk that is important to the decision to vaccinate for a particular disease or not. All kittens and cats deserve this thoughtful analysis, and deserve for this analysis to be repeated regularly as risk factors change throughout a cat's life.

Certainly, vaccination against infectious diseases will continue to be an important part of health maintenance for all cats. The single most important thing kitten owners can do for the health of their youngsters, however, is to commit to an indoor life for their pets. Keeping one's cats indoors alone or as part of a stable group of healthy felines will do more to ensure that every individual enjoys nine long, healthy lives than any other measure possibly could.

11

Litter-Box Training for Perfect Habits

Kittens, like their older brethren, are naturally fastidious animals. No cat wants to soil its living area, and each will seek opportunities to maintain a spotless environment. This is the cat's basic nature, so why do so many kittens and even older cats break training, even occasionally? This is a question most veterinarians hear often from their cat-owning clients. Failure to use the litter box consistently is one of the most troubling problems cat lovers face, and it is one that can even end an otherwise loving relationship between a cat and its family.

Off to a Good Start

(see www.phsspca.org/training/litterbox.htm)

I have personally raised a great many kittens from birth through litter training and into young adulthood. I am convinced that, under ideal conditions, this training is virtually effortless and complete by the age of four to five weeks for every emotionally normal kitten. While it seems likely that at least some of this training comes from a kitten's mother before weaning, I have seen many orphaned kittens learn the skills needed for perfect litter box use without a female to teach them. Given easy access to almost any kind of litter material, young cats will come to prefer using such material when they need to relieve themselves. This preference seems quite well established at about four weeks of age in most kittens, although I have seen many start to use litter consistently as young as three weeks of age.

Many sources, such as the link listed above, provide the basic dos and don'ts for making sure your kitten is consistently litter box friendly. Such things as keeping the box easily accessible and clean (emptied daily) seem self-evident. If a cat cannot easily get to the box, or if the box is usually dirty, even the most well-trained cat will find alternative spots for relieving itself. This is only logical but overlooked in many cases, unfortunately. A litter box should also be roomy. Most cats want enough room in their boxes to turn around and cover their deposits. If the box is small and forces the cat to step in soiled areas in the box, this can be very off-putting to these naturally clean pets. Many cats like covers on their boxes, and I recommend such boxes for both sanitary and privacy reasons, but kittens unaccustomed to a covered box may take time to learn to accept this style. Provide both at first, and allow the cat to learn that the covered box has distinct advantages. Placing the box far away from food dishes and bedding is important to prevent contamination of these areas with litter.*

Although the usual rule of thumb for numbers of boxes is one per cat, it may be necessary to have more than this number, at least at first. The litter-box area should be ac-

---

*There are many different types of cat litters available to the pet owner. Personally, I prefer wood-pellet litter (cedar or pine, usually), because it has a wonderful aroma and my kittens adapt quickly to it. It doesn't track through my home the way clay or some clumping litters do, and it degrades with use into sawdust, which is biodegradable and disposed of easily. Automatic litter boxes usually require clumping litter, which is fine. I have never used the "crystals" that are also available, but have clients who use them and like their odor-controlling properties. I do not recommend the use of clay litters because those are generally dusty and can cause respiratory problems in especially sensitive kittens.

cessible, but also out of the flow of heavy traffic in the home. Most kittens and cats like peace and quiet around the box, and will avoid boxes that are in noisy, congested places in the house.

So, your kitten or cat has its own large, familiar box, full of clean litter and strategically placed in a location that provides privacy and quiet, but still has accidents outside the box. What now?

An example of this problem happened recently with one of my Ocicat kittens. I had placed a fourteen-week-old female with a family in a nearby town. They had a six-month-old female Abyssinian kitten already, and two young daughters. The kitten I placed with this nice family had never had a single litter box accident since the time she and her siblings had started exploring the box at about three weeks of age. Because of this, I was quite astonished when I received a call from the father about two weeks after the adoption, asking me what he should do about the kitten's failure to use the litter box.

We talked for a while and I asked about the kitten's environment: How did she and the older kitten get along? What about the girls? How did they handle the kitten? I learned that the older kitten was very active and chased the younger kitten in play almost constantly. I also learned that the daughters sometimes fought over the kittens. The baby I had raised in a calm home with other kittens its own age now found itself in a strange and, at times, oppressive new environment in which it was the smallest, most vulnerable individual. Small wonder that this little kitten became confused and frightened.

I made some suggestions for helping the kitten to feel safe and welcome in its new home. These included preventing rough play between the two kittens until the younger one could assert itself more, and instructing the daughters in how to handle a young, insecure cat so that it would feel less vulnerable. A slower pace of introduction into the family was clearly needed. These suggestions worked well over the next several weeks, and today the kitten is a happy, well-adjusted member of its new family.

The Other Causes of Poor Litter-Box Habits

As we discussed in chapter 6, the indoor life provides the safest lifestyle for a cat, but it can place stresses on a kitten or cat that may result in misbehavior. The period in which a kitten is weaned and adopted into a new home is an especially disruptive one for a young cat. During this transition, a kitten with previously perfect litter habits may forget those habits in the confusion and turmoil of adjusting to entirely new circumstances.

Whenever a kitten, or even an older cat, comes into a new home, there will be a period of time in which that cat must make a substantial emotional adjustment to its new territory and other animals in the home. Such a transition is easiest when the kitten or cat is already confident of its ability to handle change. Even the best socialized cat will have difficulty accepting its new home if that home is excessively noisy or busy, however. If there are other, established pets, especially other dominant cats, the adjustment to the new territory may be even more difficult. When you adopt a new kitten or cat into your home, remember that this adoption may create significant stress for the newcomer. To minimize this stress and reduce the chance of misbehavior, make the new home as welcoming and safe as possible for your new pet. The overwhelming majority of adopted cats will adjust well over a short time to a warm, welcoming environment, becoming full-fledged, happy members of the family for years to come.

Although it is unusual for a young kitten to have organic disease such as bladder problems as a cause of litter-box misbehavior, we can never rule this possibility out entirely. This is especially true if the misbehaving kitten has a self-confident personality, and the new home is quiet and nonthreatening. It is a good idea to consult with your veterinarian whenever litter-box misbehaviors persist or if the kitten seems to lack appetite or energy. An older cat that relieves itself outside the litter box should always be examined by a veterinarian for signs of urinary tract disease. If you have been feeding your cat or kitten dry cat food, make an immediate switch to canned food as part of preventing primary urinary tract or kidney problems (see chapters 23 and 27).

If you adopt a kitten that is feral (previously homeless and living on its own), or is very young with no training in how to use the litter box, the best approach will likely involve confining the kitten in a relatively small area (a bathroom, small bedroom, or utility room work well) with a suitable litter box and litter, a bed, and food and water dish. Be sure to provide toys in this first space as well. Take the kitten from this area for supervised visits to the rest of the house, but return it to this area whenever you cannot watch closely for signs that the baby needs a bathroom break. Cats, even kittens, are almost always unwilling to soil any area that they occupy. A kitten that might have an accident in a roomy living room will be reluctant to do so in a smaller area where it must eat and sleep. Most kittens will show perfect litter habits within their own little area. Once this habit is established, which will take several days or more, you can allow the kitten longer periods in the rest of the home. Usually, the young one will return to the litter box each time the need arises after such a period of training. Any kitten that persists in having accidents after such confinement must make a visit to the vet to rule out disease.

One of the most appealing characteristics of cats as pets is their astonishing fastidiousness. This cleanliness is hardwired into the instincts of all cats. Once established, these habits will usually last the entire life of the cat, and you will be able to trust your pet without reserve.

12

Should I Spay or Neuter My Kitten?

Without question, one of the most important steps you can take to insure the health and happiness of your new kitten is to have it altered (known as *spaying* in females and *neutering* in males) at the right time of its life. Altering removes the reproductive organs of the pet and provides invaluable benefits for the pet and for the community in which that pet lives. Many organizations, including the Humane Society of the United States and the American Veterinary Medical Association, have published strong recommendations for altering of all puppies and kittens before their first reproductive cycle, which usually occurs at about six months of age in kittens. This first heat cycle can occur a bit earlier for some and a bit later for others depending on genetics and the season of the year.

The Importance of Altering Your Kitten

(see www.hsus.org/pets/pet_care/why_you_should_spay_or_neuter_your_pet.html and www.catsinternational.org/articles/feline_care/benefits_spaying_neutering.html)

During the 1960s and '70s, some experts believed that early altering of male cats caused narrowing of the cat's urethra. The urethra is the tube that channels urine from the urinary bladder to the outside of the body through the penis. This narrowing of the urethra was thought to predispose some cats to the development of urinary tract obstruction later in life. We now know, however, that this effect does not occur, even in kittens altered as young as six to eight weeks of age. Urinary tract disease and obstruction is the result of other factors, most prominently consumption of dry cat foods; and altering of young male kittens is safe and recommended by all veterinarians and cat welfare groups today.

Altering your male or female kitten before it reaches puberty all but eliminates the possibility of reproductive tract cancers in adulthood. This includes mammary cancer (breast cancer), a very malignant and hard-to-treat cancer of adult cats. This protection against these malignancies is greatly diminished when the kitten is not altered until later, after it has become fully sexually mature. Further, early altering before the age of about six months prevents troublesome sexual behaviors such as spraying (both unaltered males *and* females can spray) and erratic personality changes that occur in the unaltered cat once it is sexually mature.

Your Most Important Responsibility

An extremely important reason to alter your kitten is the prevention of pregnancies that will produce new generations of unwanted kittens that will find their ways into the streets and shelters in your community. If you have ever been to such a shelter full of unwanted cats and dogs, most of which will be put to sleep because there are too few homes for them all, you know the misery and hopelessness of this situation. It is a great gift to adopt one of these innocent, homeless creatures, but it is an even greater gift to make sure that dozens more never spend a night in such a place because of human carelessness. You give this gift to all cats when you make sure that your new kitten spends its life in your home, altered and happy to be your companion, rather than desperately seeking to roam outdoors in search of a mate with which to create those hopeless generations.

Contrary to the old belief that a female cat "needs" to have a litter before being spayed, there is absolutely no benefit for the male or female cat in producing kittens. As a matter of fact, allowing children to witness "the miracle of birth" by permitting a pet to produce kittens is often counterproductive. Things do not always go smoothly in the birth and rearing of kittens. Sometimes kittens are born with birth defects, or the first-time queen may accidentally or deliberately kill one or more kittens. These unexpected tragedies can be extremely hard for young children to understand, leaving them traumatized rather than enlightened. If there are not enough good homes to accept all of the kittens, you might be forced to surrender them to a shelter. This provides further trauma to children, and is tragic for the kittens. The best lesson for children is to show them by example the benefits of spaying or neutering their pets before they produce new generations of homeless pets. It is simply not possible to overstate the importance of accepting this most central responsibility of pet ownership.

Studies have shown that the life span of altered cats compared to unaltered cats is longer by many years. This is due to the safety of the indoor life enjoyed by altered cats, the prevention of diseases such as cancer and reproductive tract infections, and the stable, sociable behaviors of altered cats. Unaltered cats not only roam the streets more often than altered cats, but are also more likely to be surrendered to shelters or abandoned because of destructive habits that owners find they cannot tolerate.

In contrast, when spaying and neutering procedures are performed properly in competent facilities, there are absolutely no negative effects of having your kitten altered. Even very early spay and neuter procedures are clearly safe when performed properly. If you adopt your kitten from a shelter, it will undoubtedly already be altered when you take the baby home. Shelters have learned over the decades that some adoptive homes will fail to have their new kitten altered by six months of age. Experience has shown that too many of these unaltered cats then go on to produce "accidental" litters of kittens, a futile situation for the already overcrowded animal shelters. To be certain that every kitten adopted into a permanent home never contributes to the seemingly endless stream of homeless cats, rescue groups and shelters now alter all unaltered strays before those pets go to adoptive families. The adoption fee you pay for a kitten from one of these facilities will include the cost of this vital surgery.

If you happen to adopt an unaltered kitten, see your veterinarian for an exam and make an appointment to have the kitten altered as soon as your veterinarian recommends.

Preventing Obesity in the Altered Cat

Veterinarians have recognized for years that the altered cat has a much greater tendency to become obese than the unaltered cat. This effect is due to changes in the altered cat's activity level and hormone balance. Once thought to be inevitable, obesity is actually easily prevented in all cats (see chapter 20). While real changes do take place inside the altered cat's body, the real culprit in the almost universal fattening of the altered pet is high-carbohydrate foods. Much as human adults seem to gain extra pounds in middle age as their metabolism changes, so too do altered cats begin to accumulate excess weight with no apparent change in lifestyle. The truth is that the kitten consuming lots of high-carbohydrate junk food in the form of dry kibble seems to tolerate this poor diet full of unnecessary "carb calories" much as a human teenager with a junk-food diet often can. Once metabolism changes, however, the altered cat loses that tolerance, and foods high in processed carbohydrate begin to pack on the pounds.

In my practice, most of the adult cats I see for the first time are overweight, and many are morbidly obese (so overweight that their health is damaged). The histories of these cats invariably include a slow but unchanging weight gain after the time they were surgically altered. All of my overweight patients ate dry cat food as kittens and continued to do so as altered adults. This health-damaging weight gain does not occur when altered cats eat low-carbohydrate foods as adults. It is a good idea to feed even unaltered kittens canned food and/or raw meat even before they are spayed or neutered. This will eliminate the need to change foods after altering, and obesity prevention will be automatic.

Whatever wet food you choose for your altered cat, do not free-feed additional dry food alongside. Many owners make this mistake. Cats do not need to "graze" on a constant basis as though they were cattle. The natural feeding behaviors of the cat dictate intermittent feeding when prey is successfully located and killed. In the wild state, cats do not eat constantly; they eat periodically depending on the availability of prey and their ability to catch that prey. Twice-daily meal-feeding of wet food at about 3 to 4 ounces of food per meal simulates the cat's free-roaming feeding behaviors as closely as is reasonably possible and allows the cat to maintain a healthy adult weight throughout its life.

13

Help...My Kitten Is Clawing the Furniture!

Second only to house soiling (see chapter 11), destructive clawing of furniture, drapes, and other household possessions by kittens and cats is a common complaint from my clients. Occasionally, the complaint about a cat's indiscriminate use of its claws comes from an elderly person or a cat owner with an immune-compromising disease who cannot risk being scratched by a pet cat. In all cases, the question of whether to declaw a kitten is full of ethical and practical considerations.

To Declaw or Not to Declaw?

(see www.cfainc.org/health/declawing.html and
www.marvistavet.com/html/body_declawing_and_its_alternatives.html)

Let me begin this discussion by saying that I am fundamentally opposed to declawing of cats for a number of reasons. Foremost among these is my strong belief that almost all cats can be trained not to damage home furnishings. Only rarely does an owner who is willing to train a kitten or cat have to make the choice between having a cat with claws or having intact furniture. I do not declaw my own cats and I require that those who adopt my Ocicat kittens sign a contract in which they agree never to declaw the kitten they adopt from me. When clients ask my opinion about declawing, I always say that this behavior can be very transient in a young cat's development and I strongly suggest alternatives to surgical declawing.

The natural exploration behaviors of kittens four to sixteen weeks of age includes the experimental use of claws in various types of materials in their environments. It is during this time that a kitten learns how to use those claws to climb, defend itself, entertain itself with toys, and sharpen its claws for future use. The destructiveness of clawing behavior can be diminished greatly by clipping the tips of the claws on a regular basis. Once-weekly trimming of at least the front claws will keep them blunt and teach the youngster to accept this procedure without struggle. If you are not comfortable with performing nail trims on your kitten, have your veterinarian show you how to do this and practice regularly. Mastering this procedure will save you, your cat, and your home furnishings inestimable grief over the life of your cat.

Owners must also provide good alternative surfaces for the natural scratching tendencies of the kitten. Scratching posts wrapped with sisal rope should be distributed around the house. Cats also love to scratch carpeting, so providing cat trees with carpet coverings will attract the cat to these surfaces and away from furniture. A sharp "No!" whenever a kitten starts to scratch at forbidden areas can be quite helpful along with these other measures. Kittens generally avoid disapproval from humans, and as long as that disapproval does not include physical punishment, there is little danger of causing fear or aggression behaviors in response.

My own home sees a variety of cats of all ages living underfoot with access to all of my furniture. Despite this, even my oldest furniture is in excellent condition, with only a few strands of scratched fabric here and there as evidence of some errant kitten's experimentations. I keep my kittens claws trimmed and have many tall, carpet-covered cat trees around my house. I have also learned that leather-covered furniture is much less attractive to cats as scratching objects than are fabric-covered pieces. For some reason, the smooth finished surface of leather is less appealing for sharpening claws, so I have mostly leather furniture. Leather can also be more resistant to stains, another advantage to this kind of furniture around animals (as well as children and sloppy adults).

Of course, owners must discourage the kitten from scratching people as well as furniture. I have had clients complain to me that their kitten scratches them often during play, only to learn that some members of the family roughhouse with the youngster. Humans should not engage in play with a cat that elicits both use of claws and biting by the kitten. One of the most important lessons for the kitten is that humans are not to be bitten or scratched. It is impossible to teach this lesson if owners allow rough play at some times and not at others. Rough play with simulated fighting occurs naturally between a young cat and its fellow animal playmates, but the biting and scratching of humans is not permissible. When a kitten begins to play rough with family members, play should stop immediately accompanied by a stern "No!" The young cat will quickly associate this undesirable result with the bad behavior, extinguishing that behavior.

As a kitten becomes an adult, the training provided by regular nail trimming, ready access to lots of authorized scratching areas, and regularly reinforced disapproval of unauthorized clawing, including the scratching of humans, will produce a pet that has an excellent set of scratching behaviors. In almost every case, the question of whether to declaw or not to declaw need never even arise. In some rare cases of especially stubborn scratching tendencies, a product known as Soft Paws nail caps may be the answer. These soft plastic nail covers, held on with glue, fit snugly over the trimmed nail and can last several weeks before they need to be reapplied. In situations where immune-compromised humans or elderly family members simply cannot risk even the occasional accidental scratch, I find these nail covers work very well. They are usually applied in the grooming shop or veterinary clinic, but owners who have good cat-handling skills can learn to apply them at home as well.

There are several techniques for surgical declawing of kittens and cats. All of these techniques, even the newest techniques using a surgical laser rather than a stainless-steel scalpel blade, cause pain and mutilation of the cat's paws. No decision to declaw a cat should be made lightly or before all other efforts to limit the objectionable behavior have been completely exhausted. In some cases, these efforts might even include finding a new home for a pet where the objectionable behavior is more easily tolerated.

There is considerable social disapproval of declawing of pet cats today, and rightly so. This is the same social disapproval that has caused dog owners to start rethinking the long-standing traditions of ear cropping and other elective cosmetic surgery for their canine companions. Just as we are obligated to feed our cats the foods that they are designed to utilize, not the foods we humans find most convenient, we are also obligated to act responsibly when we consider making drastic and mutilating alterations to a cat's anatomy for our own purposes.

14

Toys and Treats—
Spoil Your Kitten in a Good Way

There are few activities more enjoyable for pet lovers than playing with a kitten. The endless energy of the young cat, coupled with its astounding agility and inquisitiveness, can provide hours of captivating entertainment for its human family members. There is another important reason to play with your kitten, however. Cats kept indoors, as all should be today, can suffer from mind-numbing boredom if their environment fails to stimulate their natural curiosity and playfulness. Outdoors, cats find an endless supply of moving, chirping, rustling, rattling objects to chase and explore. Inside the safety and comfort of the home, however, the kitten may lack those experiences of life that would naturally develop its fun-loving, self-confident personality. In cats, as in humans, intelligence is only partly genetic. Much of an indoor adult cat's outgoing, environment-engaging behaviors must be cultivated through "enrichment" of its environment.

Making Life a Cabaret for Your Kitten
(see www.indoorcat.org/need.php)

Most of the published information that is available about the importance of environmental enrichment for captive animals applies to zoo species kept in zoological parks or research species housed in institutional facilities. While these groups of animals clearly deserve this attention to their special habitat needs, "captive" house cats also need such attention from owners. The stereotype of the indoor cat is generally that of a Garfield kind of pet, an overweight, sluggish couch potato with little interest in activities other than sleeping and eating. To the extent that this stereotype is accurate, it is unnecessarily so. No cat need grow up overweight, inactive, and uninvolved in its home environment. I deal elsewhere with the issue of diet-related obesity in cats. While an active lifestyle is unquestionably important to keeping your cat svelte throughout its life, proper diet is, in fact, the single most important factor in this aspect of health. See chapter 20 for more on this problem.

More than just burning off calories, enrichment of your kitten's environment is all about keeping it interested and engaged in the life of the family. Providing that crucial stimulation is neither difficult nor excessively time-consuming.

If you watch kittens in a group as they interact with one another, you will observe a number of different kinds of hardwired action behaviors. Without being taught to do so, kittens romp around their allowed space, usually at high speed. They explore their territory, often repetitively, seeking anything new in their world since they last looked around. They play with their peers (other kittens at or near their own age), often in mock fights with fangs bared and partially sheathed claws, grasping any part of their adversary that is available. They take turns winning and losing these mock battles. When they are not battling with one another, they chase each other back and forth across the territory, again taking turns chasing and being chased.

Kittens love to play hide-and-seek with one another. Any large object can serve as the fort behind or within which they will hide from one another, waiting to pounce on the unsuspecting adversary or pretend prey. Between sessions of chasing and fighting with each other, kittens will find objects that roll when swatted that can be chased. Often, the entire group will join in the chase after the rolling "prey." They attack inanimate objects with hilarious ferocity, building their own sense of self-sufficiency and safety.

Even kittens that grow up alone will attempt to develop these same skills, using humans or dogs as playmate surrogates. These behaviors mimic exactly the play activities seen in youngsters of wild species; they help to prepare both groups for active adulthood in which such behaviors will equip them to survive on their own. The indoor cat has little ultimate use for the skills and experience it acquires in youthful play. It will never have to evade an attacker, and it will never have to hunt and capture its own breakfast or dinner. Inside that young captive cat, however, the spirit and drive to remain alert, watchful, and athletic within its environment will struggle to find an outlet. Building an environment that draws out those naturally active tendencies is one of the key responsibilities of the conscientious cat owner.

Providing a varied assortment of toys is central to this environmental enrichment. Happily, the world is full of every imaginable type of cat entertainment, including large exercise wheels (yes, some cats will use these and seem to love running in place); videotapes that allow cats to watch and listen to birds, squirrels, and other "animals of interest" on television; and small flashlight pointers that can keep a kitten chasing the mysterious red light dot across the floor and up the wall for hours. My own cats adore very simple items such as colored paper strips on the tip of a stick making a kind of safe "sparkler," as well as more complicated pieces, such as small motorized toys that move much as a small prey animal would. Catnip-filled plush toys are a favorite with some cats. If you put the search terms "cat toys" into your Internet browser, you will pull up dozens of sites offering an astonishing selection of delightful playthings for your cat.

One type of toy that I especially like is the small hollow plastic ball that can be twisted open and filled with pieces of food treats. When this ball is rolled across the floor, pieces of treats fall out on the floor. This allows the cat to learn how to control the availability of treats while playing with the ball. It is amazing how quickly a kitten will figure out how the ball works and successfully feed itself! I have one caveat about treats. While kibbled cat food fits neatly into the ball, dry cereal-based cat kibble or kibbled cat treats should not be used in this treat-dispensing toy. These foods are poor quality for cats under all circumstances. Instead, I use small pieces of freeze-dried meats like chicken, fish, or beef (see page 95). Properly sized, these pieces of pure meat will fall out of the ball as it rolls, just as high-carb kibble does, without filling the kitten with junk food.

One note of caution: kittens *can* ingest very small balls, marbles, and the like. Avoid providing toys that are so small that they can be swallowed during play. Also avoid providing string or yarn as toys, as these can be swallowed and cause a surgical emergency or even death. Although cats are much less likely than puppies to "eat" their toys, I have on a few occasions had to surgically remove small toys or string from a kitten's stomach or intestinal tract. Your veterinarian is an excellent source of advice about safe cat playthings.

In addition to having toys, it is important that a kitten's living and play areas have high and low places for resting, "lying in wait," and just plain adding variety and interest to its everyday activities. Like the multitiered children's play areas at today's fast-food chains, the ideal kitten play and living areas have nooks and crannies galore for the youngster to master on its way to self-confident adulthood. If possible, provide a variety of cat trees of differing heights in the kitten's home territory. This will have the added benefit of drawing the kitten away from the furniture. In my experience, the time a kitten or cat will spend on sofas, chairs, and tables will decrease in direct proportion to the availability of other, more intriguing, cat-attractive places to play and sleep.

For the most realistic environmental enrichment, consider purchasing or building an indoor/outdoor habitat situation for your kitten or cat. By this, I mean setting up an area where the kitten can enjoy true unsupervised outdoor privileges within an enclosure that closely adjoins the home building. This play and relaxation area can be reached by the cat at will (weather permitting, of course) through a small door leading from the interior of the home. I have seen some very ingenious custom-built arrangements for accomplishing this, and there are some excellent modular units available through the classified section at the back of most cat magazines, as well as the Internet. This concept of free, safe, access to the outdoor world for the indoor cat is adaptable to homes of all sizes, and even apartments with balconies or patios.

Be sure to spend time with your kitten. Although toys and cat trees are important features of the enriched environment, nothing can take the place of gentle human contact during the kitten's playtime. Cats are creatures of habit. If a kitten is accustomed to prolonged pleasurable interactions with a variety of humans, especially associated with play, it will enjoy these same interactions as an adult. A kitten that is left to its own devices during playtime will mature into an adult cat that also prefers its own company to that of the family. It is unreasonable to expect that a kitten deprived of the family's time and attention during its youth will be anything but reclusive and shy as an adult cat.

Finally, I believe that almost all kittens are happiest when they can grow up with another kitten or young adult cat. Growing into adulthood with a feline buddy develops the kitten's personality to its fullest, and prevents the inevitable loneliness a cat feels when left alone during the day. If the newly adopted kitten joins another, older cat already in the family, this can also result in a wonderful friendship between the two. The new kitten will likely be shunned by the resident cat for a short period, but who can resist the wiles of a kitten? Most youngsters can win over even the most skeptical older cat, to the benefit of both. Be patient and introduce the two (or more) cats to each other gradually, and never allow them to be together unsupervised until their friendship is established as evidenced by such behaviors as grooming each other, playing together, and sleeping together. We humans enjoy, even crave, the companionship of others of our species, and cats are no different.

What About "Candy" for Kittens?

Candy and snack food are an everyday occurrence for human children, but what about allowing kittens to have "treats"? It is a fact of life that people use food to express affection, and they enjoy showing affection to their pets by offering especially tasty treats. This practice can be harmful, or healthy, depending on what kinds of treats are involved and how often you treat your pet.

Pet food aisles are filled with snack products that will make your cat sit up and beg. Almost all of these treats are not good for your kitten, unfortunately. As we have discussed earlier, foods that are full of highly processed carbohydrate are inappropriate for an obligatory carnivore like the cat; treats with these substances are similarly poor choices for your kitten's "fun food." Some will argue that the occasional carb-filled snack cannot be so harmful. After all, we humans indulge in foods that we know aren't good for us now and then, don't we? The answer is yes, we all eat poor-quality foods ourselves, but this is hardly a good reason to offer snacks to our kittens that they would not eat if they were able to choose healthier options. And there *are* better options. My own cats are crazy about freeze-dried meat snacks, and I recommend these to all of my clients. These freeze-dried treats are pure cooked meat, without artificial colors, flavors, salt, or any carbohydrate added to make them crunchy. They are crunchy because they are freeze-dried. They are extremely palatable, and some of my clients even jokingly call them "kitty crack" because their cats enjoy them so much.

Several companies market these excellent treats for cats (and dogs) in pet stores. The treats are also available online (see www.samsstore.com/livalittles.html and www .sitstay.com/store/edibles/treatswl.shtml, for example. There are many such sites). They may seem expensive when compared to the usual, kibble-type treats, but these products are very concentrated nutrition, and pets need less of them to be satisfied. They will not interfere with the other good nutrition habits the kitten is learning. These freeze-dried bits can be used as rewards for good behavior, during playtime for more fun (kittens and cats bat them around as playthings), or even during travel when it is difficult to feed the kitten its usual food.

We know intuitively that the happy kitten will grow into the happy, healthy, well-adjusted adult cat that lives for decades as a treasured member of the family. A small amount of creativity and effort on your part can make your kitten into that long-lived, irreplaceable pet.

15

What If Your Kitten Becomes Sick or Injured?

Without question, your veterinarian is the best source of information and assistance whenever your kitten seems to be sick or injured. Like human children, kittens are prone to many kittenhood illnesses and can become injured through their inquisitive explorations as well. It is good for kitten owners to have some idea of what to watch for and how to deal with emergencies when they first arise. The following advice is not intended to replace the hands-on, expert assistance of your veterinarian, but will prepare the owner to make good decisions about when to take the kitten to the doctor.

Is My Kitten Really Sick?

SIGNS OF THE "STOMACH FLU"

The normal demeanor of the healthy kitten is that of high activity, good appetite, normal urine and stool output, and rapid growth. Even the healthy kitten, however, can have an "off" day. A kitten may sleep more than usual for a day or so, but if its appetite and eliminations are normal, there is little cause for concern. Even moderate fluctuations in appetite, if they last only a day or two, are not cause for alarm. Any prolonged change in these important measures of a kitten's good health should signal that something may be wrong.

Kittens vomit rarely, and never repeatedly, unless there is something amiss. Parasites, gastrointestinal viral or bacterial infections, poisoning, and gastrointestinal blockage can all cause frequent vomiting in a kitten. All of these conditions require the assistance of a veterinarian if the kitten is to return to health. If your kitten does vomit once or twice in a short period, but retains its good appetite and activity level, the problem will likely resolve on its own. Do not medicate your kitten for vomiting with any over-the-counter or prescription drugs unless your veterinarian tells you to do so. If your baby vomits repeatedly and becomes lethargic and unwilling to eat, consult your veterinarian immediately or seek emergency help if this happens after hours.

Like vomiting, diarrhea is a very nonspecific sign in the kitten. Many minor and major problems may manifest with this sign. A onetime occurrence of loose stool may signal nothing more than a bout of indigestion that will disappear on its own. If diarrhea lasts for more than twelve hours, however, a veterinarian's help is needed to resolve the problem and prevent the kitten from becoming dehydrated and debilitated from loss of fluids and electrolytes. Bloody diarrhea in the kitten is an emergency signal to seek professional assistance immediately. If you can take a fresh sample of the abnormal stool with you to the clinic, that will assist your veterinarian in making the diagnosis and treating the problem correctly.

A kitten that refuses to eat for an entire day is a sick kitten, unless the refused food is new to the youngster. Even so, it is very unusual for a young cat to lose its appetite entirely, even for short periods. You might want to offer a kitten that is not eating some meat baby food, as a test of its appetite for very palatable food. Kittens typically love meat baby food. If the kitten refuses even this treat, seek the help of your veterinarian as soon as possible. If the loss of appetite is accompanied by vomiting and/or diarrhea, do not delay in getting help from your veterinarian.

JUST A LITTLE "HEAD COLD"?

Kittens are susceptible to upper respiratory infections (URI), just as human children are. Even those that are vaccinated against some of the viruses that cause feline URI can still start showing typical sneezing, congestion, discharge from the eyes, and the like. This is because there are many microbes that can cause URI for which we have no effective vaccine. So, what should you do if your kitten gets a cold?

Although many colds in kittens are caused by viruses, not bacteria, cats will often develop secondary bacterial complications in association with viral URI. For this reason, it is wise to treat URI signs in kittens with an appropriate oral antibiotic. Few young cats with significant clinical illness of this type will recover without help. In fact, without treatment some kittens will become extremely sick and may even die. A percentage of untreated kittens will become chronically infected and show signs of URI continually or periodically throughout their lives. I never adopt a wait-and-see attitude with my patients that have URI, but prescribe an antibiotic such as Clavamox or azithromycin for at least ten days after I examine the kitten and rule out any other cause of the illness.

Of course, kittens can go through a period of sneezing because of irritants in the air or environment. If your baby sneezes repeatedly over a day or two, especially during windy times, but shows no evidence of discharge from the eyes or nasal passages and continues to eat well, you can wait for a few days for the signs to subside. If you see inactivity, lack of appetite, or significant discharge or congestion, seek help right away.

In addition to antibiotic therapy for URI, I recommend that my clients nebulize their kittens, three to four times per day, for about ten minutes per session. This process for the kitten is exactly like the process of nebulizing a congested child. The machines for use with children can be used for kittens as well. Placing the kitten in a small room or cage with a nebulizer producing humidifying cool steam can greatly relieve congestion and enable the kitten to clear its nasal passages and lower airways of harmful bacteria and mucus. It is important not to overnebulize, however. Never leave the kitten in the steamy environment for more than ten to fifteen minutes per session. I usually provide my clients with sterile saline solution with a dilute Gentocin concentration (2 mg/cc) to use in their nebulizer. This provides additional bacteria-fighting support right on the infected nasal passages. Plain saline solution can be effective as well. Consult with your veterinarian about what kind of solution to use for your kitten's treatments.

Serious Respiratory Disease

Sometimes, a kitten will begin to have great difficulty breathing from advanced URI, pneumonia, or other very serious diseases such as congenital heart disease or even FIP (see chapter 9). Whenever your kitten begins to breathe rapidly or seems to be laboring to breathe, or is panting for extended periods, it is a medical emergency and you must seek veterinary assistance immediately. No disease that causes a kitten or cat to have this kind of problem can be ignored; it will not resolve on its own and is life threatening. Pneumonia from advanced upper respiratory disease may be treatable with appropriate support, but young cats with pneumonia are very sick indeed. Congenital heart problems that lead to respiratory distress usually have a guarded prognosis, and fluid accumulation in the chest from any cause must be diagnosed promptly if there is to be any hope of recovery.

Poisoning

Fortunately, kittens are generally less likely to ingest household chemical poisons than are puppies or toddlers, although some common chemicals, like antifreeze, do have pleasant tastes that may attract the young cat. Occasionally a youngster will consume drugs like Tylenol or other human painkillers during play. Of course, all such substances must be kept well out of reach of all pets as they can be deadly, even in small doses, for pets as well as for children. If you suspect your kitten may have consumed *any* amount of any prescription or over-the-counter drug, including dietary supplements meant for humans or other animal species, call your veterinarian immediately. Most poisoning can be treated if treatment comes in time.

Outdoor cats may be exposed to poisoned rodent bait or pesticides. Prevention of poisoning with such toxins is one of the many reasons to keep your cat indoors except under the strictest supervision. Because of their fastidious grooming habits, cats can become intoxicated with poisons, including household cleaning chemicals, that contact their coats or feet when they clean themselves. Never leave chemical powders or liquid spills where your kitten or cat can inadvertently walk through, inhale, or roll in them. When using cleaners on floors, counters, or any other surfaces available to your kitten, be sure to remove residue completely. Poisoning can be successfully treated in most cases if it is detected early and treated promptly. *Always* advise your veterinarian of all potentially harmful substances that are kept or used in the cat's environment, indoors or out.

In my experience, the most common cause of intoxication for kittens is poisonous houseplants. Lilies of all types can be very harmful for the kitten that chews on leaves or flowers of the plant. A number of other highly poisonous plants are commonly kept as home decorations, and kittens love to chew on greenery around the house. Not only is this chewing of plants potentially deadly for cats, it is quite hard on the plants. I have given up on live plants around my house, and keep only the artificial, silk variety myself. At the clinic, we have several very attractive arrangements, all silk. Silk plants are not nearly as interesting to cats, and they withstand the occasional munch from the inquisitive clinic cat without much disfigurement. They last much longer than live plants, and require only the occasional dusting to keep them looking bright and decorative. If your cat seems attracted to even artificial greenery consider eliminating these or removing them to cat-safe locations. This includes real and artificial Christmas trees.

Sudden, repetitive vomiting or profound depression and lethargy in a kitten may signal poisoning. If you see signs like this, contact your veterinarian immediately. Make a swift search of the kitten's environment for signs of any plant or substance the kitten may have ingested. This information will be invaluable to your veterinarian in managing your kitten's problem.

Injuries

Kittens are very agile creatures. Although they love to jump from high places and frolic with abandon around the house, they are much less likely to sustain major injuries from falls or sudden stops against furniture or walls than are puppies. Even so, kittens can strain, sprain, or even fracture their limbs in some especially disastrous mishaps. If your kitten should suddenly become lame for more than a few hours, or if you notice blood or extreme pain in any part of a kitten's body, see your veterinarian right away. Lacerations can become infected and blood loss from a bleeding wound can be substantial for a small cat if serious injury is ignored.

Most major injuries to kittens and cats occur outdoors. Automobile accidents and attacks from other animals are the most common source of serious injury to cats allowed outdoors. Kittens may also rarely miscalculate the distance to the ground when they jump from high places outdoors, resulting in broken bones or dislocations. Older cats almost never make this kind of mistake, although any cat that is running for its life can become injured in the dash through or over fences, balconies, trees, and the like.

Abscesses from fights with other cats may arise after a period of time after an outdoor adventure. Abscesses show up as painful swellings on the body, or even as draining wounds once the abscess has broken open. Abscesses require a veterinarian's care as soon as the problem becomes evident. Keep your kittens and cats indoors. It is the single most important accident-prevention measure we can take with our felines. In any case of suspected injury, call your veterinarian for guidance about whether a visit is necessary. Kittens are resilient, elastic little animals, with a great capability to recover from trauma, but they may need help for complete, rapid recovery.

An owner's vigilance is the most important health aid for all cats. Like children, kittens need supervision of their day-to-day well-being if they are to grow up healthy, happy, and safe from permanent harm.

16

I Found an Orphaned Kitten— What Do I Do Now?

I am often contacted by distraught people who have found a very young orphaned kitten outside their home or during their daily activities. These compassionate individuals have taken the baby into their care but don't know how to rear the little one. Today, with many unwanted pregnancies in homeless, unspayed females living outdoors, such situations are all too common. When the new mother is killed or wanders off, the abandoned newborns are very vulnerable and do not survive unless they are found quickly by a sympathetic human. Fortunately, there are a number of cat rescue groups composed of very dedicated cat lovers with lots of experience with raising young orphans (see www.cats-central.com/cat_clubs.htm and www.petplace.com/article.aspx?id=305). These groups are happy to assist with specific situations. Also, many pet shops, pet food warehouse retailers (e.g., Petsmart and Petco), and veterinary clinics can provide contact information for cat rescue groups in their immediate area.

Where Do I Start?

If the orphaned kitten is still relatively vigorous, there is a good chance you will be able to nurse it along and save its life. If the baby's eyes are open, the youngster is at least nine to fourteen days old and may do well with diligent care. If its eyes are not open and it weighs less than three to four ounces, saving it will be much harder, although not impossible. Newborn kittens are unable to maintain normal body temperature without a warm environment. This role is ordinarily filled by the mother-cat's body. The orphan will need a warming blanket, warm water bottles, or the like to stay warm. Use traditional heating pads with great caution. It is very easy to overheat, or even kill, a kitten with the old-style heating pad, as they become excessively warm with electric heat. The kitten will be unable to move away from this heat and can be injured easily. If such a pad is the only option, use several layers of towels or blankets on top of the pad to protect the kitten from overheating. Place the heating device and padding in a box or other container to prevent the kitten from becoming displaced away from the warm environment.

Food and water are the next most important needs for the orphaned kitten. There are several choices for the milk the orphan should receive. Cow's milk is not a good choice for kittens because it has nutrient levels that are very different than cat's milk. Goat's milk is often used and seems to support good growth in kittens. I prefer the commercial milk replacers for cats because they are easy to find in most pet stores and simulate the mother-cat's milk quite well. Most come in powdered form, which is economical and easy to store and use as needed. Several companies provide these replacers along with directions about how to reconstitute the powdered product (see www.petplace .com/article.aspx?id=305). The kitten will require about one to two teaspoons of milk replacer per ounce of body weight total per day during the first two weeks of life, and about 50 percent more during the third week. This amount should be divided into five to eight feedings throughout the day. Younger kittens should receive smaller, more frequent feedings than older ones.

There are a number of types of baby bottles available at most neighborhood pet stores or large pet supply stores. These can work well for feeding the nursing kitten. I prefer bottle nipples that are long and tapered, rather than the shorter, "snub-nosed" type. These allow more efficient feeding of the milk or milk replacer. Just as you would do if you were bottle-feeding a human infant, make sure that the amount of fluid that comes out of the nipple tip is not too much, but comes easily into the kitten's mouth when it sucks. If the kitten has to work too hard to get liquid out of the nipple, it will become exhausted and discouraged. If the liquid comes too freely, the kitten's mouth will become overfilled and the baby may choke. The flow rate will vary depending on how old and how large the kitten is. It is a good idea to weigh the kitten every few days to make sure it is gaining weight steadily.

If you have a kitchen scale that weighs in grams, this is ideal as you will be able to detect small gains or losses on a frequent basis. Each ounce of weight is equivalent to about 28 grams. Newborn kittens weigh about 75 to 110 grams (or about three to four ounces) and should double their weight in the first two weeks of life. At one month, a kitten should weigh about one pound, or about 450 grams. Typically, a normal kitten will gain about a pound per month after that.

At about three weeks of age (or about eight to twelve ounces of body weight if the age of the kitten is not known), you should begin to introduce the kitten to solid food. Meat baby food or canned/pouched kitten foods of most brands are fine for this. It may help to mix a bit of the milk replacer into the new food for its familiar taste. Place the food on a small flat plate or saucer (kittens are leery of putting their faces into deep bowls) and place a small amount of the food on the kitten's upper lip. This will cause it to lick the food from its lip, and it will probably become instantly interested in this new, good-tasting stuff. If it takes a few days for the kitten to show interest in feeding itself, don't worry. Make sure you offer the new diet before you feed the milk replacer, so the kitten is hungry when you offer the solid food. If at any point the kitten begins to refuse food of any kind, see your veterinarian right away.

Cleaning Up

The mother-cat cleans the eliminations from her kittens several times a day by licking their hindquarters. The very young orphan kitten will generally not eliminate urine and stool without this stimulation. Fortunately, substituting for the mother in this task is not difficult. Simply moisten a cotton ball or soft cloth with warm water and gently massage the rectum and penis (males) or vulva (females) until the kitten urinates and defecates.

This process should be repeated several times daily. The kitten will urinate several times daily, but may only defecate one to three times daily. The stool should be a yellow–orange–light brown color and have a puddinglike consistency.

At about three weeks, the kitten can be introduced to the litter box. Remarkably, most kittens seem to know what to do in the box, even if they haven't had Mom around to set the example. Cats of all ages are by nature fastidious; once the kitten uses the box successfully a time or two, this part of your responsibility will be over. Keep the litter area clean and easily accessible, and the kitten will continue to use it consistently. Some kittens may develop diarrhea during the transition from liquid to solid food. If this persists, or if the stool becomes watery, ask your veterinarian for advice about how to resolve this. There are a number of medications that can take care of this. It may be necessary to deworm the kitten at this point as well. Parasites are a common cause of loose stool in the weaning kitten.

Once the orphan is six to eight weeks of age and growing well, it will be time to check with your veterinarian about what vaccines it will need and when they should be administered. See chapter 10 for more information about this. As discussed in the next chapter, canned food is an excellent diet for the kitten as it grows and also after it becomes an adult. It is my opinion from raising hundreds of kittens that dry cat food is inappropriate for cats at any age.

Raising an orphaned kitten can be a very emotional and difficult job. If the baby does not do well, it can be stressful and even tragic. As anyone who has completed this important job can tell you, however, the rewards of providing a future for an abandoned kitten are great, and you can be very proud of your commitment to this worthwhile labor of love.

PART

 # 3

The Glorious Years of
Young Adulthood

17

Your Cat's an Adult—
What to Feed It Now?

Now that your kitten is a full-grown cat, you may be wondering what changes you should make to keep your special friend as healthy in adulthood as it has been during its first months of life. Certainly you should have your cat spayed or neutered, if you haven't already done that. You will plan to have your youngster examined by your veterinarian annually without fail. You may think that your cat's diet should change at this time as well, but that is not so. Just as wild kittens that become cats do not change the prey they hunt, your young adult cat should continue to eat the same, high-protein, low-carbohydrate food that provided such excellent nutrition for it in babyhood. However, if you are presently feeding your cat a dry kitten food, now is the time to make the switch to a food that will keep your cat healthy for the rest of its life.

The Fallacy in the Life-Stage Concept

For a number of years now, many pet food companies have marketed their dry and canned cat foods in accordance with a "life-stage" concept. The theory goes that kittens need a certain type of nutrient profile (the combination of protein, fat, carbohydrate, vitamins, and minerals in a diet); adult cats need a different nutrient profile; and older, "senior" cats need another, different nutrient profile in order to achieve and maintain optimum health. This concept has met with wide acceptance, or at least has met no real resistance, among veterinary nutrition experts. This acceptance is remarkable, because it flies in the face of a number of obvious contradictory characteristics of cat foods and cats themselves.

In the wild, neither small nor large cats change the nutrient profile of their diet as they age. Once feral kittens of all cat species are weaned, they begin to eat the same foods that their adult role models hunt and eat, small mammals, birds, lizards, bird eggs, insects, and the like. Kittens eat right alongside, or after, older cats. During the lifetime of the cat, we see no difference in the diet that younger and older cats choose to hunt and eat. To the extent that the diet of the cat changes over time, it does so as a result of increasing or decreasing availability of the various prey in the environment. The age of the cat does not play a role, even here.

We know that the nutrient profiles of the foods kittens eat naturally are identical to the profiles of the foods that adult feral cats eat. After all, a mouse or a bird or a lizard is nutritionally the same whether caught and eaten by a youngster or an older animal. While kittens need more protein and calories per unit of their body weight than do adult cats, they meet this increased need by consuming a greater amount of food per unit of their weight. This is exactly the method used by the pregnant and lactating queen to meet the temporary increase in nutrient needs imposed by reproduction. The pregnant queen eats more while she is pregnant and lactating, and then decreases her intake after the kittens are weaned.

Conversely, as cats grow older and their needs for calories and some nutrients decrease, this change in needs is accommodated by decreased intake, per unit of body weight. This is the natural manner in which a species whose available diet is uniform in nutrients adjusts the intake of nutrients as its requirements fluctuate. Life-stage concept–based pet foods ignore this fact of a cat's life. Further, pet food companies that insist cats must be fed according to their life stage are inconsistent in their own application of this principle. Canned and dry forms of a kitten diet will have widely varying amounts of protein, fat, and carbohydrates, the energy nutrients. For example, the dry formula of one of the most popular kitten foods on the market has 37 percent dry-matter protein and almost 28 percent dry-matter highly processed carbohydrate. The corresponding canned kitten formula has 49 percent protein but much less carbohydrate than the dry product, with about 15 percent. Considering that the digestibility of these energy nutrients is greater in the canned formulas than in the dry, the difference in protein content become's even greater from the point of view of the cat eating these foods.

If we look at the adult formula, dry and canned, from this same company, we see something similar. The adult dry formula has 33 percent dry-matter protein and over 36 percent dry-matter highly processed carbohydrate. The canned adult food has more protein, at over 36 percent dry matter, but significantly less carbohydrate, at about 28 percent dry matter. This inconsistency is evident across all of the canned and dry products of all pet food companies. Why would these foods for the same life stage have such different levels of key nutrients when made by the same company? Do cats have different needs depending on whether they are eating dry or canned foods? The answer is no.

In fact, it is the food technology of canned and dry foods, not feline nutritional principles, that dictates the energy nutrient levels of these two forms of food. Dry pet foods are made with breakfast cereal and human snack-food technology called *extrusion*. Like the breakfast cereals and snacks, like corn chips that are made for humans, extruded pet foods must contain large amounts of starch to manufacture them into crunchy tidbits. Canned foods do not impose this requirement for starch, although some canned foods do still contain high levels of carbohydrate as "filler," as we see in the example above. Dry cat foods are loaded with cereals so that they will pop out of the extruder in the form of kibble (see chapter 20). The life-stage requirements of the cat have nothing to do with it.

Studies done to determine the energy composition of small mammal prey have shown that such prey generally contain about 55 percent dry-matter protein, about 35 percent dry-matter fat, and less than 2 percent carbohydrate. Clearly, many commercial foods are not even remotely similar to the natural foods of cats, and dry foods are the worst offenders in this regard. Fortunately, although the canned food described above does not qualify as having a natural energy-nutrient profile, there are commercial canned foods on the market with much better profiles.

So, What Do I Feed My Adult Cat?

Because of what we know about the cat's natural life-stage feeding habits, you should *not* vary the profile of the food you feed your adult cat as it matures. Given a diet that is high enough in protein and fat to be health-promoting, the kitten and adult cat will consume enough canned food or raw/cooked meat to meet its needs at every life stage, and will stop eating when this level has been reached. We do not see this self-limiting food consumption with dry food for reasons that are discussed in chapter 20, on obesity in cats.

Look for a canned food that has high protein, ideally above 40 percent on a dry matter basis (see appendix I for how to read a pet food label), moderate amounts of fat, ideally 25 to 35 percent dry matter, and low carbohydrate, ideally below 10 percent dry matter. One dry food on the market has only 7 percent carbohydrate, according to the manufacturer. Chemical analysis of this food shows that its carbohydrate level is actually about 13 percent. Although I had hoped that this product would be a satisfactory dry food option for my patients and my own cats, it has proved very disappointing in tests I have conducted. This food can promote obesity in spayed and neutered adult cats, just as its much higher carbohydrate dry food rivals do, and it cannot be used by diabetics. Feeding this food to a diabetic in remission causes a lapse out of remission. This food uses potato as its starch component for extrusion; apparently potato, with its very high simple sugar content and high glycemic index (corresponding rise in blood sugar), still causes the adverse effects in the cat that higher levels of less sugary carbohydrate ingredients do. Other "no cereal" dry foods containing novel starches like tapioca are in development. These foods will also fall far short of ideal foods for cats.

Recently, at least one company has started marketing a dehydrated powdered cat food. Along with some meat protein, this food contains an extraorindary amount of vegetables, fruits, and even honey! As a result, the carbohydrate content on a dry-matter basis exceeds 30 percent. This food is nothing more than powdered kibble, containing as much processed carbohydrate as the kibbled dry cat foods we have criticized in this and earlier chapters. The company attempts to obscure this fact by insisting that consumers consider only the carbohydrate content *after* water is added to the powder. On a wet-matter basis, the carbohydrate content is greater than 7 percent. Pet owners should not be misled by this, however. On a wet basis, dry kibbled cat foods also have 7 to 10 percent carbs. This is a dangerous level of processed carbohydrate for felines. Good quality canned cat foods have about 2 percent or less carbohydrate. So, no matter how you compare this food with other types, such a high-carbohydrate powdered food is a poor choice for feeding any cat. Avoid it.

For now, dry cat foods are not appropriate for the adult cat at any age. Rather, I recommend canned cat foods that have energy nutrient profiles as close to the cat's natural prey as possible. Certainly, you should avoid carbohydrate levels above 10 percent dry matter. Many manufacturers' kitten life-stage products will satisfy this requirement, although not all will, as we see in the example above. Kitten life-stage foods that have 15 percent carbohydrate or more are not appropriate for kittens *or* adult cats. Some canned lines do not have life-stage positioning, but are one-size-fits all products. The most popular small-can "gourmet" cat food product is in this category. These foods are usually meat-based and low in carbohydrate.

The ingredients in a canned food can be very instructive about how much carbohydrate is in the can. If you see such ingredients as cornmeal, corn grits, corn flour, rice flour, potato, sweet potato, carrots, apples, berries, or the like, you can be reasonably certain the food is too high in carbohydrate to be a good food for your adult cat. To avoid the ingredients in commercial foods that are unnatural for the cat's diet, many owners are turning to raw-meat diets. I personally feed raw meat to my cats, but it is not essential to do so to provide a very healthful diet for your kitten or cat. I recommend to all of my clients canned foods that meet the low-carbohydrate requirement, with good results.

18

The Annual Health Checkup—
Dos and Don'ts

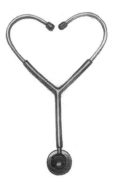

One thing about which all cat care experts can agree is the importance of regular veterinary exams for your cat throughout its entire life, from kittenhood through the senior years. If your veterinarian has a genuine interest and expertise with cats, the annual exam can be a crucial weapon against insidious disease. Even young cats can develop cancer and other serious or equally life-threatening conditions. A regular thorough evaluation of your cat's general well-being, and a discussion of any usual signs you may have observed since the last exam, can make all the difference in your pet's continued good health.

What to Look for in a Veterinarian for Your Cat

Because you expect to have a close relationship with your cat's veterinarian over decades, it is imperative that you choose a professional who has an interest in cats. No veterinarian, the author included, has the same level of interest or expertise with all species. Some veterinarians in practices that serve several species have much greater skill with dogs, or exotic species, than with cats. Some veterinarians do not feel as comfortable handling cats as they do handling dogs or other animals. There is a knack to handling cats in a way that is calming and reassuring to the cat, and veterinarians with this knack are better able to perform a good exam. Not all veterinarians have excellent cat-handling skills.

In addition, cats and their medical needs and problems are *very* different from those of other animals, even dogs. Veterinarians who see large numbers of cats and who intensively study their problems will be more adept at diagnosing and treating those problems. This skill and up-to-date understanding of feline medicine will make all the difference to your cat's health over its lifetime. It is completely reasonable for you to interview any veterinarian you consider for your cat's doctor, before you make a selection. Questions about the individual's experience with cats and comfort level in handling cats are fair, but of course, you should ask such questions in a polite way, with no implied judgment. Good veterinarians will appreciate your carefulness in choosing your cat's health-care provider. If your questions meet with defensiveness or irritation, you may wish to keep looking.

The first exam with your cat's veterinarian, whether it occurs when your cat is a kitten or an adult, is a critical time in the relationship between you and your cat's doctor. Be sure to make your expectations clear about the kind of care you wish for your cat. For example, if you want to be able to call your veterinarian with questions between exams, and hope to speak with the veterinarian personally, say so. This kind of expectation may or may not be something every veterinarian can meet. Regardless of the answers to your interview questions, good communication at the outset of your relationship is the key to your satisfaction with the care your pet receives, as well as your veterinarian's ability to meet your expectations. Good veterinarians want you to be pleased with the care they deliver. You are more likely to be pleased if you express what you want, and allow the veterinarian to respond to your expectations. Just as importantly, your veterinarian will understand the commitment you have made to the well-being of your cat and can make the same commitment.

If at any time you believe that your veterinarian is not the right doctor for your cat, you must feel free to seek a referral to another veterinarian, or choose another one yourself. The concept of "second opinion" is a time-honored one in human medicine and it should also be perfectly acceptable in veterinary medicine. No one veterinarian has all the answers, as any good one will tell you. You should never feel intimidated about seeking another opinion about your cat's case, or even about changing to another veterinarian's care altogether. You must feel entirely comfortable about your choice of health-care providers for your cat.

Having said that you have a right to expect expert care for your pet, I would also urge you to do your part to maintain strong ties with your cat's veterinarian, once you have made a lasting selection. Relationships are two-way streets. When you find the doctor in whom you have confidence, maintain that relationship by following all medical instructions completely, observing all recommended recheck exams, reporting complications and good results of treatment faithfully, and showing a regard for your doctor's schedule by keeping appointments on time. A good veterinarian who cares deeply about your pet is invaluable to your cat's health. When you find that person, be sure to hold up your end of the relationship.

Talk About Vaccines

The annual exam is the time when the subject of vaccination comes up. The days when all cats received all available feline vaccines are over. There are many products that protect against diseases that do not present risk for your cat. You and your veterinarian must discuss, in detail, which of these many vaccines are right for your cat's circumstances (see chapter 10 for more information on this). The schedule of administration of those vaccines has changed over the past decade as well. We know today that the protection from some common vaccines lasts longer than just one year. Your objective, and your veterinarian's objective, is to vaccinate your cat against only those diseases which pose a risk for your particular cat, and to vaccinate against those diseases only as often as absolutely necessary.

Talk About Your Cat's Teeth and Gums

One of the many things your veterinarian will check during the annual exam is the condition of your cat's mouth, gums, and teeth. Even in young cats, examination of this part of the body is extremely important. By the time your cat is four to six years old, tartar and plaque accumulation on your pet's teeth can become excessive, requiring a thorough cleaning. When a cat's teeth and gums are kept clean with regular prophylaxis, it is quite possible for the pet to retain all of its teeth, all of its life. Starting at about five years of age, most cats will do very well with dental cleaning every other year. This may become an annual requirement as the cat ages; your veterinarian can advise you about this.

Whatever the schedule, fighting gum disease and keeping your cat's teeth bright and clean through regular professional care is essential to your cat's general health as well as the health of its mouth. It is well known that oral infections in humans can lead to kidney damage, heart disease, and problems throughout the rest of the body. We strongly suspect that this is also the case in pets, including cats. Regular dental care can prevent these kinds of serious complications of periodontal disease, and keep the cat's teeth right where nature put them, for decades on end. Many veterinarians urge their clients to brush their pets' teeth on a regular basis at home. There are a number of brushing devices and pet-safe toothpastes available for this purpose (see online sites such as http://cats.about.com/cs/healthissues/a/dentalcareplan.htm). We know that even merely wiping the surfaces of the teeth with a finger-cot (a thimblelike device) or towel is helpful for removing plaque buildup and saving teeth. Starting this process with your kitten will increase likelihood of success as it becomes an adult.

If clients will commit to regular home oral care, and their cat will permit it, I encourage this wholeheartedly. Unfortunately, this is not particularly practical for the majority of my clients and patients. I have found that insisting on home care when the circumstances simply will not permit it is futile and results in frustration for everyone. I would rather my clients commit to having their pet's teeth and gums examined regularly, and allowing regular cleaning procedures as needed in my clinic, than to nag them about brushing their cat's teeth at home. Clients are not bad "parents" for their cat if they are unable to accomplish this task on a regular basis at home. Unfortunately, feeding "dental-care" type dry foods does not prevent the chronic buildup of plaque and tartar as promised, and regular checkups remain the main line of defense against deterioration of a cat's oral health. Depend on your veterinarian for this important aspect of total preventive care. See chapter 19 for more information about dental issues.

The Weight Check

One of the simplest but most important aspects of the annual checkup is weight assessment. Whether a cat is at optimum weight, or has gained or lost weight since the previous visit, this measurement is a source of invaluable information for the veterinarian. Creeping weight gain is evidence of overfeeding, or feeding the wrong foods. Obesity is as dangerous in the cat as it is in humans, and may affect as many as 50 percent or more of cats from two to ten years of age. It must be dealt with aggressively to avoid damage to the overweight cat's general health.

Conversely, unexplained weight loss may be a sign of deteriorating health from underlying causes and should be worked up with a complete series of tests. Of course, if the obese or overweight cat is losing weight gradually due to a dietary change from dry cat food to canned, that information usually means that the patient is in better health today than before. Taken together with the rest of the physical exam, your cat's weight today, compared to its weight one year ago, is an important piece of your pet's health puzzle. Your veterinarian can do a body condition assessment and record that along with weight. These objective data can point the astute clinician in the right diagnostic direction if disease is present. Be sure to ask your veterinarian to compare all of your cat's prior weight readings and body condition scores with the present one, for maximum benefit.

Generally, a healthy-weight adult male cat will weigh between nine and twelve pounds and a female will weigh from seven to ten pounds. Cats that weigh more than this, unless they are very large-framed cats such as purebred Maine Coon or Norwegian Forest Cats, are overweight. Today, many cat owners have lost perspective about what normal-weight cats look like, because they may have lived with a series of chronically overweight cats without realizing it. Fortunately, veterinarians today are beginning to realize that the number of their patients that are overweight is increasing, and the health of those patients is deteriorating. They realize that they must lead the effort against this serious and common problem. Chapter 20 discuses this problem in greater depth and explains how to reverse the problem.

Assessment of Your Cat's Heart Health
During the Routine Exam

In general, cats seem to develop less heart disease than dogs do. Nevertheless, there are several types of heart problems that affect cats at any age, and your veterinarian's careful assessment of this organ is vital at each annual exam (see chapter 28). An auscultation (listening to your cat's heart sounds with a stethoscope) is a routine part of the physical exam for cats, just as it is for people. If your veterinarian hears anything amiss during the auscultation, additional diagnostic procedures, like an ECG (or EKG, electrocardiogram), ultrasound (echocardiogram), or X-rays, may be needed. Understanding your cat's heart health is crucial to the length and quality of its entire life. If you have questions about how your cat's heart sounds, or the diseases that can cause heart disease in your pet, be sure to ask!

Evaluating Your Cat's Abdomen

Another very important part of the complete physical examination is the palpation of your cat's abdomen (belly). The experienced clinician can feel almost every organ in this area of the body, and determine whether those organs are normal in size and shape, with just his or her hands during a gentle palpation. It is also possible to detect lumps in the abdomen that do not belong there, perhaps indicating a tumor or infection in this region. This ability is reduced significantly in the obese patient, however, because large amounts of abdominal fat obscure all of the normal structures in this area. Keeping your cat at its ideal weight makes a thorough physical examination easier, and less stressful for your cat.

If your veterinarian detects anything amiss in the abdomen during the palpation, additional tests may be indicated. X-rays, an ultrasound exam, and blood work can clarify anything that is unusual on the routine physical exam of the cat's belly so that real abnormalities can be ruled out.

What About Routine Bood Tests for Cats at the Annual Health Checkup?

Many veterinarians do not perform blood work and urinalysis as part of the "well-pet" checkup in animals less than seven years of age. This is a reasonable approach as long as there are no signs whatsoever in the patient history or physical exam that anything is amiss. Alternatively, some clinicians, or their clients, want a laboratory evaluation every time the pet is examined. This is also a rational approach that will, in rare cases, disclose early problems. In my practice, I offer but do not insist on this level of exam in younger adults that seem to be in excellent health by physical exam. One clear advantage to performing lab tests under such circumstances is the normal baseline of values that can be established for the individual cat. This baseline provides important comparisons for later tests if the cat becomes sick.

19

Feline Dental Health—Your Cat Can Keep Those Pearly Whites!

The Importance of Your Cat's Oral Health

(see www.sniksnak.com/cathealth/dental2.html)

In the past decade, veterinarians have become increasingly aware of the importance of clean teeth and healthy gums to the general health and happiness of their feline patients. Without regular oral exams and professional care as needed, cats not only begin to lose teeth at an early age but may also experience problems with other organs. The gums have a very rich blood supply. When the gums become infected because bacteria are thriving around the teeth (called *periodontal disease*), these infections cause inflammation and can make gingivitis and stomatitis (see chapter 24) much worse. The blood vessels in those inflamed tissues will carry bacteria from the mouth to the rest of the body, where those bacteria can set up new infections. The kidneys and the heart are particularly vulnerable to this spread of disease.

Keeping your cat's teeth and gums cleansed of this bacterial buildup will prevent these complications while also preventing gum recession and tooth loss. I have seen many twenty-year-old cats with every tooth still in place. This is the natural state for the aging cat. Although many cat owners think that cats will inevitably lose their teeth as they grow older, this is not the case. Good preventive care of your cat's mouth will safeguard the health of the entire body, and keep those valuable teeth right where they belong.

All veterinarians know that the ideal basis for good oral health in the cat is regular brushing of the teeth (see www.placervillevet.com/cat%20toothbrushing.htm). If you can start brushing your cat's teeth when it is a kitten, gently and patiently, it is likely your cat will accept this throughout its life. Some adults can learn to accept having their teeth brushed or wiped clean of plaque, but starting early is best. If you are successful in caring for your cat's teeth at home in this way, you may be able to avoid having professional cleaning done as often as is necessary for the cat not receiving this regular home care.

Unfortunately, many adult cats simply will not accept brushing at home. As ideal as regular home care is, there is little point in turning a loving relationship between you and your cat into a nightmare by battling to clean its teeth. If this is your situation, I recommend regular professional exams and thorough cleaning by your veterinarian as the next best choice. In any case, you will want to have your veterinarian check your cat's mouth at every regular exam.

What About Dental Scaling and Cleaning Without Anesthesia?

You may hear from nonveterinarians that dental cleanings can be done without anesthesia. This is not true. Dental procedures performed with the pet wide-awake cannot effectively reach and clean below the gum line, or accurately assess the health of all of the teeth. It is impossible without deep sedation or anesthesia to evaluate gum recession and a kind of cavities that cats get called *resorptive neck lesions*. When my clients ask about cleaning their pet's teeth without anesthesia, I remind them of how hard it would be for them to thoroughly brush and examine all surfaces of their cat's teeth at home. I tell them that a thorough dental cleaning is far more involved and annoying to a wide-awake cat than a simple brushing would be, and that I want to do the very best job possible without traumatizing their pet.

While sedation and anesthesia have their inherent risks, today's gas anesthetics are safer than ever. Middle-aged and older cats should have a thorough physical exam and basic blood and urine evaluation, at least, to evaluate the pet's general health status prior to the procedure. Even cats with chronic diseases can have dental work done safely. With careful preanesthetic evaluation and monitoring of the cat's condition throughout the entire procedure, dental prophylaxis is safe, and extremely important to your pet's current and future well-being. This point cannot be overstated.

What About a "Dental" Diet?

You *cannot* protect your cat's teeth and gums by feeding "tartar-control" cat food. Valid clinical trials on "real" cats over realistic periods of time have not been done to prove that these formulas result in better long-term tooth and gum health in cats. Veterinarians everywhere treat serious dental disease every day in cats eating these very formulas. These foods usually contain very high levels of highly processed carbohydrate (35 percent dry matter or more) and cellulose, a wood-derived indigestible fiber, for its abrasive effect. This fiber puts an unnatural burden on the cat's gastrointestinal tract, which is unaccustomed to handling indigestible fiber. It also increases stool volume dramatically. The cat evolved eating wet-only, low-fiber, low-carbohydrate foods. Its teeth and gums, as well as the rest of its body, are perfectly suited to this formula.

The cat in its natural state *does* get a natural abrasive action from the bone in its captured prey. This same effect is available in the form of meats with bone ground into the meat. For my patients with a tendency to accumulate plaque and tartar rapidly (as some people do), I recommend their owners feed raw or cooked meats with ground bone periodically, or as an exclusive diet. Bone does not disintegrate and deposit a carbohydrate film on a cat's teeth, as kibble does. Tartar-control treats based on carbohydrate have the same drawbacks for dental health that the dry dental diets do. Avoid them. Just as human dentists do not recommend corn chips or breakfast cereal to cleanse their patient's teeth, pet owners should not feed high-carbohydrate "crunchies" to their cats for this purpose.

As I discuss elsewhere in this book, high levels of highly processed carbohydrate are not healthful for cats. Meat-based wet cat foods do *not* promote dental disease in cats, but they do supply plenty of the nutrients the cat needs most, protein, fat, vitamins, and essential fatty acids that come naturally with meat.

Remember . . .

Perhaps the most important first step you can take to keep your cat's mouth healthy is to believe that you can make the decisions to ensure that health, and that your cat can keep its teeth for life. Tooth loss and gum disease are not inevitable, they occur when you fail to understand how to prevent them. Remember:

1. To brush your cat's teeth regularly if you possibly can
2. To see your cat's veterinarian at least annually for checkups
3. To follow your veterinarian's advice about regular cleanings under anesthesia
4. To avoid feeding "designer" dry cat foods that neglect your cat's total health

20

Obesity— The Silent Epidemic

The Problem of Obesity

(see www.catnutrition.org/obesity.html)

The majority of today's pet cats are at least somewhat overweight, and an unfortunately large percentage of these pets are *obese*. Long gone are the days when an average, medium-framed adult feline weighed a sleek ten pounds. Now, the same cat typically will weigh thirteen to fourteen pounds, and a disturbing number will even tip the scales at a whopping, morbidly obese twenty pounds–plus! I see this so often in my feline practice. Each week, proud and devoted owners present their impossibly rotund felines to me for routine checkups without the slightest idea that their healthy pets have an insidious and dangerous disease. They are astonished when I tell them that "Cleo" or

"Mr. Whiskers" is on a clear and certain path to one of many chronic debilitating diseases that almost inevitably accompany long-term obesity in the cat.

As frightening to me as the epidemic of obesity in cats is, I find the failure of owners to recognize the problem even more frightening. Most of my overweight patients live with owners that did not realize their cats had this problem before they came to me. The reason so many attentive owners don't know that their cats are fat is simple. For most of them, it has been decades since they have even seen a cat that has that natural sleek, athletic build of the truly healthy mixed-breed cat. So what happened to the fit, swift, agile feline athletes we knew just a few decades ago? How did we turn millions of cats into the lethargic, overweight, food-obsessed couch potatoes we see today? Whose fault is it anyway, and how do we change it?

Why Are So Many of Our Cats Fat?

Decades before the demand for specialized and convenience commercial cat foods began to grow, dog owners comprised a large market for dry foods for their canine family members. The pet food industry was happy to meet this demand. Unfortunately, the development of commercial dog foods was driven not just by owner demand, but also by the pet food companies' desire to find profitable uses for excess agricultural commodities like corn, other grains, and meat unfit for or unused for human consumption. Manufacturers made no real effort to use science in the design of these early dog foods. The industry was unregulated and the rush to produce products for the marketplace was a free-for-all.

As the pet food industry began to grow, the pet food companies were not required to do any real-life feeding studies. They were required only to formulate into their foods enough of the various nutrients that the National Research Council said that pets needed. Random samples of a company's diets had to meet the established minimums and maximums in a laboratory analysis. Even though this gave a minimum of assurance of the quality of these foods, the ingredient content of these foods continued to be based on the cost of ingredients, not the pet's natural diet. To meet nutrient requirements, companies merely added commercial supplements when the lowest-cost ingredient mix did not provide the right balance.

Most pet food makers knew that the cat had some unique nutritional requirements. For example, cats need preformed vitamin A because they cannot synthesize this vitamin from dietary beta-carotene as dogs can. They need high levels of certain meat-derived amino acids, arginine and taurine, because they have limited capability to make these molecules in their bodies. They need an essential fatty acid, arachidonic acid, in the diet because they cannot make their own supply of this essential fatty acid as the dog can. The pet food companies believed, however, that existing dog food rations could provide the basis for cat food formulations, with minor tweaking of those formulations to give the cat its essential nutrient requirements.

Pet food manufacturers seemed to ignore the cat's unique metabolic machinery designed for high production of energy from protein, but not carbohydrate (see chapter 1). Cat owners, like dog owners before them, seemed to prefer the dry kibble form of food for their cats because of its convenience and seeming economy. As the number of dry cat foods grew in response to cat-owner demand, they were little more than high-cereal dry dog foods, processed into smaller, cat-size kibble, with a slightly different vitamin/mineral mix added. While the number and variety of cat foods has proliferated beyond anyone's ability to imagine twenty years ago, the heavy grain basis of these dry diets is still the same.

Without anyone realizing it, the cat eating dry food was suddenly eating food more fit for herbivores. Today's commercial dry foods, even those that are "premium quality," are uniformly high in essentially predigested carbohydrate, with only moderate levels of protein (much from vegetable protein sources) and little of the fat cats desperately need to meet their requirements for essential fatty acids and digestible calories from high-protein sources.

Why Are Dry Cat Foods Nutritionally Upside Down?

Both wet (canned and pouched) and dry cat foods are the product of marketing and food technology considerations, not the science of feline nutrition. Consider that canned and dry forms of the exact same formula of any brand have very different energy nutrient profiles (energy nutrients are the protein, fat, and carbohydrates of a food). Wet products have relatively high protein (usually about 40 to 55 percent of the dry matter if moisture is removed), moderate fat (usually 25 to 35 percent of dry matter), and low carbohydrate (usually about 2 to 8 percent dry matter), with fiber, vitamins, and minerals making up the balance.

Dry foods, however, bear no nutritional resemblance to their corresponding wet versions. A dry food will usually have about 20 to 35 percent dry-matter protein, 10 to 25 percent fat dry matter, and 25 to 50 percent dry-matter carbohydrate, with the balance made up of fiber and vitamin/mineral mix. Dry foods often have relatively high fiber content (5 to 8 percent) whereas canned foods, unless they have fiber deliberately added as a separate ingredient, have almost no fiber. Why would different forms of the exact same formula have such very different energy nutrient content? Do cats have different needs depending on whether they are eating canned or dry?

The answer is, "No, of course not." The cat has the exact same energy nutrient needs (and tolerance) no matter what form of food it eats. So why the great difference in these formulas?

A Lesson in Pet Food Technology

The production of a dry kibble using the process of extrusion (the same process used in making breakfast cereal and high-carbohydrate snack foods) dictates the energy nutrient mix of dry pet foods. Extrusion is the expansion and "popping" of kibbles through a high-heat, high-pressure process that will not occur unless there is substantial starch content in the mixture that is fed into the extruder. A canned food formula will end up a damp puddle at the end of the process, rather than as fluffy, air-filled kibbles ready for drying. So, pet food companies add tons of corn, rice, wheat, oats, barley, and other grains, the less expensive the better, to the meat meal and other low-volume ingredients that make up dry pet foods, to bulk them up. Recently, a dry food containing potato instead of cereal grain appeared on the market.

Further compounding the problem, when the cereal starches in the dry kibble mixture undergo processing at high heat and pressure during extrusion, they are predigested (broken down) by these extremes of cooking, and enter the pet's bloodstream essentially as sugar. Nothing in the cat's evolutionary development could possibly have prepared it for a steady diet of this glucose-laden junk food.

Not all cereals are created equal. Some grains cause a greater rise in blood sugar when consumed and digested (this effect is called the *glycemic index*). Perhaps the most offensive of all grains used in pet foods is corn, from which corn syrup, a pure sugar, dextrose, is derived. Because it is plentiful and cheap in this country, corn is one of the favorite dry pet food ingredients used by the industry. Most of the most expensive "premium" dry pet foods contain high amounts of this ingredient. Potato, a new ingredient in dry foods, also has a very high glycemic index, and is equally undesirable in pet foods for cats. The most popular cat foods are formulated according to the food technology requirements of this very convenient, easy-to-sell form of food, not according to the cat's known evolutionary requirements.

Ironically, dried kibble is almost completely unpalatable for the typical cat when it first comes out of the extruder and drying ovens. This is not surprising; one would expect that cats would find grains unappealing as food, otherwise, they would compete with rodents for grains rather than protecting those grain harvests by hunting the rodents. Because cats will not readily eat grain-based foods, a separate industry grew up to produce potent palatability enhancers for coating pet foods. These palatability additives may be acidified yeast (cats like the taste and/or mouth-feel of acid substances), but more commonly are comprised of meat "digests." *Digests* are meat by-products like animal entrails, fermented into a liquid "soup," and then sprayed onto the outside of the dry cat food kibble.

Few pet owners and veterinarians, including those opposed to the feeding of raw foods to their pets, would be so enthusiastic about commercial dry pet foods if they knew how this ingredient was made and applied to pet foods. With digests on the outside of grain-based kibble, cats are essentially tricked into eating a food they would not ordinarily eat. This reminds me of the application of candy coatings on the outside of children's breakfast cereal to increase a child's craving for relatively low nutritional-value human breakfast foods.

Compare the formulation and production of dry cat foods with the formulation and production of wet foods. Wet-formula cat foods do not require starch in their production. Pureed, chunked, sliced, or grilled meats go perfectly well into a sealed can or pouch that is then sterilized in a high-heat sterilizer. These meat-based formulas are highly palatable for cats. Wet foods have energy nutrient profiles that are high protein, low to moderate fat, and low carbohydrate, because this is the nutrient profile of meat-based food that will not be extruded and will not require palatability enhancers.

This is quite different from the nutrient profile of dry foods, which are slave to the food technology of extrusion and the resulting need for coatings of palatability-enhancers such as fermented digest before packaging. The ingredients and nutritional value of the different forms of cat food are dictated by the requirements of food technology, not the science of feline nutrition.

Carbohydrates: The Culprit in the Feline Obesity Epidemic

Ask any pet food company scientist why they formulate such high levels of highly processed carbohydrate into their costliest dry cat foods, and they will insist that, while the cat has no known requirement for carbohydrate, there is no known harm in using carbohydrate ingredients in cat food. They will further argue that those very ingredients allow production of the most convenient form of cat food, dry kibble.

Research into the causes and management of feline type 2 diabetes, including work originated by me and later verified by colleagues at one of these large companies, suggests strongly that the blood sugar level of the cat is rapidly influenced by the energy nutrients in its diet. Sugar from highly processed cereal grains in the dry diet floods the blood that carries nutrients from the GI tract to the liver, causing an alarm to go out to the pancreas. One of the most important jobs of this small organ near the cat's stomach is to keep the blood sugar level in the cat from rising to harmful levels. The pancreas responds by producing and secreting insulin, a hormone that drives blood sugar into the cells of the body, thereby lowering the tide of sugar to more normal levels.

In the wild state, the obligatory carnivore seldom if ever encounters this state of high-sugar emergency. The foods the feral cat consumes contain 5 percent or less carbohydrate, and all of that 5 percent would be complex carbohydrates like grasses and seeds from the gastrointestinal tract of a small prey animal. Never, in its widest travels, would the cat have an opportunity to eat processed-cereal junk food of the type and quantity represented by a steady diet of dry cat food. The cat's pancreas is not prepared to cope with this daily blood sugar crisis (the consequences of this unnatural pressure on the pancreas, and related pressures on the cat's liver, are discussed in detail in chapter 21).

The normal cat pancreas tries to control this unnatural state by putting high levels of insulin into constant circulation. This high insulin level causes the accumulation of fat in the body as energy nutrients are driven into the cells, even in the absence of a need for all that energy. As high insulin levels succeed in lowering the blood sugar, the animal may even experience a relative hypoglycemia, or lower-than-normal blood sugar, which will trigger hunger and the additional consumption of high-sugar dry food. A vicious cycle starts. Many humans can experience this roller-coaster of high and low blood glucose when they eat highly processed carbohydrate diets as well.

Complicating all of this vicious cycling is the cat's unique system of signals from food that tell it that it is full and should stop eating. Because the cat evolved in an environment rich in protein and fat but deficient in carbohydrate, consumption of fat and protein evolved as the signal to the cat that it should cease intake when calorie needs are met. A high-carbohydrate diet, however, has a minimal effect on intake signals in the cat, even as energy requirements are met and even exceeded. Not only is the cat's pancreas poorly suited to handling repetitive substantial sugar loads from highly processed dry cat food, the satiety system is also unable to respond to high carbohydrate intake by making the cat feel full.

The end result is cats that overeat highly processed carbohydrate foods, spiking repeated surges of insulin from their limited carnivore's pancreatic reserve. Many become overweight, even obese. For a large number of cats, their metabolic systems eventually become overwhelmed by this unnatural chain of events and its unremitting stress on the pancreas, resulting in diabetes. Because most house cats are sexually altered, a physiologic state that reduces the cat's metabolic needs much as the attainment of middle age does in humans, the cycle becomes even more destructive and inescapable.

It is no surprise that so many of today's dry-food-fed cats are obese. What is more surprising to me is that not *all* are. The observation that some cats somehow manage to escape becoming overweight on dry-food diets is similar to the observation that not all humans that smoke cigarettes get cancer. They are the exceptions to the rule, individuals spared by good genes and a myriad of other, unknown factors from a serious, lifestyle-related harm. We don't have tests to determine which cats have the good genes and which do not. What we do know is that dry kibbled cat food is a dangerous dietary choice for all cats, especially because there are superior, readily available alternatives.

Why Should We Be Concerned About Overweight Cats?

If your cat becomes seriously overweight, is this really a problem? Are we worrying about something that is really a cosmetic issue, instead of a medical threat? Once a cat becomes greatly overweight, about thirteen to fourteen pounds for the average cat, many things change for that animal. Activity levels decrease, leading to even more weight gain. The cat loses its interest in and ability to groom itself, and its coat becomes dull and dry. Fecal residue at the rectum of the cat that cannot groom itself causes discomfort and even infection. Strain on joints causes many overweight cats to have pain when they jump, or just try to move quickly. Although cats do not seem to suffer from atherosclerosis (hardening of the arteries), excess pounds rob them of life and its quality even so. The fat cat is a couch potato, unwilling to play and interact with other animals or people, so quality of life deteriorates.

My clients with overweight cats are surprised when I advise a diet change but do not insist that they start an exercise program for their cat at the same time. The reason for this is simple. One of the first of the many positive changes owners see when their cats change from a high-carb diet to a low-carb one is an astonishing physical rejuvenation. Couch potatoes begin to play with toys and chase around the house as if they were kittens again. They become far more interactive with the family than ever before. The cat does get more exercise, and that increased activity works together with the low-carb diet to reduce weight naturally. I have seen this result in every single one of the hundreds of overweight patients I have worked with.

Further, cats on medication for arthritis can reduce or even stop medication altogether. Problems with constipation often disappear; the dull dry coat is replaced by the lustrous healthy hair of the cat's younger days. The list of benefits goes on and on.

Prevention or correction of obesity in the cat is not merely an exercise in cosmetics, although the cat at its optimal weight *is* more beautiful, more agile, and more graceful than the overweight cat. Much more than that, helping our cats remain athletic and svelte helps them remain active and healthy for many more years of life. When a cat is living its life as nature intended it to do, at the weight its frame and structure were meant to maintain, all of its systems function at their best. The greatest threat to the cat's naturally healthful state is the present day practice of feeding commercial dry cat foods.

How Have Unhealthful Foods Gained Such Wide Acceptance?

Many pet owners and veterinarians believe that commercial pet foods are safe and nutritious to feed to their pets because they have been scientifically tested through "feeding trials." The American Association of Feed Control Officials' statement you see on many pet foods guarantees that the contents of the can or bag have undergone some kind of testing to assure that it is good for your pet. This statement is extremely misunderstood by most pet owners and their veterinarians and misleads them into believing they can trust the long-term nutritional quality of the food bearing the statement.

What pet owners and their pet's health-care providers do not realize about these "feeding trials" is that they only last a few months and test foods on a small number of cats. Because they are of such limited duration, only severe toxicities are likely to be disclosed during the course of such a trial. These feeding tests typically involve young animals so that the tested product can claim safety and completeness in the sensitive growth phase of life. This means that young cats with great resilience and metabolic reserves, and relatively high metabolic rates compared to older cats, consume the tested product for a few months, entitling the product to claim safety, efficacy, and freedom from ill effects even if fed to an aging pet for decades!

Imagine if a fast-food company conducted a feeding trial with humans, in which a group of active teenagers ate only the fast food of these giant companies for a period of a few months. Let's assume that during this trial most of the youngsters involved suffered no noticeable ill effects. At the end of this trial, let's imagine that this fast-food company began to make claims that their trial proved that their burgers were clearly "complete and balanced" as sole nutrition for the lifetime of all humans. Can you imagine a more absurd claim based on a more absurd "scientific trial"?

Six months of feeding of a particular food to a small group of healthy young cats does not prove that that product will not harm such animals over a lifetime, or even over a few years. The fact is that within two to eight years of constant free-choice consumption of any dry cat food, a significant percentage of cats will be overweight, and many of these will be morbidly obese. You don't hear about this, because the pet food companies don't test for overweight and obesity. It is telling, however, that nearly all pet food companies now produce a wide variety of costly weight-loss foods to help your fat cat shed those pounds once they have acquired them. Clearly, the risk of obesity is well known to the companies that have produced the foods that made your cat fat, or they would not have spent the millions to package and market weight-loss products. Sad to say, these rescue formulas don't work; for most cats they make matters worse.

Think About It

In late 2005, a research group at the University of Pennsylvania School of Veterinary Medicine published a study that was intended to find out if a low-carbohydrate diet would support weight loss and prevent weight gain in two groups of cats consuming two dry kibbled diets. One of these diets was higher in processed carbohydrate than the other, but both were much higher in processed carbohydrate than canned commercial diets or homemade meat diets. The conclusions of the study are quite mysterious, in part because there was no truly low carbohydrate, meat-based diet used, and partly because the obese and normal-weight cats were all housed together and able to eat each other's food.

What is more disturbing than the lack of real-world conclusions from this study is the fact that *only* kibbled cat food was even studied. The so-called low-carbohydrate diet in this experiment was much higher in carbohydrates than the free-living feral cat would ever consume (see chapter 1). Further, the carbohydrates in both diets were from highly processed cereal, also a far cry from any natural diet of the obligatory carnivore. It is a mystery why this study did not even include any commercial canned food, given that, of all commercial foods, canned cat foods typically have the least amount of processed carbohydrate available to cats in commercial foods today. If these researchers were really interested in testing the effects of low dietary carbohydrate in the origins and control of feline obesity, why would they fail to feed canned cat food to at least some of the cats? This study seems to have been based upon the assumption, clearly erroneous, that dry cat foods are the only type of food available to cats today.

Why "Weight-Loss" Pet Foods Don't Help Your Cat Lose Weight

If you have ever tried to reduce your overweight cat's excess pounds using one or more of the many weight-loss foods, you know they don't work. Why not? The answer is simple. Those new expensive foods are based upon the exact same faulty understanding of the cat that allowed the original foods to cause obesity in the first place. In developing the foods to correct the obesity caused by their "regular" foods, the pet food companies have not yet come to an understanding of the unique metabolic characteristics of the cat. Instead, they have simply applied tired old human dieting theory to their feline diet foods, perhaps in hopes that the rationale will be familiar and seem sensible to the humans who buy these foods for their cats.

Feline "light" or "weight-control" foods are uniformly very low in fat, and this reduction in fat is compensated for with an increase in, you guessed it, *processed grain carbo-hydrate plus indigestible fiber.* Can there be any doubt that such a diet will fail to reverse the damage done by the cat's previous, high-carbohydrate diet? On this new diet, the cat receives even less natural nourishment because the added fiber creates constipating residue and decreases nutrient digestibility. The cat experiences even less satisfaction from protein and fat signals to its brain, and craves more food. More highly processed carbohydrate stimulates even greater overproduction of insulin, with deposition of more fat. The cycle continues. Usually, the cat does not lose weight unless portions are reduced to near-starvation levels. Worse still, the cat is always hungry and miserable.

Cats are high-meat, high-protein, low-carbohydrate creatures. For the most part, dietary fat does not make cats fat, high levels of dietary carbohydrate do. Felines are the quintessential "Atkins" species, for which high-carbohydrate foods are not simply irrational, they are deadly. We will see this over and over in the chapters ahead.

How to Know If Your Cat Is Overweight

1. If your cat is an adult female, she should weigh between seven and eleven pounds at the most. Exceptions are purebred cats of the Maine Coon, Norwegian Forest Cat, and Ragdoll breeds. Females of these breeds can weigh as much as twelve to fourteen pounds.
2. If your cat is an adult male, and not one of the larger breed cats mentioned above, your cat should weigh nine to twelve pounds at most. Males of the large breeds can weigh thirteen to eighteen pounds normally.
3. Even if your cat does not exceed the guidelines above, he or she may still be overweight. One way to tell is to stand your cat up on its back legs. Do you see a "waist" just below the rib cage and just above the hind legs? Cats should not be perfect rectangles or squares. They are designed to have shoulders and ribs that are broader then their hips, like an athletic human swimmer.
4. Another measure of a cat's degree of overweight is the fat under the skin over the ribs. If you place the palm of your hand against your cat's rib cage and can't feel ribs readily against your palm, then your cat is at least a little overweight. If you can't feel ribs even if you use your fingertips to feel for ribs, then your cat has a lot of fat under the skin there and is badly in need of a weight-loss program.

5. If your cat doesn't groom itself anymore, or can't groom areas such as under its tail, hind legs, and belly because of excess fat getting in the way, it's time for action to make your cat healthy again!

Are There No Scientific Studies About Feline Obesity and Its Cause?

Lately, we have seen a few studies about overweight in cats published in pet food company newsletters and even in one veterinary journal. These studies clearly reflect the pet food industry's growing awareness of the public's concern about high carbohydrate diets for cats. In late 2005, a research group at the University of Pennsylvania School of Veterinary Medicine published a study that was intended to find out if a "low-carbohydrate" diet would support weight loss and prevent weight gain in two groups of cats consuming two dry kibbled diets (see sidebar, page 136).

The conclusions of the study are quite muddled, in part because there was no truly low-carbohydrate, meat-based diet used, and partly because the obese and normal-weight cats were all housed together and able to eat each other's food! The study report itself concludes that "the observations of this investigation must be viewed within the context of the diets used. Specifically formulated test diets and *appropriate study design* could overcome the disparity in ingredients and control for nutrient profile." Indeed!

While this is an admirable level of candor and objectivity from the study scientists, the effect of this study's publication will be to make veterinarians believe that this research actually proved something important about carbohydrates and obesity, that carbohydrate levels in cat foods have little impact on weight gain or loss. In fact, the work proved no such thing!

In another study by the University of Georgia printed in a promotional newsletter of a large pet food company, the effects of two dry high-carbohydrate diets were studied in a small group of obese and nonobese cats for a few months. Again, neither diet could be considered "low-carbohydrate" relative to the cat's natural diet. The kibble with the lesser amount of highly processed cereal content was identified as "low carbohydrate" although it contained 23 percent highly processed carbohydrate. The editor of the newsletter, who is a pet food company representative, described the study as showing that "healthy cats appear well able to adapt to a wide range of carbohydrate intake." This is an astonishing conclusion from such a one-sided experiment. No low-carbohydrate diet was even part of the limited scope of the study, and the kinds of tests done on the cats in the research allow no such conclusion. Both of these research studies are examples of results-oriented studies, designed in advance to provide support for the position the pet food companies have already taken. Unfortunately, such "research" misleads pet owners and veterinarians to believe that genuine science supports the industry's products. It is clearly time for the opinion-leaders of the veterinary profession to stand up and conduct *real* scientific inquiry into the question of how to feed our cats.

How to Help Your Cat Lose That Health-Damaging Excess Weight

Because the cause of obesity in our house cats is diet-related, the solution is also nutritional. We must remove the carbohydrate and replace it with the much-needed protein and fat. This is easy to do, fortunately. Most wet cat foods have the right balance of energy nutrients to sustain health in the cat, as well as starting the weight-loss process. The mere act of changing from a high-carbohydrate dry diet to a low-carbohydrate canned diet will start the reversal of negative metabolic effects in the cat's body overnight. Many cats will not overeat wet foods, even if given limitless amounts. The protein and fat content of such foods (canned or homemade meat diets) send the natural satiety signal to the cat's brain when enough food has been consumed.

Some cats previously fed dry foods, however, have an acquired habit of overeating because of the nutritional inadequacies of their previous diet. For such cats, especially overweight cats, meal-feeding of set portions is appropriate. This may be less convenient for owners than merely leaving a "bottomless" bowl of dry food out all the time. The cost to the pet's health is simply not worth this convenience, however, as any concerned cat owner will agree.

Obese cats will lose from four to sixteen ounces per month, without severe portion restriction. An overweight cat, fourteen or more pounds, will need about nine ounces of good-quality wet cat food daily, to supply its calories and keep its appetite satisfied. Less overweight cats from twelve to fourteen pounds will need about six to seven ounces of such low-carbohydrate food every day. With this much food, overweight cats will lose their excess weight, gradually and safely. They will regain their former activity level and begin to groom themselves. Joint pain from arthritis will gradually disappear. The athlete hiding inside of every fat cat can come out to play once again.

Once your cat is losing weight, remember that, today, no dry diet is safe for your previously overweight cat to eat. One day perhaps, some pet food company will invent some way to make a food that combines the convenience of dry kibble with the nutrient suitability of canned foods and raw meat. That time has not yet come, even with potato or tapioca-based formulas, and your obesity-prone cat should never eat dry kibbled food or crunchy dry cat treats with their high sugar content.

The transition to an all wet food diet may take time with some cats. They are, after all, creatures of habit. I have yet to meet a cat that cannot learn to love wet food, though, and the health benefits of this new diet are well worth the effort.

How to Switch Your Cat from Dry Cat Food to Wet Cat Foods

Dry cat foods are highly addictive, especially for some cats. If your cat has eaten nothing but dry food all its life, it will probably resist a change to more nutritious wet foods. In essence, your cat is addicted to the dry kibble flavorings the way young children become "addicted" to junk food if that is all they eat for a long period. I have seen many cats like this. They do present a small challenge when owners try to make the switch to better nutrition. Fortunately, I have never seen a single cat that cannot be switched with the right approach and a little patience. I recommend my clients with dry-food-addicted cats try the following:

1. Look for and select canned or pouched cat food that has meat ingredients. Avoid foods with starchy vegetables like potato, corn, rice, or wheat in any form, carrots, and any kind of fruit. These ingredients are not only full of sugar and carbohydrate, but they also decrease palatability. Canned foods with meat ingredients will be more appealing to your dry food lover than cereals, vegetables, and fruits. Some cats really like fish-based canned foods. These can be good transitional foods.
2. Select several flavors and textures of the meat-based canned or pouched foods to increase the chances that at least one will appeal to your picky eater.
3. If your cat likes meat gravies or juice (like tuna juice from human tuna), it is okay to use this to top the wet food and create a saucy texture to increase your cat's interest in the new food at the beginning. You may also top the new wet

food with roasted meat if your cat likes meat. Use your imagination in selecting "enhancers" to put in the new food during the switch period. This won't be necessary for very long.

4. There are appetite stimulants, like cyproheptadine (an antihistamine), that give cats an appetite about twenty minutes after administration of about 2 milligrams. Because the great majority of cats will continue eating, and enjoying, wet foods once they eat just a meal or two, this kind of stimulation is needed only temporarily in those cats that need it to get started. You will need to speak with your veterinarian about this.

5. Many dry-food-addicted cats will eat meat baby food readily even before they acquire a taste for wet cat foods. Offer some of this, and even hand-feed it to your cat if necessary. You can even use meat baby food to "top" the canned or pouched cat food you are switching to.

6. As a very last resort, mix the dry food your cat prefers with canned or pouched foods. Increase the amount of wet food and decrease the amount of dry food over the course of a few days.

7. Do not allow your cat to refuse to eat anything for more than thirty-six hours. Even three to four ounces per day of a meat-based food will provide enough protein to avoid hepatic lipidosis (see chapter 22). If your cat is eating at least this amount, continue to make the diet change.

Using the techniques above, I have switched even the most resistant cats from dry cat food to wet. If your cat is already eating some wet food before you begin the switch to all-wet, you will have little or no trouble convincing it to make a complete switch to all wet, all the time.

21

Feline Diabetes— A Man-made Killer

In 1990, experts estimated that the number of diabetic cats in the United States was at least 150,000 such cases at any one time. Since then, the sheer numbers of pet cats have grown tremendously, and the negative influences causing this very serious disease have increased. Most veterinarians agree that they are seeing more and more feline diabetic patients as time goes by. I certainly am. In my practice of well over two thousand regular patients, at least fifty are diabetic at any one time, or about 2.5 percent of my patients. If this number is even close to the true incidence of this very serious disease today, the total number of cats in the country with diabetes could be 1.5 million at any one time! This is an astounding number of cats to be affected simultaneously by a very serious, often fatal disease.

Some will say that this increase in numbers of diagnosed diabetics is not only due to the increase in cats overall, but also to the increased health care that today's cats receive. Owners seem more aware of the need to take their cats to the veterinarian for regular checkups, and they more carefully watch their cats' behavior at home. Surely, now that most well-cared-for pet cats live indoors, it is easier for owners to notice when their pets are ill and more likely that they will rush to get prompt diagnosis and treatment for any disease than it was in 1990. Even if an increase in the quantity of health care pet owners give their cats were a partial explanation, though, feline lifestyle changes during the past twenty-five years have also increased the chance that any cat will develop adult-onset diabetes in its lifetime.

We know the indoor cat gets a bit less exercise than an outdoor cat. Exercise is important in preventing both obesity and diabetes in humans, and this is probably true for cats as well. Even outdoor cats sleep a great deal, however, about eighteen to twenty hours per day. Play and hunting activities take up only a short period in even the free-roaming cat's daily schedule. On the other hand, I know that my indoors-only patients that eat only low-carbohydrate foods do not become overweight, and virtually never become diabetic. Yet, they experience the same restriction on their hunting and roaming ways. The level of exercise restriction that an indoor cat experiences is not a critical factor in development of either obesity or diabetes, despite current thinking that this is the sole reason for the problems.

Cats that eat low-carbohydrate wet foods are much more likely to avoid becoming overweight and to remain active even living indoors. This is because high-carbohydrate cat foods, especially dry cat foods (which must have a lot of carbohydrate to form a kibble), create wide swings of blood sugar, as candy does for humans. This can cause a kind of sluggish feeling and reluctance to play with humans and other animals. This effect decreases exercise far more than the mere fact of living indoors (see http://petdiabetes.wikia .com).

Feline Diabetes—How Can Such a Common Disease Be So Misunderstood?

Adult-onset diabetes in the cat (type 2 diabetes) is caused when there is a release of large amounts of glucose (blood sugar) into the bloodstream without the pancreas making and releasing enough insulin to handle that sugar. In diabetics, the pancreas does not respond to rising blood sugar. When this happens, the cat begins to feel great thirst and will produce much more urine than usual. Usually, a diabetic cat's appetite also increases, but it will still lose weight over time. As the disease goes on without treatment, the cat will start to vomit, become very dehydrated, and act very sick.

The diagnosis of feline diabetes is generally easy. Blood and urine tests that show significantly elevated sugar levels, accompanied by the typical clinical signs, are all that is needed, although other tests will show how much secondary damage is present as well. Because the diabetic cat lacks enough insulin of its own making, treatment after diagnosis consists of insulin injections under the skin, just as it does for human diabetics. For decades, this has been the standard approach to treating feline diabetes. For decades, most cats have not done well after their diagnosis, even when their owners have been devoted to giving them good care and daily insulin shots.

In the 1980s, researchers studied how diet might be used to improve the quality of life for diabetic cats. They concluded that combining high fiber with a cat's normal diet would help control diabetes in cats. This high-fiber idea became popular with veterinarians, and pet food manufacturers who funded the research started making diets that had a lot of added indigestible fiber in the form of cellulose (wood fiber).

The theory was that the fiber in the diet would interfere with the absorption of dietary sugar from the intestines into the bloodstream. With this decrease in digestibility, dietary sugar would go into the bloodstream more slowly and would not cause the wide swings of blood sugar that make controlling the diabetic cat so difficult. This theory seemed logical. The diets have been prescribed by every veterinarian in small animal practice for the treatment of feline diabetes for two decades now. There is just one problem: they don't work.

There are some serious problems with the research and the conclusion that adding cellulose fiber to a cat's regular food is a good way to control its diabetes. First, the high-fiber diet research compared diets with high carbohydrate *and* fiber to diets with high carbohydrate *without* fiber. In this experiment, the high-carbohydrate diet with the high fiber did seem to provide more control than the high-carbohydrate diet without fiber. To conclude from this that a high-carbohydrate/high-fiber diet is the best dietary approach for controlling feline diabetes is misleading, however.

Imagine a study proving that candy bars with added fiber are better for human diabetics than candy bars without this fiber, because all of the sugar in those high-fiber candy bars is absorbed more slowly. Imagine concluding from such a study that human diabetics should control their disease by eating candy bars with indigestible fiber. Most physicians tell their human diabetic patients not to eat candy bars at all, because all dietary sugar, with or without fiber, makes this disease very hard to control.

If the researchers of the 1980s had studied how *low*-carbohydrate diets affect feline diabetics, instead of simply manipulating the absorption of sugar from high-carbohydrate diets, they would have discovered that taking the carbohydrate (sugar) out of the diet is a much bigger help in the control of feline diabetes than is adding indigestible vegetable residue to high-sugar diets. Cats eating a high-fiber/high-carbohydrate diet still have high blood sugar levels. Also, stool volume in cats that eat a high-fiber diet goes up greatly, and constipation sometimes occurs. As if this weren't bad enough, a high-fiber diet is not appetizing for cats, and so manufacturers have to add a lot of palatability enhancers to fool the carnivorous cat into eating a very unnatural food. The amount of such food must also be restricted, making the patient hungry all the time.

Necessity Is the Mother of Invention

In 1994, one of my own cats, Punkin, developed diabetes and started me down the road to understanding this disease for the very first time. Although I had been a veterinarian for seventeen years at that time, I had always used the high-fiber, high-carbohydrate diet and insulin injection strategy for the diabetic cats in my care. I, like all of my colleagues, knew about the high-fiber research and believed it was the best information available. Like my other diabetic patients, Punkin was very hard to regulate. His blood glucose would swing from very high to very low. He suffered several episodes of a very serious condition called *diabetic ketoacidosis*, which happens to a cat when too little insulin leads to prolonged high blood sugar levels.

Punkin also had episodes of hypoglycemia (blood sugar too low) leading to seizures. His case was a medical nightmare. After suffering with my poor cat for about a year like this, I became so frustrated that I did something that no one else I knew had done before that time. I stepped back and took a good long look at what I was doing. I asked myself, "Why is this so hard? What am I doing that is keeping my cat from getting better?"

When I asked myself these questions, I had already worked for one of the largest pet food manufactures for almost a decade. I knew quite a bit about the processing that was used to make both dry and canned pet foods, and I also knew a lot about the ingredients that went into pet foods. I knew that to make dry cat foods, a manufacturer had to use lots of cereal. Dry kibbled foods are very high in refined carbohydrates and simple sugar. The sugar is absorbed quickly from the food and goes into the cat's bloodstream, assaulting the metabolic machinery of the liver and pancreas. Making things worse, when a cat "grazes" on high carbohydrate food all day, this assault goes on and on. This is true of a high-carbohydrate, high-fiber diet just as it is true of a high-carbohydrate, low-fiber diet.

Realizing all of this, I wondered if his high-carbohydrate diet was making Punkin's diabetes hard to control. I also thought it might be what was making him act so hungry all the time. What if the food I was feeding had too much carbohydrate and simple sugar, and too little of the other nutrients Punkin needed to be healthy and control his diabetes? I decided to do a little experiment with him. I changed his diet from one of the high-carbohydrate, high-fiber dry foods, to one of the canned kitten foods on the market. This canned kitten food had very little carbohydrate and sugar but lots of the protein and fat that Punkin's body needed so badly. My experiment worked better than I had dreamed it could. Punkin's blood sugar levels fell immediately after only one day on the canned diet. I had to stop giving him the high doses of insulin he used to need. If I had left the insulin dose the same as before the diet change, he would have had serious low blood sugar problems. Within five days on the new diet, Punkin didn't need any insulin injections at all. He had good blood sugar levels just by eating the canned kitten food alone.

I was delighted. What a sensational result. But Punkin was only one cat, and one cat does not even begin to make a complete experiment. I knew I needed to try my experiment on other diabetic cats. Luckily, I knew other veterinarians in practice who were willing to try my new approach in some of the diabetic cats they were trying to treat. Working together, we switched a dozen diabetic cats to the new diet. It worked, every time. We found that every cat needed a lot less insulin when it ate the canned diet than when it ate a high-carbohydrate, high-fiber diet. Many, like Punkin, went off insulin shots altogether. Gradually we switched more and more cats to canned cat food, and found the same result. This was definitely a big step forward for cats with diabetes—and for their owners.

With help from friends at Heska Corporation, a veterinary biotechnology company in Colorado, I applied for a patent on the new idea. At first I was doubtful you could get a patent on such a simple "no-brainer" idea. I knew that this was not rocket science, only a simple, logical approach that seemed so obvious once I took the time to think about it. But it was a truly novel idea that no one else had ever put into writing, so the United States patent office issued my patent in March 2001 (patent # 6,203,825; text available online at the U.S. Patent Office Web site).

What Causes Diabetes in the Cat?

For many years, veterinarians have known that obesity in cats seemed to make the obese patient more likely to get diabetes. In fact, most of us thought that overweight actually *caused* diabetes. Today, I do not believe excess pounds in a cat are a cause of this condition. I believe that obesity in the cat and feline diabetes have the same parent causes, but are not a cause of one another. Although we do see many feline diabetics that are also quite overweight, these cats are probably genetically predisposed to get *both* of these problems from the same root causes. Because we often see cats that have one, but not both, of these conditions, this is undoubtedly because of each cat's unique genetic makeup. The significant numbers of always-slender cats that have full-blown diabetes suggest that being proper weight does not protect from this disease. Also, we see very overweight cats that become diabetic, but then recover from their diabetes easily on proper diet and insulin, long before they lose the weight they need to lose.

If obesity doesn't directly cause diabetes, then what does? Well, with cats just as with people, it definitely pays to have good genes. Some cats simply have genes that make them more or less likely to get diabetes, and more or less likely to get lots of other diseases as well. The story doesn't stop there, though. Other environmental factors play a big part in either getting or avoiding a disease such as diabetes. Without question, for the cat (and for most humans as well), the most important environmental factor that causes diabetes is diet.*

Because today's indoor cat is almost always eating dry cat food, with its extremely high sugar content, a cat with any genetic tendency to become obese and/or become diabetic will do just that when sugar is a large part of its diet. In my many years of practice, I have never seen a diabetic cat that was eating canned food or a homemade meat-based diet only. Also, I have never seen a significantly overweight cat that was eating such low-carbohydrate diets only. The onset of obesity and diabetes is triggered by constant flooding of the cat's system with refined carbohydrate from the dry diet, day after day, month after month, and year after year. In many cats, this steady sugar rush finally exhausts the small pancreatic capabilities of the carnivore because the cat's evolu-

---

*In rare instances, diabetes in cats is accompanied by or may even be caused by other primary diseases of the endocrine system. Hyperthyroidism, Cushing's disease, and acromegaly are examples of other hormonal diseases that may complicate diabetes. Diabetes that is exceptionally difficult to manage using the priciples described in this chapter must be evaluated by the attending veterinarian for evidence of one of these complicating diseases.

tion never prepared it for a constant high-sugar diet. In many cats, these relentless sugar surges cause the cat pancreas to turn that sugar to fat (see chapter 20). Obesity, with or without diabetes, follows.

Why Are Dry-Food-Fed Diabetics So Prone to Hypoglycemia?

Many diabetic cats on insulin experience periodic episodes of hypoglycemia when their blood sugar plummets. These cats, like Punkin, become weak or even comatose, and may even have a seizure. These signs all result when the cat's brain isn't getting enough sugar (glucose). This serious complication is all too common in dry-food-fed diabetics. However, we do not see clinical hypoglycemia in diabetic cats that are eating low-carbohydrate wet foods. Why?

To answer this question, we have to understand how the pancreas and liver in the cat work together. As we have discussed, one of the pancreas's most important jobs is to make sure that the cat's blood sugar level does not go too high. On the other hand, one of the liver's most important jobs is too make sure that the blood sugar level does not go too low. The pancreas and liver work together as a team to keep the blood sugar level steady in the normal range for health. The pancreas produces constant small bursts of insulin over the course of the day in response to rising glucose and it produces another hormone, glucagon, in response to falling glucose levels. Glucagon acts on the liver to cause it to release its small stores of glucose (glycogen) and to cause it to produce larger amounts of glucose from amino acids in a process called gluconeogenesis. In the healthy cat, these two organs work seamlessly together to keep the cat's blood sugar in balance at all times.

In the normal cat, when the pancreas and liver sense that blood sugar is dropping significantly (as when a cat exercises vigorously), greater amounts of glucose (blood sugar) are produced in the liver. This is a very well-developed liver activity in this species, because the cat in nature gets very little of its sugar from its food. Dietary protein and amino acids are the sugar reservoir in this species.

As we have discussed previously, dry cat food has high levels of carbohydrate and sugar. These levels stress the pancreas, causing some cats to become diabetic. This is not the only derangement in the dry-food-fed cat, however. When the cat's diet is high in carbohydrate and sugar, the function of the patient's liver also becomes abnormal. Instead of responding to small drops in blood sugar with production of sugar, the liver in the dry-food-fed cat fails to respond. The constant high dietary sugar load has caused the liver to lose some of its ability to respond quickly to the event of falling blood sugar.

Thus, in the dry-food-fed cat, the pancreas cannot respond to high sugar any more, and the liver does not respond to low sugar as it normally would. There is no research in the cat which shows us just what changes occur to make the liver less able to respond to falling glucose in this species when dietary carbohydrate is high. Perhaps pancreatic production of *both* insulin and glucagon in the dry-food-fed cat are suppressed by hyperglycemia. In such a case, neither of the glucose-regulatory hormones of the pancreas would be available to maintain the normal range of blood glucose in the animal. It is also possible that the liver itself becomes unable to respond to glucagon in an environment flooded with excess blood sugar.

In any event, the cat has become a complete carbohydrate "cripple." This crippled cat is completely dependent upon exactly the right amount of insulin from the outside. It is extremely difficult to provide such precise amounts of injected insulin. This is why owners find it extremely frustrating to try to manage the dry-food-fed cat.

Why Do Low-Carbohydrate Foods Work So Well in Diabetic Cats?

One thing was puzzling. It was not a surprise that cats eating foods with a lot less sugar would have lower blood sugar levels (just like human diabetics who do not eat candy or other high-sugar foods), but it was a bit surprising that many of them would stop needing insulin shots. I, like other veterinarians, had always thought that a diabetic cat's pancreas had stopped doing its job forever. No diabetic cats I had ever treated with high carbohydrate diets, with or without fiber, had ever stopped needing insulin. What was going on? It was certain that the diabetic cat's pancreas had started to work again, or the cat eating even a low-carbohydrate canned diet would always need the insulin injections, at least at low doses. But so many of our cats didn't need any insulin from the outside, their pancreas was working. This was very exciting; it meant that many diabetics, maybe almost all of them, could actually be cured of this disease. This has turned out to be true, but cats are individuals, as any cat owner knows. Every cat responds just a little bit differently, as the following cases show:

Maggie Dunbar

Maggie was a ten-year-old female white long-haired cat. Like almost all of my patients, she had eaten dry food since she was a kitten. Occasionally her owners would feed her some canned food as a special treat, but during the day she ate many small meals of a "premium quality" dry cat food. She had been healthy for ten years and was not overweight at eight pounds. One day, Maggie's owners noticed that she seemed to be losing weight. Her backbone seemed more noticeable to them, even through her long coat. She wasn't eating very well and was drinking a lot of water. When I saw Maggie, she was dehydrated and weighed only seven pounds. A blood test showed that her blood sugar level was 410 mg/dL (this is a measure of how much sugar is in each one-tenth liter of blood; a liter is about a quart). Normal resting blood sugar levels for the cat range between about 50 mg/dL and 120 mg/dL. Maggie also had sugar in her urine.

We hospitalized Maggie and started feeding her canned food only. Maggie was ecstatic; she was getting her special treat food twice a day and she loved it. By the second day, Maggie's average blood sugar was 180 mg/dL, and, by the third day, it was 100 mg/dL. We sent Maggie home with no insulin and told the Dunbars to feed her only canned food. A week later, Maggie had been completely normal at home and her blood sugar level was 90 mg/dL on average. With her owners only feeding her canned food twice a day, Maggie remains normal to this day (two years later) and has never needed insulin injections. She has gained back the lost pound and is doing great.

Goldstein Murphy

Goldstein is an eight-year old neutered male domestic short-haired tabby cat whose owner is completely devoted to him. Mr. Murphy is single and Goldstein is his roommate and best friend. Mr. Murphy adopted Goldstein from the local animal shelter as a kitten; the two had spent eight years hanging out together and keeping each other company, and Goldstein ate commercial dry food exclusively all his life.

One day, Mr. Murphy noticed that Goldstein was spending a lot of time near his water bowl. This was very unusual for the cat, as he usually spent his days sunning near a large window in the house. Goldstein was going to the litter box almost every hour as well. This also was unusual for him, so Mr. Murphy brought Goldstein to me for examination. Goldstein was overweight at fourteen pounds (I told Mr. Murphy he should weigh about eleven pounds) but was in good condition otherwise. He was still eating his dry food well and was relatively active. We took a blood and urine sample for analysis; Goldstein was very diabetic, with lots of sugar in his urine and a blood sugar level of 490 mg/dL.

We hospitalized Goldstein and started feeding him canned food. He liked the new food and ate it well. By the next day, Goldstein's blood sugar level was down to 300 mg/dL without insulin. The diet alone had helped him a lot. We added 1 unit of insulin twice daily (I always use a special kind called protamine-zinc insulin, or PZI, which works best in cats), and, by the third day, Goldstein's blood sugar was between 100mg/dL and 150 mg/dL throughout the day. We sent Goldstein home with a prescription for a 1-unit PZI insulin injection every twelve hours and a canned-food-only diet.

A week later, at Goldstein's weekly blood sugar check, we discovered that his sugar level was 60 mg/dL. This meant that Goldstein was in the low-normal range for blood sugar, and needed to have his insulin reduced or even stopped. We stopped his insulin for twenty-four hours, rechecked his blood sugar, and it was still 60 mg/dL. We sent Goldstein home and instructed Mr. Murphy not to give any more insulin until we checked Goldstein again in one week. One week later, Goldstein's blood sugar was still low-normal. He has not needed any insulin injections for over a year now. He is healthy and happy and has lost almost two pounds in that year. Mr. Murphy knows never to feed his cat any dry food ever again. The following story shows why...

Punkin Hodgkins

My own cat, Punkin, the one whose out-of-control diabetes had caused me to start thinking about what we veterinarians might be doing wrong with our feline diabetic patients, was doing great. His blood sugar levels had been in the low-normal range for almost two years, without any insulin injections. He ate low-carbohydrate canned cat food happily and had lost a pound from his earlier twelve-pound frame. My husband and I decided to board Punkin at a local cat boarding facility while we took a weeklong vacation. We instructed the manager of the facility that we wanted Punkin to eat only canned food that we brought along for him and nothing else during our time away.

When we returned from our vacation, we took Punkin home. We immediately noticed that he was very thirsty and filled up his litter box with urine the first night he was home. I tested his blood for sugar and found his level was 400 mg/dL! Punkin was diabetic again! I was devastated. I started giving him small doses of insulin again and called the boarding facility to ask about Punkin's stay there.

After much discussion, the manager of the kennel told me that she had been concerned that Punkin wasn't getting enough to eat with just the canned food we asked them to feed him morning and night. She thought that cats needed to "graze" (a term that applies to cattle, not cats) during the day as well, so she gave him some premium-quality dry food along with his canned food. She had meant well, and I appreciated her concern for my cat, but she had caused him to become diabetic again, and very quickly.

Fortunately, after two weeks on doses of insulin that I decreased as his blood sugar levels started to become normal again, Punkin was able to keep his blood sugar in the normal range all by himself and I stopped giving him insulin. Punkin never got dry food again and never needed insulin again, either. This was an important lesson for me and all of my diabetic patients. Cats that have been diabetic will always tend to become diabetic again quickly if they eat high-sugar foods, even if they have been "normal" for long periods. They don't have the ability to resist the effects of high-sugar foods, even for short periods, like they did before they became diabetic.

We have seen many cases like Punkin's where a recovered diabetic cat eats dry food again and immediately starts to need insulin again. I make it a point to emphasize to my clients that their recovered diabetic cat will never be able to have high-carbohydrate foods again in its lifetime.

Although many cats recover from their diabetes quickly, as Maggie, Goldstein, and Punkin did, some are much slower to become normal. Unfortunately, cats that have been diabetic for a long time seem to take longer to improve. Many of these will still go off insulin eventually, but the longer a cat is diabetic before its diet is changed to low-sugar foods, the harder the process of recovery:

Rascal Simon

Rascal was a six-year-old neutered male short-haired cat that weighed twenty pounds when I first saw him. He was at least eight to nine pounds overweight for his frame. Rascal had been diagnosed as a diabetic by a veterinarian two years earlier in another state where the Simons lived at the time. Rascal had been getting 6 units of Humulin™ Lente insulin (this is a type of human insulin, not PZI that I prefer) twice a day and was eating one of the high-fiber, high-carbohydrate dry foods for diabetic cats. Rascal's owners were not happy with his lack of progress during the two years of his treatment for diabetes. His previous veterinarian would check his blood glucose and fructosamine once each month and adjust Rascal's insulin dose depending on those tests. Sometimes

Rascal's blood sugar was very high, as high as 520 mg/dL, and the insulin dose would be increased. Sometimes his blood sugar would be lower, as low as 100 mg/dL, and his insulin dose would be decreased. Once, Rascal even had a seizure because his blood sugar dropped all the way to 25 mg/dL! When this happened, Rascal's owners rushed him to the vet's and he was hospitalized for three days while his doctor gave him IV fluids and adjusted his dose of insulin again. It was a never-ending seesaw. The Simons were about to give up, when they moved to Orange County, California, and a neighbor told them to bring Rascal to my clinic.

When I first saw Rascal, he weighed twenty pounds, and was obese. His coat was dull and he had dry, flaky dandruff coming off his skin. The Simons told me that Rascal drank lots and lots of water, and went to the litter box to urinate at least ten times a day. Every day they had to empty all of the litter and what seemed like quarts of urine from the box. Rascal was always starving; he begged for food whenever his bowl was empty, and would steal any human food, even pretzels and potato chips that he was able to get to. He never seemed content and didn't socialize with the family at all. The Simons were giving him six units of Humulin insulin every twelve hours.

We hospitalized Rascal and found that his blood sugar ranged between 300 and 450 mg/dL throughout the day, even though he was getting so much insulin every day. We stopped giving Rascal any insulin at all, and changed his diet to low-carbohydrate canned food only. At first, he ate only a small amount of the canned food. Rascal was "carbohydrate addicted" and wanted his dry food. Even so, his blood sugar the first day off dry food, and with no insulin, ranged from 250 to 375 mg/dL, a respectable improvement for a cat without insulin injections. We started him on variable units of PZI insulin every eight hours, and, within two days, his blood sugar levels ranged from 125 to 200 mg/dL. His excessive thirst and urination stopped altogether, and he started eating the canned food well. We taught the Simons to home-test Rascal's blood glucose with a human glucometer two to three times per day, and sent him home with a scale of doses of insulin to give to him every eight hours depending on the blood glucose reading at each of these test times (see appendix III).

Using this home-testing technique, the Simons found Rascal's glucose ranged during one twelve-hour period between 60 and 150 mg/dL. We stopped giving him insulin for one day and his blood sugar started rising to over 200 mg/dL at the highest. We started insulin back according to the sliding scale. This process of readjusting Rascal's insulin as he responded better and better to the canned diet and insulin continued for another two months. Eventually he was getting less than one-half unit of PZI every twelve hours, and finally, after three months of proper diet and the right insulin, Rascal went off insulin altogether.

Rascal has been off insulin for eight months now, has lost three of the eight pounds he needed to lose, and his coat is starting to shine. He uses the litter box three to four times daily, and drinks very little water because his food has most of the water he needs. The dandruff is gone, and the Simons can't believe how active Rascal has become. He no longer begs for food all the time, eats his canned food at mealtime only, and is more affectionate than ever. Rascal's owners continue to home-test him once a week.

Unfortunately, some cats, a minority in my practice, never go off insulin no matter what we do. These are always cats that have had their diabetes for a long time, usually several years, and that have been out of control for all that time. For all cats, making the right diet change early in the course of the disease is critical to the future normalcy of the patient. It is a mistake to switch a diabetic cat to a high-protein, high-fiber, high-carbohydrate *dry* diet, even though such diets claim to be good for the management of feline diabetes.

Even when a cat does not go off insulin, low-carbohydrate foods are a must for keeping a cat's blood sugar as low as possible and avoiding ketoacidosis, a serious condition where a diabetic cat becomes quite ill from too-high blood sugar levels; and the lows of hypoglycemia, where the patient becomes weak, disoriented, and may even have a seizure. All dry cat foods, even the high-fiber dry foods marketed for years for the diabetic cat, cause these problems. Even newer, high-protein dry foods made especially for diabetic cats cause persistent insulin dependency and the potential for ketoacidosis and hypoglycemia, because they contain excessive amounts of carbohydrate. It is not the level of protein in the dry food, but the high amount of carbohydrate, that makes all dry foods deadly for diabetic cats.

What About Insulin?

If a diabetic cat needs to have insulin shots, the choice of insulin is as important as the choice of food. The several human insulin types are not good choices for cats because the cat's own insulin is quite a bit different in structure from human insulin. Animal-derived PZI insulin is either bovine (cow) or a combination of bovine and porcine (pig) insulin and, while it may seem odd, this insulin from cows or pigs is closer in structure to the cat's own insulin. Because of this similarity, PZI works better to regulate the diabetic cat until the patient can begin to make its own insulin again. Because PZI is so much more effective at lower doses than the human insulin types (including a new human insulin called Lantus), the feline diabetic on PZI insulin is easier to regulate down into the normal range. This allows the cat's pancreas to reactivate and start providing insulin from within the cat's own body.

The Good News

Cats previously on dry foods respond extremely well to the switch from high-sugar dry diets to low-sugar canned foods. Obese diabetics begin to lose weight even though canned foods often have higher fat than dry high-fiber foods do. With less sugar flooding the system, less insulin needs to be injected into the diabetic patient to cope with that sugar flood. Remarkably, the "exhausted" feline pancreas seems to be able to recover some or all of its ability to make its own insulin, and probably glucagon as well, once that constant sugar flood from the diet stops. High blood sugar seems to damage the cat's pancreas in ways we don't understand completely at this time, but it is undoubtedly related to the cat's evolution as a strict meat-eater, and it *is* reversible in most cats.

This is tremendous news for diabetic cats and their owners who once were doomed to a lifetime of never-ending insulin shots, increasing illness with dangerous highs and lows, and eventual death from this uncontrollable disease. We now know how to do a much better job of treating and even curing diabetes once it happens. When we use this knowledge, rather than simply following the old, ineffective methods, we have the ability to give back health to the hundreds of thousands of cats that live with diabetes today. What is just as exciting, however, is the chance to *prevent* diabetes in the millions of cats that will share our lives in the coming years by feeding them the proper diet for the obligatory carnivore. This is new hope for actual prevention of a very old and hopeless disease.

Feline Diabetes: What to Look For

1. **Diabetic cats have a history of eating dry cat food.** In my experience with hundreds of feline diabetics, every single one has eaten a steady, often exclusive, diet of dry cat food. Most of my patients have eaten the very best, most expensive brands, so even "premium" diets predispose to diabetes. Dry foods have lots of predigested carbohydrate and some (so-called "light" or weight-reducing type diets) have high fiber. High-fiber dry diets do not keep a cat from getting diabetes and do not control diabetes once it occurs.

2. **The cat with diabetes will usually drink more water than usual and flood the litter box.** If you notice your cat showing these signs, a visit to the vet is in order, right away. Your cat's doctor can take a blood sample and a urine sample and tell whether your cat has this disease. The sooner diabetes is detected and treated, the better your cat will respond. You may also notice your cat eating more than usual, or less than usual. Some diabetics start to vomit frequently and begin to lose weight. Don't ignore any of these important signs of illness!

3. **Many diabetics are neutered males that are at least moderately overweight.** If your cat fits this profile, be especially suspicious of any changes in the amount of water he drinks and the number of trips he makes to the litter box. Some diabetics even have "mistakes" outside the litter box because they are producing so much urine that they lose control occasionally. These signs signal a trip to your veterinarian right away.

What to Do If Your Cat Is Diabetic

Once your veterinarian determines that your cat is a diabetic, I advise the following:

1. If your cat eats dry food of any kind, stop this immediately! Your cat cannot become healthy again on any dry diet. This advice may run counter to your regular veterinarian's advice if he or she is unaware of the facts about how dry cat food makes diabetes hard to control. Remember, your veterinarian may well be following recommendations from experts based on studies done years

ago. We know more now, but changes in scientific thinking come into practice very slowly. Discuss the importance of getting sugar out of your cat's diet with your cat's doctor; you can help educate your veterinarian and improve care for many other cats.

2. Your veterinarian may recommend a canned food that is made for diabetics. These canned foods are generally good for this, but some cats won't eat them. Fortunately, most canned foods available at the grocery store or pet food warehouse-type stores are very appetizing for cats and will work very well to stop the flood of sugar into your cat's system. If your cat is an early diabetic, this may be all that you need to do. Your veterinarian can check your cat's blood glucose to see if your cat needs insulin along with a diet change. Avoid canned foods with corn, rice, potato of any kind, carrots, and apples and any other fruit. Select a meat-based food for the lowest sugar content (see www .sugarcats.net/sites/jmpeerson/canfood.html)

3. If your cat needs insulin after the switch from dry food to canned, suggest to your veterinarian that you'd like to use the animal-source insulin called PZI (protamine-zinc insulin) for your cat. PZI insulin was once off the market because the invention of human insulin made it unnecessary for use in people. It is now readily available again for cats from a number of sources, but your veterinarian may not know this. This is your opportunity to be an active participant in your cat's care by sharing this information. Avoid using noninsulin glucose control oral medications such as glipizide. There is evidence that this drug may cause further damage to the pancreas.

A study conducted in the late 1990s at the University of California-Davis and published in 2001 has been used recently by one PZI manufacturer (Idexx Laboratories) to justify very inadequate dosing recommendations they make for their product. Those dosing recommendations run contrary to my own tight regulation protocol (see Appendix III). Today, this decade-old study is out of date and cannot be used as a guide for managing feline diabetes because it predated more progressive work done by myself and others which shows that proper diet is the key to success in diabetes management and prevention (there were no dietary controls of any kind in this trial). This study also used a very outdated method of determining adequate doses of PZI insulin, timing of doses, and the importance of owner hometesting to insure good blood glucose control throughout each day.

Recently, a small study from Australia has shown that glargine (Lantus) insulin caused normalcy in a few new feline diabetics *when they were also put on a high-protein, low-carbohydrate diet.* This study does not really show that glargine is better than PZI, however. Glargine has a longer time to onset and duration of action than other types of insulin such as PZI. The use of PZI insulin in this study was suboptimum for maximizing the effectiveness of this type of insulin. Further, new diabetic patients that are switched from high-carbohydrate dry foods to low-carbohydrate wet foods very often become normal on almost any type of insulin, and sometimes without any insulin administration at all, so the findings in this narrow study did not necessarily demonstrate any superiority of glargine in a broader group of affected cats.

PZI insulin is not available in Australia, so the scientists that conducted this study were attempting to validate a type of insulin that patients outside the United States could readily purchase. In my experience with innumerable diabetic cats, and all of the many types of insulin, including glargine, I have not found any insulin equal to or superior to bovine-source PZI insulin for managing those cats that require insulin for any period of time.

Consider buying a diabetes home-testing device (called a *glucometer*) from your local human pharmacy so that you can test your cat's blood sugar at home, without the stress of taking your cat to the veterinarian. Home-testing does not replace regular veterinary visits, but gives the pet owner a good deal of good information between veterinary exams (see *www.felinediabetes.com/bg-test.htm*). All human diabetics test their own blood sugar daily, and the glucometers they use are extremely easy and painless for you to use for your cat. More and more owners are opting for this; about 90 percent of all of my clients test their own cats at home and then phone or e-mail me with results. The accuracy of home-testing glucometers is quite good in the experience of my clients, and allows good results with much less stress on the patient.

If your cat is a new diabetic, following this plan may help your cat become normal within a few weeks or months (see www.yourdiabeticcat.com).

What to Do If Your Cat Is Not Diabetic . . . Yet

1. If you are feeding your cat dry cat food, stop! The longer your cat eats dry cat food, the more likely it will become diabetic and obese, and addicted to the special flavorings in dry cat foods. Most cats will switch to canned foods willingly, some are very happy about the change. If your cat seems stubborn about

this, you may need to add a few kibbles of the old dry food on top of the canned food for a few days to entice your pet to try the new food. See the section in chapter 20 about switching your cat from dry food to wet (also see www .catnutrition.org). Your veterinarian may also have some suggestions about how to make a switch with a carbohydrate-addicted cat. It is absolutely necessary for you to make this positive change in your cat's lifestyle right away, *even if you have to be a little creative in convincing your cat to make this change.*

2. Become a label-reader when you are shopping for canned food for your cat. Some canned foods have cereal and other nonmeat ingredients in the ingredient list. Cereal, vegetable, and fruits are unnecessary, poor-quality ingredients in canned foods, and you will want to avoid any wet food with such fillers. Your cat is a strict carnivore; the best diet will be full of meat ingredients, not grain, fruits, or high-sugar vegetables such as potatoes, carrots, fruits, and the like. The more you and other cat owners demand and buy canned foods with meat ingredients and no fillers, the more of these kinds of choices you will have in the future.

3. If your cat is overweight, the change to a canned diet will automatically help your cat lose that excess weight gradually without having to go hungry. Most adult cats will be very satisfied with about 3 to 4 ounces of canned food twice daily. This is the amount in a smallest-size can. Larger-size cans are 5.5 or 14 ounces, so feed those accordingly. More obese cats (fourteen to twenty-plus pounds) may need a little more food to be satisfied, and you may feed yours 4 to 5 ounces twice daily until your very overweight pet is less than fourteen pounds.

4. The usual cat treats that you buy in the store are very high in carbohydrate and sugar, just like dry cat food. Do not feed these to any cat. If you enjoy giving your cat a treat for doing tricks or at special times during the day (like bedtime), look for treats that are freeze-dried meat, with no fillers. These are available in chicken, beef, liver, and fish flavors, and cats just love them!

Today, we have an opportunity to stop a deadly epidemic in its tracks. Well-meaning people, owners, and pet health-care professionals and scientists alike have been working together for decades to give pet cats better lives. It was inevitable that we would take some wrong turns in that journey. The feeding of overprocessed, high-carbohydrate foods was just such a wrong turn. Now that we know we have taken that wrong turn, it is time to turn back and get on the right road once again.

22

Hepatic Lipidosis and Pancreatitis—More Dietary Diseases

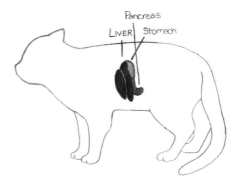

wo conditions we see with some frequency in cats are hepatic lipidosis (HL) and pancreatitis. We know a great deal about HL, but less about pancreatitis in this species. Both conditions are invariably linked to inappropriate, carbohydrate-rich diets fed to the cat, an obligatory carnivore. High carbohydrate diets assault the sugar-controlling functions of both the liver and the pancreas, and such diets cause the obesity that predisposes the overweight cat to hepatic lipidosis.

Hepatic Lipidosis

(see http://maxshouse.com/Feline_Hepatic_Lipidosis.htm)

Hepatic lipidosis is a condition in cats that causes mild to severe signs of liver function impairment requiring prompt medical treatment. We know that, at its root, HL is caused by the accumulation of fat in the cells and tissues of the liver. This clogging of the liver with excess fat is what leads to the failure of the liver's normal functions. We also know that the vast majority of cases of HL occur in overweight or obese cats that stop eating for a period of days or weeks. Because almost all cats that develop HL are overweight, the major predisposing cause of HL is the state of obesity. Once again, I cannot overemphasize the importance of preventing obesity in the cat by avoiding dry cat foods for the entire life of the cat.

When the overweight cat stops eating for any reason, for longer than a few days, HL becomes likely. As the cat starves, large amounts of the fat that is stored in the cat's body are released from those stores and begin to travel to the liver through the bloodstream. This is a normal response to starvation in all animals, and allows the survival of the animal until food becomes available again. Normally, this fat is processed into protein-wrapped "packages" and then sent through the bloodstream to the tissues of the body that require them for energy. In the cat, however, particularly the overweight cat, so much fat floods the liver at a time when protein for this packaging process is unavailable, that the fat simply builds up and begins to disrupt the liver's normal activities.

The accumulation of fat in the liver, with the resulting liver dysfunction, makes the cat even less willing to eat. Even if the original reason for the patient's lack of appetite has resolved, the cat is now ill from its HL, and a vicious cycle is under way. The longer the starvation and HL continue, the more critically ill the cat becomes. Veterinary care is imperative to reverse this process! Sometimes an underlying disease process, such as an infection or tumor, will have caused the original lack of appetite. If this is the case, the veterinarian must treat both the underlying disease and the secondary HL if the patient is to recover.

In the majority of HL cases, however, the original problem that caused the cat to stop eating is never identified because it will have resolved by the time HL develops. In these cases, treating HL alone will provide recovery. Logically, the focus of management for HL is to provide the protein the patient needs to allow its liver to liberate the excess fat from its cells. This makes treating HL very straightforward. The mainstay of HL treatment is to feed the patient, ensuring that sufficient protein and calories are available for the liver to begin to do its job of moving fat through the body once again. Liver-supportive supplements, like SAM-e (S-adenosylmethionine) and milk thistle, are also usually prescribed for the patient recovering from HL until the functions of this organ have returned to normal as reflected in the patient's blood test values.

Diagnosing Hepatic Lipidosis

The cat with HL will invariably have a history of poor appetite or severe food restriction in the days and weeks before the owner notices more severe signs. Often, the patient will actually have a yellowish cast to the skin. This is called *icterus*, or jaundice, and it is caused by the accumulation in the skin of waste substances (bile pigments) normally processed by the liver. These pigments are usually secreted into the GI tract and eliminated in the stool. As the liver loses its ability to process these substances, they accumulate in the bloodstream and eventually start to "stain" the tissues a yellow/orange color.

Even before this yellowing is apparent, the HL patient will show signs of profound illness. Owners will notice lethargy, vomiting, diarrhea, and other indicators that the cat feels very sick. The veterinarian will often detect dehydration and significant weight loss in the cat with HL. Although these latter signs are typical of a great many feline maladies, blood tests, urinalysis, X-rays, and ultrasound examination will help diagnose the primary problem as HL. Once the diagnosis is made, and underlying diseases complicating the HL are identified, if they exist, the veterinarian will begin treatment by providing the fluids and nutrition that will reverse the process started during the patient's starvation.

When I graduated from veterinary school in 1977, HL was an almost universally fatal disease in cats. This was because we did not understand why and how this disease occurred. Today, we know that if we can provide enough protein and calories to the patient, the liver will return to health and the cat will survive. It is really that simple. Of course, because the cat with HL is usually quite ill, simply putting a bowl of food down will not work to start the recovery. Cats with HL do not want to eat. So, to make sure lifesaving nutrients get to the inside of the patient, a feeding tube to deliver food directly into the GI tract is often necessary. This may sound ominous, but the use of feeding tubes in cats is relatively simple and easy. The cat can even return home with the tube in place and owners can feed their pet through the tube with little instruction. Nutritious, pudding-consistency "recovery" foods, high in protein and low in carbohydrates, can be pushed by syringe down the tube and into the cat's stomach every few hours, helping the patient's liver to recover.

If the tube has been placed in the esophagus, the cat can and will begin to eat on its own "around" the tube. That is, the patient's normal appetite will begin to return as the liver becomes healthy again and the cat will start to eat voluntarily even though the tube has not yet been removed. When this happens, the veterinarian will remove the tube and the patient will continue to recover. If the patient loses the excess weight and continues to eat low-carbohydrate, high-protein foods, HL will not recur.

Feline Pancreatitis

Feline pancreatitis (inflammation of the pancreas) is a poorly understood condition. It is harder to diagnose in feline patients than in dogs and the direct cause is almost never discovered. While trauma, poisons, tumors, and infections that arise in the pancreas or spread to the pancreas from elsewhere in the body are possible causes, these account for few cases of this condition.

The clinical signs of feline pancreatitis are often subtle. The affected cat may have a fever, refuse to eat, and seem pained in the abdominal area. Sometimes the patient has a history of vomiting and is dehydrated as well, but just as often the cat is presented to the veterinarian just for being a bit "off." Unfortunately, there are fewer laboratory blood tests for diagnosing this disease in the cat than in the dog, and the diagnosis is best made through an ultrasound examination of the affected organ and the abdomen in general. There is a relatively new test, called the PLI, which may be useful in pinpointing feline pancreatitis. Unfortunately, this test is costly and takes many days for results. Even when the PLI verifies that the patient's pancreas is inflamed, the disease requires the same symptomatic treatment after diagnosis that was appropriate before diagnosis.

Treatment of pancreatitis attempts to manage the vomiting, dehydration, and pain the patient may be experiencing. Removal of any toxin, infection, tumor, or other obvious causative factors is imperative, of course. Traditional methods of treating cats with pancreatitis also call for nutritional support with a low-fat, high-carbohydrate diet. This part of the usual treatment is, unfortunately, misguided. Most veterinarians will agree that "the cat is not a small dog" but, when it comes to pancreatitis, we still have a tendency to manage feline pancreatitis as we would manage the condition in dogs, where it is well known that dietary fat can cause or aggravate this problem.

There has never been any convincing proof that cats with pancreatitis are intolerant of dietary fat. Further, we have discussed at length in several earlier chapters how unwise it is to feed high-carbohydrate foods to the cat. The pancreas of the cat is not adapted to a high-carbohydrate diet, and these are harmful to even the normal, healthy feline pancreas. Foods with high amounts of processed carbohydrates will be even more harmful for the debilitated pancreas. The feline pancreatitis patient, like all other cats, should have a high-protein, low-carbohydrate diet, to avoid further irritation to this organ from carbohydrate.

Pancreatitis may be accompanied by diabetes (lack of insulin secretion from the pancreas) or lack of pancreatic enzymes that allow digestion in the GI tract. In fact, cats with diabetes typically have at least low-grade pancreatitis at the same time. Inflammatory damage to the pancreas can destroy the ability of this organ to perform its normal functions. If these deficiency conditions are present, the patient will require supplementation with insulin injections or enzymes added to the food until the affected organ can resume secretion of these vital substances.

Discussions of the causes of feline pancreatitis in veterinary references do not consider the effects of constant poor nutrition, in the form of high-carbohydrate dry cat foods, on the healthy cat pancreas. This failure to consider the most prevalent pancreatic toxin for the cat, high-dietary carbohydrate, is the stumbling block in our efforts to understand this problem. Until researchers begin to explore the relationship between lifetime diets containing inappropriate amounts of processed dietary carbohydrates and pancreatic inflammation, this condition will continue to confound veterinarians and defy good treatment and prevention.

23

Feline Bladder Problems— Never Again!

After obesity, bladder disease, also called *urinary tract inflammation* (UTI) or *cystitis*, is the most common nutritionally caused problem in the adult cat. For years, veterinarians have struggled with this seemingly mysterious problem, with very limited success. The affected cat strains to urinate, may have blood in its urine, and can even become blocked and unable to urinate at all. This becomes a life-threatening emergency situation that requires immediate veterinary attention.

Why Do Cats Develop Urinary Tract Problems?

Cats are a very successful and naturally healthy species. Left to feed themselves, cats generally do not have major urinary tract problems. Yet, in the 1970s and '80s, veterinarians began to see very large numbers of cases of cystitis (bladder inflammation and infection), bladder crystal and stone formation, and urinary blockage in their feline patients. Many cats died when their blockage caused acute renal failure and treatment arrived too late. Veterinary surgeons even developed a new surgical procedure, called a *perineal urethrostomy*, in which the male cat's urethra is amputated to better allow urine with crystals to flow from the bladder to the outside. This surgery was lifesaving for chronically affected cats, but painful and disfiguring. Unfortunately, this surgery and other less drastic medical treatments were not always effective over the long term.

Sadly for millions of cats, the analysis the experts applied to this problem was flawed, and the solution faulty. The rise of urinary tract diseases in the cat coincided exactly with the increasing use of dry kibble to feed cats. In fact, in previous times when cats consumed meat-based foods, commercial or otherwise, they simply did not develop UTI. Scientists at the pet food companies studied the problem and concluded that it was the magnesium in commercial pet foods that caused UTI. They concluded this simply because the major type of crystals formed in affected cats were made up of a magnesium salt. The experts reasoned that the amount of magnesium in the foods of affected cats must be too high, causing magnesium levels in the urine to be too high. Their theory went that high magnesium in the bladder caused stones to form. The experts failed to consider that the natural prey diet of cats also contained significant magnesium but was composed of entirely different types of ingredients.

The pet food scientists did notice a key difference in the urine of dry-food-fed cats. The urine of such cats was alkaline in its pH, rather than acid. Magnesium crystals form in alkaline urine, not acid urine. They reasoned that if they added acid to the food of these cats and removed the magnesium, the problem would go away. Many different "prescription-type" foods appeared on the market and were available through veterinarians as treatment or prevention of UTI. This approach was only partially successful, however. Many cats with UTI that were managed with these diets still had recurrences of their disease. Worse, some of them developed a different type of crystals, made of a calcium salt (calcium oxalate), because their urine had become too acid. For these cats, the cure was as devastating as the original disease.

Dry diets also cause UTI because of their very low moisture content as compared to wet foods. Even healthy cats that eat dry diets and have access to plenty of fresh water have consistently more concentrated urine than those that eat wet foods. Although dry-food-fed cats drink extra water, they do not make up for the lower moisture of their food by drinking enough free water. This situation is most likely the result of the cat's evolutionary origins in the desert and other types of arid environments. The cat's thirst drive for nondietary water is not strong. It never needed to be strong when the animal was eating high-moisture foods. When we deprive the cat of dietary water, we invariably cause a state of relative dehydration, with disastrous results.

The studies that were done to find a cat food that would eliminate the UTI problem never included a low-carbohydrate, meat-based wet food as one of the options to be studied. The test diets in these studies were usually low-moisture, carbohydrate-based foods with different kinds of acidifying ingredients and different levels of magnesium. The role of high levels of highly processed carbohydrate in dry form was never questioned or studied in the nutritional research into this disease. We have seen this oversight before in the studies involving diets for diabetic and obese cats.

In those studies, the scientists looked for ways to modify cereal-based foods to make them effective in managing these medical conditions (see chapter 20). They did not, however, even consider that meat-based, wet foods might provide the best solution for the problems. Their conclusion that high-carbohydrate foods with indigestible fiber were more effective in dealing with obesity and diabetes than carbohydrate-based foods without indigestible fiber might have been correct as far as it went, but it certainly did not solve those terrible problems in cats because it never included the real dietary solution.

Similarly, when research to solve the problem of UTI in cats also failed to even consider that the cat's natural nutrient profile might be the logical solution, it failed to solve the problem. The artificial urinary-tract-disease-fighting diets that were developed are costly for the pet owner, often do little to provide relief from disease, and may even cause other diseases. In fact, cats began developing UTI in epidemic numbers purely and simply because their carnivorous metabolic requirements were being met by feeding a diet suited for herbivorous/omnivorous animals.

So, Where Are We Now?

For the past twenty-five years, no additional progress has been made in dealing with UTI in cats. Veterinarians and cat owners have resigned themselves to the existence of this common and very serious problem, with nothing available to prevent it or cure it satisfactorily. Every week I see new patients that have been on special diets for this problem, without success. Although the numbers of cats that must have the painful and mutilating surgery for UTI have decreased, this surgery is still recommended for many cats that continue to relapse on their diets of expensive "prescription-type" dry cat foods. Many of these cats are diagnosed with a form of UTI called *idiopathic cystitis*, which means "bladder inflammation with no known cause." Veterinarians reason that if the special diets cannot control the problem, then the cause must be complex and mysterious, beyond understanding and solution.

Ironically, the means to eradicate UTI from the feline population has always been right in front of us. Plant-based cat foods, specifically dry cat foods with their very high amounts of processed cereal and very low moisture content, *cause* UTI, pure and simple. Even the special, additive-containing foods for UTI cats can, and do, continue to promote this terrible condition. On the other hand, cats eating meat-based wet foods simply do not develop UTI. The problem is not, and has never been, the level of magnesium in the diet of UTI cats. The problem is the extremely low-moisture, alkaline-urine-producing, high-processed-carbohydrate formulas of dry cat foods.

How Do Plant-Based Cat Foods Cause Urinary Tract Disease?

As we have discussed in previous chapters, cats are obligatory carnivores, adapted over millions of years to the consumption of meat, not plant materials. Because predators like the cat consume plenty of bone along with meat, the metabolites of the carnivorous diet include lots of minerals, including magnesium. Magnesium in the cat's diet is not, and never was, the problem. The problem is dry cat foods because:

1. The urine of carnivores consuming meat is acid (below a pH of 7.4), not alkaline (above a pH of 7.4). Dry cat foods, with their high plant content, cause a very alkaline urine pH. This is an unnatural environment in the cat's bladder, leading to inflammation. The consumption of meat creates a healthy bladder environment.

2. Dry cat foods provide almost no moisture, whereas a natural prey diet provides 75 to 80 percent moisture. The cat has a low thirst-drive to consume free water because of its evolutionary origins. Thus, the dry-food-fed cat is usually subclinically dehydrated, and its urine is very concentrated. This unnaturally

high concentration of minerals and other constituents in the urine, along with an alkaline pH, leads to UTI.

3. When a cat consumes a wet, meat-based diet, the resulting urine has a natural acid pH and is more dilute than the urine of dry-food-fed cats. These conditions do not allow the formation of crystals and stones, and eliminate inflammation.

As I explain to my clients, if you put the wrong fuel in any engine, you can expect poor performance. If you own an automobile with a gasoline-burning engine, and you put diesel fuel in that engine, the system will run very badly. This is exactly what we do when we feed plants to a cat. We are putting the wrong fuel in the cat's engine, and the engine does not run normally. Had the pet food companies understood that plant-based foods were the wrong fuel for cats, they might have made a better decision about how to solve the emerging problem of UTI.

Just as it would be foolish for you to try to rectify the problem of diesel-fuel in your gasoline engine by pouring additives into the tank along with the diesel fuel, it was foolish to try to provide corrective additives to dry cat food to make it "work" in the cat. The simple and complete solution to the problem was to back up and feed the cat a diet of natural ingredients in a natural form.

I know this simple solution works, and works extremely well, because I have treated without any special diets whatsoever every single UTI cat I have seen in my clinic. Here are some examples of such cases:

Missy Forbes

Missy was a two-year-old spayed female domestic short-haired calico cat with previously perfect litter-box habits. She was in good body condition at nine and a half pounds. Her diet was a "premium" brand dry cat food with occasional "treats" of wet canned food, which she loved. A week before I saw Missy, she had started to have "accidents" outside the box, and her owners were understandably distressed about this. There were no obvious new stress factors in her life, and her basic physical exam was normal in all respects. Missy's complete blood count and chemistry panel were also normal. We performed a urinalysis, and discovered that Missy had a small amount of blood and protein in her urine, with a urine pH level of 8.0. Her urine was quite concentrated with a specific gravity of 1.055. This is a highly concentrated and alkaline urine for the cat. There were no crystals in Missy's urine, and no bacteria. We concluded that she had a urinary tract inflammation secondary to the concentrated high urine pH. Missy's bladder lining was not designed to handle such alkaline urine, and it was becoming quite inflamed as a result of this abnormal condition.

We immediately changed Missy's diet to an all-wet, meat-based commercial cat food, with no corn, potato, carrots, or fruit ingredients. Her owners were instructed to allow no dry cat food whatsoever. Missy herself was very happy with this change. We also prescribed a short course of an anti-inflammatory drug to help reduce the urinary tract inflammation and give Missy relief from the irritable bladder sensations that were making her urinate frequently and indiscriminately. Within three days, Missy was back to her old perfect litter-box habits, and two weeks later when we rechecked her urine, there was no trace of blood or significant protein, and her urine pH was 7.0. The specific gravity of her urine was 1.036. A month later, Missy's pH was 6.5, a very acceptable level of acidity. Missy has done extremely well, and has been normal now for over a year on nothing more than an exclusively wet-food diet of over-the-counter commercial cat foods.

Roger Bowman

Roger was a six-year-old, neutered male domestic long-haired cat with a history of recurrent UTI. Roger's first episode of bladder problems started when he was three years old. He had been fed a diet of grocery store dry cat food exclusively up to that point. His previous veterinarian had prescribed a special acidifying diet for treatment of UTI after that first episode, and Roger had been on that diet ever since. About every six to eight months, Roger would develop blood in his urine and start to strain to urinate in the litter box. His owners knew what this meant, and each time this happened, Roger would go to his veterinarian for treatment. Fluid therapy and antibiotics seemed to resolve the UTI episodes for a time.

Roger came to us because his owners had moved from their previous residence in another state. After the move, his UTI flared up again, and his owners sought help for the problem, once again. Roger was overweight at sixteen pounds at presentation. He showed painfulness in his bladder area during his physical exam, but was otherwise normal physically. Rogers baseline blood work was normal, but his urinalysis showed significant blood cells and protein, an acid pH of 5.5, small numbers of calcium-salt crystals in his urine, and a concentrated urine with a specific gravity of 1.052. There were no bacteria in his urine.

We treated Roger as he had been treated before, with fluids and antibiotics, and added anti-inflammatory drug therapy as well. The most important thing we did for Roger was to educate his owners about the role of the acidifying cat food in the recurrences of his disease. They were confused because they believed that the special diet they were feeding was supposed to prevent the crystals from forming in Roger's urine. We explained that Roger's urine was actually too acid now, because of the diet he was eating. The amount of acidifying ingredients added to that diet caused Roger's urine pH to become too low, and a new type of crystal was forming there in the concentrated urine caused by the low-moisture of the dry diet. We instructed them to feed Roger any wet, meat-based commercial food without high carbohydrate ingredients from plants. This would naturally correct the problems Roger had been experiencing.

Because he had been on dry foods all his life, Roger resisted this change for a few days. His owners offered him a number of different canned and pouched foods, and found some that he liked well enough to eat at least 3 to 4 ounces per day. Within a week, Roger was eating 7 to 8 ounces of wet cat food per day and his UTI signs were gone.

We rechecked Roger at two weeks, four weeks, eight weeks, and six months. Within a month, he had lost almost a pound of his excess body weight and had no blood, protein, or crystals in his urine. His urine pH was 6.5 and had a specific gravity of 1.035. At six months, Roger had lost over four pounds and looked like a new cat. His activity level had never been higher, his owners were delighted. Eighteen months after his diet change, Roger has had no new recurrences of his UTI, and his urinalysis rechecks have been normal.

Morris Cassidy

Morris was a ten-year-old domestic short-haired neutered male cat. Morris's owners reported that he had been acting lethargic for several days and refused to eat his normal dry cat food, a "premium" brand, for the last two days. On physical exam, Morris was moderately dehydrated, and his bladder was large and very hard to the touch. He was painful in the abdominal area around his bladder. We determined immediately that the flow of urine out of Morris's bladder was completely blocked. He was in a life-threatening crisis. We immediately passed a catheter into Morris's bladder and began to empty very bloody urine out of it. We drew blood for testing and began to give Morris intravenous fluids.

Morris had a large amount of blood, protein, and magnesium-salt crystals in his urine. His urine pH was 7.5 with a specific gravity of 1.060. He was in acute kidney failure as well, because he had been blocked for a few days at least. This had caused all of the toxins the kidney normally filters from the blood to accumulate in the body. Fortunately, once the flow of urine from Morris's body was restored and his dehydration was corrected with intravenous fluids, all of the signs of kidney failure resolved quickly and he even began to have an interest in food again. Because of the large amount of crystals in his urine, though, we had to leave Morris's urinary catheter in for four days after his initial treatment began to make sure that he did not become reblocked. His urine remained very bloody for several days. Ultrasound exam of Morris's bladder showed a markedly thickened, "angry" bladder wall, in reaction to the constant irritation of alkaline pH and concentrated urine full of crystalline "sand."

Once Morris was eating the regular commercial wet cat food we offered him, his urine pH dropped to 6.5 and the amount of urinary crystals in his urine samples dropped to low levels. Within six days, his urine no longer had visible blood; only trace amounts were detected on the urinalysis. One week after presentation, Morris went home a much happier cat than we had seen seven days earlier. We rechecked Morris every few days after that, to make sure he continued to do well. Eight months after his brush with death, Morris was healthy with no signs of a recurrence of his blockage or permanent kidney problems. He now eats only commercial canned or pouched cat foods with no carbohydrate-containing ingredients such as corn, rice, potato, sweet potato, carrots, or fruit of any kind. I know that I will never see Morris again in my clinic with this problem as long as his owners feed him like a cat!

In domestic cats, true UTI is a disease with a nutritional basis. Rarely, we see cats in our clinic that have stress-caused litter-box problems that do not resolve with a diet change. These cats do not have the typical changes in their bladder environment that we see with real UTI. The problem in such cats is behavioral, not physical. Overcrowding, aggression among cats, significant changes in a cat's environment, and the like can trigger urine marking or spraying outside the box. Such cats are "acting out" in response to psychological stressors.

In such cases, although a change from dry to wet food is still appropriate, it will also be necessary to identify the source of the stress that is causing the misbehavior. If at all possible, the owner must alleviate that stress. In those cases where the owner cannot resolve the environmental problem entirely, there are drug therapies that may help to reduce the affected cat's anxiety level enough for normal behaviors to return. These drug therapies may not need to be lifelong. In some cats, a few months of treatment may be enough to change the bad habits. In others, longer-term but low-dose therapy may provide good management. Your cat's veterinarian can determine if your cat has a behavioral problem rather than a purely physical one, and suggest an approach for dealing with the behavioral issue. There are also a number of good resources for information on this subject (see www.sniksnak.com/cathealth/marking.html).

24

Inflammatory Bowel Disease— Disease of the Decade

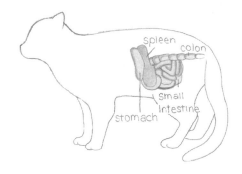

Within the past ten years, the number of new cases of feline inflammatory bowel disease has increased perhaps more than any other chronic medical problem. Thirty years ago, when I graduated from veterinary school and began to practice small animal medicine and surgery, this disease process was uncommon. Today, chronic diarrhea in adult cats, sometimes accompanied by chronic vomiting, is commonplace. These patients often undergo extensive, expensive medical workups, including biopsy of their gastrointestinal tracts, with the final determination that they have IBD (inflammatory bowel disease) or IBS (inflammatory bowel syndrome). Subsequent treatment is often less than successful. Fortunately, there is a simple explanation and solution for this condition.

What Is IBD?

(see http://maxshouse.com/inflammatory_bowel_disease.htm)

Inflammatory bowel disease, or inflammatory bowel syndrome, is not a definitive diagnosis but a pathologist's description of very general processes occurring in the tissues of the cat's gastrointestinal organs. What is clear is that in cats with this problem the tissues of the intestines, and sometimes the stomach, are involved in a chronic (long-term) immune system stimulation that disrupts normal digestive functions. Fluids are secreted into the intestines, resulting in diarrhea. Excessive motility (movement) through the inflamed tissues adds to this problem, and also decreases the assimilation of nutrients from food. If the stomach is involved, the cat vomits as well. Over time, the tissues of the GI tract become swollen and visibly abnormal in X-ray and ultrasound tests.

Because IBD is an immune-reaction disease, we assume that some immune system stimulation in the GI tract is causing this reaction. Most experts agree on this point. Food is by far the most likely stimulant of this "allergic" reaction because the ingredients in the cat's food are the major substances that contact the surface of the stomach and intestines. Proteins and other molecules in the diet cause the surface of the GI tract to react as though those molecules were foreign invaders. To solve the problem, it is logical that we need to change the kinds of substances that the cat's GI organs have to process.

How Is IBD Treated?

Up to now, IBD has been treated with immune system–suppressing drugs like prednisone, and so-called hypoallergenic diets. This idea is logical because IBD is a immune-reactive condition, but the results are seldom, if ever, highly satisfactory. The immune-suppressing drugs have side effects, and most of the commercial hypoallergenic diets are far from hypoallergenic. These commercial diets attempt to use novel protein source ingredients, like lamb and rice, to achieve the desired results. Unfortunately, the form of diet used is almost always dry. The reality is that the cat with IBD is reacting to many of the highly unnatural ingredients in the commercial food, especially the dry form of the food.

Almost everything contained in commercial dry foods, and even most commercial wet foods, is capable of causing an allergic reaction in the cat. As we have discussed repeatedly in earlier chapters, there is nothing about the ingredients or formulation of dry cat foods that make them suitable for the cat. It makes little difference whether the protein sources of such foods come from chicken, beef, lamb, fish, soy, vegetable glutens, or any other protein ingredients. If the cat with IBD doesn't react to the protein ingredients, it can and will react to the dozens of other ingredients in combination with those proteins.

In recent years, some pet food manufacturers have developed "second-generation" hypoallergenic foods. In these very expensive cat foods, all of the protein has been broken down to amino-acids, the basic components of protein. The theory behind these foods is that if you reduce dietary protein to its basic amino acids, you would have the ultimate novel protein. While the idea on paper has merit, it does not work well in the cat itself. These diets have many of the same limitations and abnormal formulation characteristics that normal cat foods do. Because the pet food company formulators do not understand the basic problem with all commercial dry foods, and even wet foods with ingredients that can cause allergy in the gastrointestinal tract of the cat, they have ignored the most obvious solution.

The diet change that would have entirely solved the problem has never been recognized by those making pet foods for cats, so the right way to correct the problem has never been used in most commercial cat foods for the IBD cat. There are a small number of hypoallergenic *canned* foods that do not contain high-carbohydrate ingredients (I prefer canned Innovative Veterinary Diets). These can be helpful in mild cases of IBD if they are used early in the allergic process. These hypoallergenic canned foods do not resolve more severe cases, however. In such cases, I have found that the best, most complete cure for this problem is to go back to the basics of the cat's natural diet. Cats with IBD are especially sensitive to the artificiality and overprocessed nature of commercial foods. They need their natural fuel to run well. I recommend a diet of raw meat for all of my patients with moderate to severe IBD that does not respond to the better canned hypoallergenic diets. Before I describe this dietary approach, however, we need a good discussion of raw or cooked meat feeding in general because, for most veterinarians, this is a completely unacceptable practice (see chapter 25).

25

Feeding Raw Meat to Your Cat— Is It Safe and Sensible?

(see www.catnutrition.org)

Ask most veterinarians whether a raw meat diet is a good idea for your cat and you will almost certainly receive an unqualified "No!" as the answer. I was once one of these individuals who believed that such a practice was a recipe for disaster. I worked for many years for one of the very largest "premium" and "prescription-type" food manufacturers, and I believed that feeding any kind of noncommercial foods, much less raw meat, was a dangerous and seriously flawed nutritional approach. I was told that such practices would lead invariably to rampant food poisoning from bacterial contamination, as well as serious nutritional imbalances in pets so fed. In reality, there is actually no scientific basis for this extreme bias against feeding the cat its evolutionary natural food, but it took me fifteen years to understand that fact.

Today, when I hear veterinary nutrition experts speak against the mere concept of raw meat diets for cats, without any qualification, I am astonished. The simple fact is that the cat we enjoy as a pet today developed as a highly successful and prolific species on that very diet over millennia of time. Long before the pet food companies decided to go into the business of providing convenient cooked and processed foods for feeding those cats, this animal had figured out how to be healthy on a diet that had no pet food company fingerprints upon it whatsoever.

In previous chapters, we have discussed the anatomy, physiology, and metabolism of today's cat, and how those characteristics clearly describe a top predator, in a class along with big wild cats, raptors (birds such as eagles, hawks, falcons, and the like), most sharks, wolverines, and piranhas, to name just a few. For such animals, meat from natural prey is very clearly a highly desirable diet. There can be no debate about this, and there should be no unqualified bias against feeding raw meat to the cat, perched as it is atop the food chain with its top-predator brethren. Day in, day out, month in, month out, for thousands of years before Western civilization saw light of day, the close ancestors of the cat caught and ate meat, and those ancestors always ate it raw.

What About Contamination?

If there can be no fundamental objection to the mere *idea* of raw meat as a diet for the cat, what legitimate objections might there be about the practical aspect of feeding raw meat to felines? The first objection would be the possibility of food poisoning from bacterial contamination of the meat. While this is certainly a possibility, just as food poisoning of humans who eat raw meat (I love sushi and sashimi!) is always at least a possibility, the reality is highly controllable and clearly overstated, in my opinion and the opinion of many others. Human-grade ground and whole raw meats for pets are available today because of the growing popularity of the practice among pet owners (see www.omaspride.com and felinespride.com). These meats are handled carefully by the processor, and frozen immediately after processing.

In my hands and the hands of my clients who elect to feed raw meat, the diet remains frozen until immediately before feeding. All of the logical precautions against bacterial contamination that we observe in handling meat for our families apply to the practice of feeding this meat to our cats. While many will argue that these precautions are not entirely foolproof, I can only respond that my approach has worked, without a single case of even low-grade gastroenteritis in my cats or those of my clients, for many years now. I genuinely believe that the evolution of the cat has prepared it for the consumption of low levels of bacteria with its food. It is unimaginable that an animal that hunts, kills prey, and then eats that prey off the ground, sometimes hours or even days after the kill, is incapable of resisting food poisoning of the type that most critics of raw meat feeding are concerned about.

Further, my own cats will decline meat that is truly tainted. I have deliberately tested this, and believe that the same instincts that lead a cat to consume meat in the first place, also tell it when not to eat a particular piece of meat in those instances where it senses danger in that meal. The notion that only commercial pet food producers can nourish our cats properly, after all these years of evolution before there *were* commercial pet foods, is just plain illogical.

I recently read a newly published article by a board-certified veterinary nutritionist in which the author condemned raw meat as a food for pets. This individual acknowledged that raw meat feeding proponents believe their pets do not suffer from food poisoning. She went on to point out that veterinarians treat many transient gastrointestinal problems symptomatically without a positive diagnosis. It was this expert's opinion that such cases are no doubt often mild food poisoning, but are simply never identified as such. I couldn't agree more. The fact is, however, that this expert failed to appreciate and account for the all-but-universal practice of feeding pets *commercial* foods today. Although raw meat feeding for both cats and dogs is a growing practice among progressive pet owners, commercial pet foods continue to be the most prevalent diet for pets in the United States and many other industrialized countries. If veterinarians are unknowingly treating numerous cases of food poisoning in their practices today, most if not all of those cases are coming from the feeding of commercial pet foods!

As I write this chapter, a widely published news story in the national press tells of a massive canned cat food recall by several major pet food manufacturers. This recall is in response to the deaths of cats from kidney failure when consuming the implicated foods. A year earlier, we witnessed a similar recall involving dry cat and dog foods due to poisoning of pets by a liver toxin produced by fungus growing in the corn used in the food. These recalls are not isolated events, but they illustrate the fact that contrary to common belief within the veterinary profession that commercial pet foods are absolutely safe and nutritious, this absolute safety and trustworthiness is simply not the case. *Commerically prepared pet foods are no more inherently safe to feed than are homemade foods for pets, or even human foods for humans!*

The illusion that the FDA and AAFCO are watching the pet food industry to prevent these kinds of problems is just that, an illusion. Unfortunately, only when large numbers of pets become ill and die do we learn that commercial foods can and do become seriously contaminated. I believe it is true that lesser problems with commercial foods are treated by veterinarians every day, with never a suspicion that the food in the bag is to blame. Yet the outrage against feeding clean raw meat to pets goes on, scientifically unexamined by those who express this outrage.

We live at a time when our own physicians and human nutritionists are insisting that people must eat more fresh, whole foods to establish and maintain their health. At the same time, we see frightening examples of how unsafe commercial pet food products can be under some circumstances. Despite all this, we continue to hold fast to the idea that our cats (and dogs) *must* eat commercial products that are far less fresh and whole than raw meat, and are clearly not safer from contamination. Dry cat foods, full of processed carbohydrates and sugar, and coated with fat and fermented liquids from animal entrails, sit on the shelf, exposed to air, for weeks, months, or more. How can anyone believe that such a food is likely to be free of contamination? This is completely illogical, and nothing more than an unexamined belief that must be reconsidered.

What About Nutritional Adequacy of Raw Meat Diets?

The second criticism of raw meat diet for cats that authorities advance is the potential nutritional inadequacy of such diets. They argue that commercial pet foods are "complete and balanced" for all life stages, or certain stages, as certified by feeding trials outlined by the AAFCO. Raw meat diets, with or without supplements, are not so tested, they insist, so cannot be trusted to be good nutrition for pets.

The problems with this argument are many. We have discussed in chapter 3 the serious limitations of the AAFCO feeding trials, and how these trials have failed to disclose serious, even fatal, nutritional inadequacies in commercial pet foods in the past. Veterinarians and experts who believe that the adequacy testing done on commercial pet foods meets any reasonable scientific standards are mistaken. In reality, no food, be it raw meat or commercial canned or dry, has been rigorously and scientifically tested in long-term feeding studies prior to use in pets. In that regard, commercial foods have no advantage over homemade ones.

The long-term feeding trials needed to establish the safety and adequacy of pet foods are, sadly, conducted in owned pets after their owners purchase the foods. In effect, every cat is a guinea pig. This is not a good situation, but it *is* the situation we have. These unmonitored feeding trials for commercial cat foods, particularly dry cat foods, are terrible failures in which the "test subjects" (our own pets) are suffering from obesity, diabetes, urinary tract disease, inflammatory bowel disease (IBD), and many other allergic conditions, to name a few of those conditions we know about. Had these foods been tested in long-term tests prior to release for sale, as they should have been, they would not have passed those tests.

How are raw meat diets doing in *their* "feeding trials"? I would say that raw-meat diets, properly designed, are proving considerably more nutritionally complete and balanced than their commercial dry-food rivals. In fact, in my practice, I can correct with raw-meat diets virtually all of the problems caused by commercial dry foods. I have never seen a single case of serious obesity, diabetes, urinary tract disease, or IBD in a cat fed meat instead of commercial dry foods. Many other people have seen the same results. Further, I do not see nutritional deficiencies in cats fed properly balanced raw-meat diets.

In the case of my own Ocicat breeding program, I have worked with more than five generations now of kittens, pregnant queens, and adult cats fed *only* raw meat, plus a single comprehensive vitamin/mineral/amino acid supplement. My kittens are born alive and thrive, my queens are robust and maintain excellent body condition throughout pregnancy and lactation, and my adult cats have amazing health and muscularity that I have never seen in dry-food-fed cats. In the more distant past, I fed dry food to my cats, as so many cat-owners still do. Then, I saw all of the nutritional problems I list above in those very cats. Now that I feed raw meat to may cats, I do not have these problems. The very same is true of my clients who now feed raw. I want to emphasize a point here. The incidence of these problems has not just declined on a raw-meat diet, they have entirely disappeared. These results are too dramatic to ignore.

Would I prefer that there were published long-term feeding studies of cat foods conducted by an impartial third party to settle this controversy once and for all? Definitely, I would. I fully expect that as this debate grows, such studies on all forms of commercials foods as well as homemade diets, done properly by unbiased scientists, will be funded and get under way. Unfortunately, it will be years before we know the results with certainty, because such studies will have to be truly long-term to satisfy everyone, including me. In the meantime, my own experiences in working within the pet food industry, and as a veterinarian and cat breeder, have convinced me that properly designed raw-meat diets are both safe and complete and balanced for health in all cats.

See appendix II for a discussion about how to feed a healthful raw meat diet. See also www.catnutrition.org.

Think About It

To illustrate how strong and automatic this bias against feeding of meat to cats is, I once asked a veterinary colleague of mine, a good friend and a very capable practitioner, to consider a pair of hypothetical patients. The first patient is a three-year-old male neutered cat that comes to the clinic for vomiting and diarrhea for the past two days. This cat eats only a "premium" dry cat food. The patient is in good condition and normal on physical exam and laboratory workup except for some possible low-level discomfort in the abdomen. I asked my friend whether he would consider the diet a likely contributing cause of the problem. He responded that he would not consider diet at all at this time. He allowed that if the cat failed to respond to conservative treatment, he might be forced to consider a possible food intolerance problem, or allergy, but he would not be concerned about food poisoning or any kind of food contamination at any point.

I then asked him to imagine another cat, identical in all ways with the first cat, except this one gets ground raw chicken as part of its diet, which also includes "premium" dry cat food. I asked if he would be concerned about the ground chicken in the diet. My friend said that he would put food poisoning at the top of his list of causes of the cat's problem, even if the cat lived with other completely unaffected cats that ate the same diet! I asked him why he was so trusting of commercial dry foods and so mistrusting of raw meat. He responded honestly that he had always been taught that it is unwise to feed cats raw meat because of its contamination, while no one had ever suggested to him that commercial foods could be contaminated and cause gastrointestinal disease. He had never thought about the potential problems with carbohydrate-rich kibbles that were coated with animal fat and fermented meat juice, and stored in the presence of air for weeks or months before feeding.

My colleague's beliefs had no scientific basis and no basis even in his own practice. He, like almost all other veterinarians, had almost no clients who fed raw or cooked meat to their cats. His views were not formed by careful observation of documented food poisoning in meat-fed cats and a corresponding absence of such cases in commercial-food-fed cats. By his own admission, all cases of vague gastrointestinal disease that he treated in commercial-food-fed cats could not be food poisoning, simply because of his blind trust in the safety of commercial foods.

IBD Is an Allergic Reaction

Significant, chronic diarrhea in cats, with or without vomiting, can be presumed to be allergic in nature once other causes of this sign, such as parasites, tumors, and other metabolic diseases, are ruled out. IBD is nothing more than allergic gastrointestinal disease, because the term *inflammatory bowel disease* is nothing more than a description of a chronic inflammatory process in the GI tract. I prefer to use human-grade raw or lightly cooked meat to manage and even cure this condition rather than resorting to immune-suppressive drugs, because it has essentially no side effects compared to drug therapy.

I have found that cats with even the most intractable and long-standing IBD will respond extremely well to ground rabbit meat as a starting diet (see appendix II for recipe). The change in such a cat is almost beyond imagining. When clients come to me, sometimes as a last resort, with a pet that hasn't had a normal stool for years, they are often considering euthanasia because of the stress and strain of this condition on their cat, their home, and their pocketbook. They are at wits' end, more often than not. The satisfaction that my staff receives in returning such a cat to normalcy within just a few days is indescribable. Even though this has happened many times in my practice, we continue to be thrilled every time. Often, we can eventually switch these patients to other kinds of raw meat, such as ground chicken. In almost all cases, we can avoid immunosuppressive drug therapy.

The solution to the problem is, as is the case with other nutritionally caused diseases, simple and easy to understand. Even though the so-called hypoallergenic diets available in commercial formulations attempt to deliver the correct solution in the form of foods with low allergic potential, they simply cannot do the job, especially if they are dry kibble. The ingredients used in commercial pet foods aren't really hypoallergenic to the majority of patients. These ingredients are processed in industrial plants that produce dozens of other products with very different ingredients. Cross-contamination between hypoallergenic and nonhypoallergenic products is a very real problem. The number of steps, the number of machines, and the number of hands that are required to produce the hypoallergenic foods make it all but impossible for these kinds of diets to deliver the results they promise, even if the nonprotein ingredients and processing methods weren't also part of the problem. As we have already discussed, there is no scientific evaluation of the effectiveness of these foods compared with more simple, less processed foods, so their failure remains a shadowy secret.

As is the problem with all "prescription-type" foods, especially the dry ones, hypoallergenic products simply attempt to retrofit a bad diet to make it less offensive to the cat's system. The real solution is to go back to the basics of cat nutrition. Dry kibbled cat food is not an inevitable reality for our cats, as some experts and pet food companies seem to believe. There are reasonable and easy alternatives that provide more effective and sensible solutions to serious, even life-threatening conditions such as IBD.

Cats That Need Drug Therapy Along with Diet Therapy

Some feline IBD patients have such long-standing disease that they require short-term or long-term treatment with certain immune-suppressive drugs along with diet. The most common drugs that veterinarians use in such cases are corticosteroids (steroids), usually prednisone, prednisolone, or dexamethasone. Steroids can dampen the exhuberant inflammatory reactions that are occurring in the GI tract of cats with IBD. The goal in using these medications is to find the lowest possible dose that will still control the signs of the disease, because steroids can cause serious side effects if used in too-high doses over long periods. It is particularly important that the cat receiving steroids avoid high-carbohydrate dry cat foods, to reduce the likelihood of one of the most serious side effects of steroid use, diabetes.

Another drug that may have a role in managing IBD is cyclosporine, also an immune system–depressing drug used in organ transplant technology in humans. While the use of cyclosporine in allergic disease in dogs and cats is new, early results with this drug in these conditions are very promising.

Some cats with IBD actually have a very early or precursor form of *gastrointestinal lymphoma*, a type of cancer that affects this organ system. Such cats may be manifesting the effects of chronic, severe irritation of the stomach and intestines, with the transformation of an inflammatory condition into a cancerous one. An analogy in humans would be the chronic irritation of the respiratory tract in the cigarette smoker, with eventual development of lung cancer.

Sometimes, the type of cancer that develops in some IBD patients is only mildly cancerous, called a *low-grade malignancy*. These types of cancer can be much easier to manage than the much more aggressive forms that also arise in felines, with or without prior IBD. Biopsies of the feline patient's gastrointestinal tract can provide the information the veterinarian needs to decide whether treatment for cancer is required in any particular patient with IBD. Some patients may not have full-blown cancer yet, but the pathologist may find evidence of a precancerous state that will transform into cancer in the patient's future. In these cases, treatment with chemotherapeutic agents such as chlorambucil (Leukeran), along with corticosteroids, can be lifesaving. I have seen a number of cats with precancerous disease and low-grade cancer of the gastrointestinal tract recover almost overnight when diet and drug therapy, including chlorambucil, are combined.

26

Your Cat Has Allergies—
What Now?

We have already discussed one of the conditions that occur in the allergy-prone cat. Inflammatory bowel disease is a common manifestation of a serious allergic reaction in the feline patient. Other common signs of allergy in cats include allergic skin disease, asthma, stomatitis (allergic gum disease), and allergic otitis. I would point out that these conditions, while they may occur alone in any particular cat, are really related problems. While we may think of the skin as merely the outside covering of the body where fur appears, the reactive cells that participate in allergic reactions are found in many areas, and can cause problems in those diverse areas even when the allergic reaction originates elsewhere. I prefer to think of skin allergies, IBD, stomatitis, asthma, and allergic otitis as multiple manifestations of the same basic process, often triggered by the same allergy-causing substances.

Allergic Skin Disease

Many cat owners have had experience with a pet that is constantly scratching its skin or pulling out its hair because of constant itchiness. Every week in my clinic I see patients with this problem. Sometimes the cat has merely "barbered" its fur with the abrasive surface of its tongue, leaving "buzz-cut" areas that appear to have been thinned and shortened as if a razor blade had been used. The skin in these patients is otherwise normal. Some patients have removed all of the hair and scraped down to the skin itself, leaving areas of rash or even open sores. We see these areas of hair loss and self-injury on the hind legs, the belly, the area around the top of the tail and the base of the spine, the front legs, or almost any other area or combination of areas.

Reaction to flea bites is one of the most common causes of allergic skin disease. Cats, like dogs, can react to the saliva or other allergens (molecules that can cause an allergic reaction) from fleas with intense itchiness of the skin and self-mutilation in response to that itchiness. The pattern of hair loss that we see *usually* in flea allergy involves the hindquarters, the area around the tail and top of the back, and the belly. Any cat with this distribution of hair loss without a history of good flea control must be suspected to have this allergy as at least part of its allergic problem. Fortunately, if a patient does have fleas, or may have had fleas in the past, the offending allergic substance can be eliminated by eliminating the fleas with good flea control. Your veterinarian can advise you about how to do this.

In the case of a cat with hair loss due to itchy skin, multiple allergens may be contributing to the problem. I often see cats with significant skin allergy yet no reason to suspect fleas as the cause. Most experts consider nonflea-allergic skin disease to be caused by inhaled allergens. Undoubtedly, the cat is capable of reacting to many molecules that are inhaled from the air in the environment. And that reaction certainly can manifest in the skin. It can also localize in the lungs and present as asthma, because the lungs are the tissues that most directly contact the allergens in inhaled air. It can spread to other parts of the body from the skin, such as to the ears. I also see cats with allergic gums, along with their skin signs and ear inflammation.

In my personal experience, skin allergies in cats usually have many allergens as the basis of the problem. Inhaled substances may well play a role, but I believe that reactions to food are almost always involved as well. I believe this because many of my skin allergic patients respond at least in part to a change to a canned or raw hypoallergenic diet. Even in cats that are allergic to several allergens, inhaled and others, decreasing the amount of total allergen that a cat must face will often relieve the signs of disease, even if some allergens remain in the environment. It is often impossible to identify and remove all of the substances that a cat is allergic to, but diet is always something we can modify to reduce the antigen load below the level needed to make the patient sick.

I have not found allergy testing, as is done in humans, to be helpful in cats. I know veterinary dermatologists who agree that this kind of testing is not as well developed for the cat as for humans and dogs. I also have not experienced good results with allergy shots (hyposensitization therapy) in cats, for the same reason. We simply do not understand the cat's immune reaction in allergy well enough, and have not done enough research in this area, to have good diagnostic and therapeutic approaches as we do in other species. These tests and injections are expensive, and seldom yield results good enough to justify this expense.

If this is true, how can we manage the skin allergies at the cat? As we have already discussed, we must first be sure that fleas or other parasites are not contributing to the problem. Once fleas, ticks, fungus, and the like are ruled out, I change the diet of my patients immediately. Dry cat foods and canned foods with fish, beef, or significant amounts of cereal are the most likely culprits that contribute to allergic skin disease. About 50 percent of the mild skin allergies that I see will have a good improvement with a change to a low-carbohydrate diet with a single source of protein, such as rabbit meat (see appendix II), or to one of the better hypoallergenic canned diets. Whether or not my patient's allergies can be treated entirely with diet alone, this diet change is the foundation of allergic disease management and good health in any case.

When my patients do not respond completely to diet change alone, I will start a course of an antihistamine, such as cyproheptadine or Benadryl. Diet and antihistamines allow good control of another percentage of cats over the first several weeks of therapy. If antihistamines are not able to resolve the problem, I prescribe a relatively new drug in veterinary medicine, cyclosporine, for my patients with the most difficult skin allergies. This drug has been used in humans for decades, mostly in organ-transplant medicine and surgery. It is an immune-suppressive drug used in humans to prevent organ rejection in patients undergoing organ transplantation. Within the last couple of years, this drug has been approved for use in animals, and it is proving to be a valuable tool in treating certain allergic conditions in pets, including cats. Your veterinarian can decide if this drug might be helpful in your particular pet.

Many veterinarians use corticosteroids to manage allergies in dogs and cats. While these drugs, usually prednisone, prednisolone, and dexamethasone, are extremely effective in the allergic patient, they have significant side effects. Among those side effects are liver problems and diabetes mellitus in some cats. I do use these drugs in some of my cases, especially some cancers and certain severe immune-system diseases such as pemphigus and autoimmune anemia. In some cases, corticosteroids are absolutely vital, and the potential side effects are worth risking because of the benefit that these drugs provide. I do not, however, believe in using long-term corticosteroid to treat common skin allergies, unless these cats do not respond satisfactorily to diet change, antihistamines, or cyclosporine.

Shula Zenda

Shula was an eleven-year-old spayed female domestic short-haired cat with a long history of periodic skin allergies and loose stool. Her diet was a "premium" dry cat food. Her owners were moving to a retirement community in another state and, although they were not clients of my clinic at the time, they brought her in to be put to sleep before they moved. Shula's owners felt they could not keep her with them in the new residence and didn't believe they could find a new home for her with her current problems. They had tried a number of treatments to control her seasonal itchiness and diarrhea. We examined Shula and determined that, other than her allergic signs, she was otherwise healthy. She had inflamed ears and ear infections, and she was over-grooming herself on her belly and the backs of her legs. Her weight was good and her baseline blood work was all normal.

I wanted to work with Shula because I believed she could be a normal cat if her diet was changed. This approach had never been tried with her. We asked the Zendas if they would be willing to sign Shula over to me personally, rather than putting her to sleep. I explained that I thought I could help her and that I would be willing to keep her as a clinic cat, or find her a good new home, if I could get her allergies under control. Shula's owners agreed to transfer ownership of their cat to me, and asked me to keep them informed about her progress.

Shula was a good eater and right away accepted the canned hypoallergenic diet I switched her to. We fed her three ounces twice daily. We cleaned her ears and started putting medicated drops in each ear twice daily. Within a week, her ears were less infected, and her stools, which had a puddinglike consistency when she first came to us, became much firmer. At the end of the first month on the new diet, Shula was much improved. Her stools were not firm yet, and she still scratched at her ears periodically, however. I started her on a diet of raw ground rabbit with bone, plus a vitamin/mineral/amino acid supplement. Shula loved the rabbit. She was in heaven. Even better, her stools became completely normal immediately. Two weeks after starting the ground rabbit, Shula was entirely normal.

Six months after we adopted Shula, one of our clients asked if she could give Shula a new home. We explained how Shula needed to eat a diet of rabbit plus a vitamin/mineral/amino acid supplement only, to remain healthy. The client agreed to follow this diet. We placed Shula in the new home, thinking everything would go well. Three weeks later Shula was back at the clinic. Her allergic-skin problems had returned and the new owner reported that she had loose stools and was not using the litter box. The new owner's son had been house-sitting for his parents during their summer vacation. He had purchased grocery store canned and dry food to feed Shula while he was caring for her. Within three days of starting this diet, Shula was showing all of her previous signs of allergy. We all agreed that Shula should return permanently to the clinic.

Shula was put back on her ground rabbit diet and, once again, returned to normal within a week. Her litter habits also returned to normal. Today, Shula lives the life of the much-loved clinic cat, happy and healthy.

Allergic Otitis (Ear Inflammation with or Without Infection)

While most pet owners are well aware that dogs commonly have chronic problems with ear infections, few realize that ear inflammation and infection are not at all rare in the cat. One of the most common underlying causes for this condition in the cat is allergy. Other causes include ringworm (actually a fungal infection of the skin in or near the ear), ear mite infestation, and tumors of the ear. If your cat is acting as though its ears are painful or itchy, or if you see crusting on or in the ears or discharge from inside the ear canal, your veterinarian is the one to examine the affected areas and make the correct diagnosis.

If all other causes of otitis are ruled out, your cat may have allergies that affect the ears, called *allergic otitis*. Allergic otitis is really an extension of more generalized allergic skin disease. The ears, and the canal of the ear that leads down to the eardrum and middle ear, is covered with tissue essentially like the skin covering the body. When we see allergic skin disease, we often see inflammation of the ears as well. Sometimes this inflammation is manifest merely as redness in the tissues of the ear, but equally often we see an active bacterial or fungal infection deep in the ear canal. This infection is secondary to the accumulation of fluid and debris that occurs when inflammation lasts for a long period. Bacteria and fungus (usually yeast) thrive in this kind of environment.

We also see small, fleshy growths, called *polyps*, in the ear canals of allergic cats. These growths are just advanced evidence of the irritating, inflammatory nature of allergic otitis. Your veterinarian will examine your cat's ears with an otoscope to evaluate whether infection or polyps are present. Also, culture and microscopic examination of the material in the ear canal is very helpful in deciding whether bacteria or yeast are present.

Once such a secondary infection is set up in allergic ears, it can be challenging to cure these infections, especially if they have been present, untreated, for weeks or months. If polyps are present, they will usually need to be removed before any infection will resolve. To manage and cure allergic ear problems we must, of course, eliminate the allergic process while we treat the ears with the right antibiotic or antifungal medication. We must also make a plan to remove at least some of the allergens that are causing the problem in the first place.

Many of the same allergens that cause more generalized skin allergy will be causing the problem in the cat with allergic ears, even if there are minimal signs of diseases on the rest of the cat's body. So, we take the same approach with these patients that we take with those cats that have more widespread skin inflammation. This includes a diet change, from any dry cat foods or canned foods with beef, fish, or cereals, to a good-quality canned hypoallergenic diet or an all-meat diet, as we discussed above. I will also use medications containing a corticosteroid in these ears, to control the allergy aspect of the disease. Because the steroid in ear drops does not enter the cat's circulation to any great extent, I believe we can use them in the treatment of this problem without the same concerns about side effects that we have when we use corticosteroids by pill or injection for more widespread allergic skin disease.

I have found that it is rarely necessary to treat simple allergic otitis with such medications as cyclosporine or corticosteroids. If the allergic process extends from the ears to other areas of the body, as it often will over time if the process is not successfully controlled early, your veterinarian may need these drugs. Never ignore signs that your cat's ears are causing pain or itchiness.

Allergic Stomatitis (Allergic Gums and Mouth)

(see www.gla.ac.uk/companion/stomatitis.htm)

Allergic stomatitis, also known as *feline lymphocytic-plasmacytic stomatitis*, is a mild to severe reddening and ulceration of the gums around most or all of a cat's teeth, the roof of the mouth, and the tissues at the back of the throat. While we also see a milder form of gum disease and inflammation in cats that have extensive plaque and tartar on the teeth, cats with allergic stomatitis are more painful and often have very little plaque or tartar. The basis of the problem lies in an immune system reaction to an allergen or allergens. This is evident from the type of cells that play a part in the inflammation that occurs. Those allergens may be in food, and they may also enter the cat's body elsewhere and trigger the allergic reaction from a distance. Infection with the feline immunodeficiency virus (see chapter 8) can also cause mild to severe stomatitis.

Some experts believe that viruses like calicivirus (see chapter 8) may play a role in causing allergic stomatitis in cats. I believe that diet must also be considered a likely contributor, if not the sole cause in at least some cases, especially in those cats that do not have other primary infections. Unlike most other allergic conditions in the cat, corticosteroids are not particularly helpful in cats with allergic stomatitis, and some experts believe that they may even be harmful. In the past, many veterinarians have extracted all or most of a cat's teeth in a desperate attempt to relieve the severe discomfort affected patient's experience. While some cats do have some resolution of their disease with this drastic approach, I have not found it to be necessary in the vast majority of cases.

Once again, I find that switching from a dry diet to a good canned hypoallergenic diet or homemade meat diet is the fundamental approach with these cats, just as with other types of allergy. Dry cat foods are highly abnormal in their nutrient content and ingredients as compared to the natural diet of the cat, or even good commercial wet foods. Such foreign diets are far more likely to expose the mouth of the cat to contact with dietary substances that are allergenic for this species.

Further, dry cat foods have very acidic coatings sprayed on the outside of the kibble to increase their palatability. Because they are generally available to the cat around the clock, dry foods can create a persistently acid environment in the mouth, with possible damage to the teeth and gums. This acid load may also explain the change in the types of resident oral bacteria we see in many cases of this condition. Unfortunately, most veterinarians and veterinary dentists are not aware of this aspect of dry food technology. As a result, dietary changes away from dry cat food is not part of the "mainstream" treatment of allergic stomatitis . . . yet.

In addition to a change in diet, I also recommend a course of antibiotics specific for oral infections, such as clindamycin. I have also successfully used cyclosporine in cases of stomatitis. Some veterinarians prefer to use interferon to treat this condition. Interferon is a protein produced by the body's own cells during certain infections. It has been used in human and veterinary medicine to fight some cancers, and research suggests it can be effective in allergic stomatitis. The exact method of its action in this disease is not well understood, but it is well worth trying in severe cases that do not respond completely to other therapies.

Some cats will require gum surgery to assist the healing of the sores and infection in the mouth. Veterinary dentists are expert at performing this kind of surgery. The laser "scalpel," which can quickly and safely remove diseased tissue, may be used during this surgical procedure. In short, there are many approaches to the management of this very difficult type of feline allergic disease. Most cats do not need to have all of their teeth extracted if several of these approaches are used according to the individual cat's degree of disease, and the individual veterinarian's preferences and experience.

Feline Asthma (Allergic Respiratory Disease)

(see www.marvistavet.com/html/body_feline_asthma.html, and

www.felineasthma.org/overview/index.htm)

Asthma, or an asthmalike condition that closely resembles this disease in people, also occurs in cats. Cats with this problem have a persistent deep, hacking cough, with episodes of coughing that last for an extended period. Owners observing their cats in the throes of an asthma attack become quite frightened, and may assume the cat is choking. In a way, the pet is choking, but there is no foreign material in the airway. The signs are the result of the airways of the cat's respiratory tract closing down and making it difficult for air to move into and out of the lungs. Some cats with asthma have episodes of shortness of breath along with or instead of the coughing attacks.

Of course, cough is a sign that may signal many feline diseases besides asthma. If your cat coughs frequently within any few hours or days, you must consult your veterinarian immediately. There are upper respiratory infections (URI) that result in cough, although cats with asthma are generally fully adult animals while URI is more common in kittens. This rule is not absolute, however, so URI must be ruled out in any coughing cat. Feline heartworm disease can also cause coughing. Many pet owners are familiar with this parasitic disease in dogs, but don't realize that heartworms can also infest cats, although to a much lesser degree than in dogs. In those areas of the world where heartworm disease is very prevalent in dogs, it must also be a strong suspicion in the coughing cat. Your veterinarian can test your cat for this problem very early in the workup for a cough.

There are other respiratory conditions that cause asthmalike signs in cats. These include lungworms, respiratory tract cancers, and heart problems. Your veterinarian will rule all of these other problems out before concluding that your cat has feline asthma. X-rays, blood tests, and samples of the cells and fluids in your cat's respiratory tract are among the diagnostic tools that can be used in the cat with a cough.

Once a diagnosis of asthma is made, there are a number of therapies that will allow you to manage your pet. Experts currently believe that inhaled allergens from the environment play an important part in allergic respiratory disease. Some of those same experts also believe, as I do, that dietary allergens play an important role as well. Asthma, like skin allergy, likely involves several or many different allergens from different parts of the environment. If pollens, air pollutants, house dust mites, and other common humans allergens are triggers for your cat's disease, these may or may not be easily controllable. Diet, on the other hand, is one of the most easily modified of the various environmental influences and, in my view, should be the first potential source of allergy-causing substances that we change.

All allergic cats in my practice, the majority of which are consuming dry cat food prior to diagnosis, are switched to a hypoallergenic commercial wet food or home-made diet. I will then use drug therapies such as antihistamines or inhalant steroids, or bronchodilators (drugs that cause the airways to enlarge, rather than constrict, during an attack), with an inhaler especially designed for cats to control the acute attack episodes. The available inhalers that have been adapted especially for cats (see www .winnfelinehealth.org/health/asthma.html) allow owners to treat acute asthmatic episodes at home in almost all cats. Cats on a hypoallergenic diet and inhaler therapy often will have fewer and fewer episodes of their asthma or breathing difficulties, so that treatment with the inhaler can be greatly reduced or even stopped altogether.

In those patients that do not respond satisfactorily to a diet change and inhaler therapy at home, or in patients with asthma *and* other signs of allergy like skin disease, I will use cyclosporine to control the signs of allergic reaction. This immune-system-suppressive drug can be a virtual godsend in managing difficult allergies. The use of this drug has not been thoroughly tested by the manufacturer in cats because of the high cost of such testing, but many veterinarians, including veterinary dermatologists and allergists and practitioners such as myself, are using it in cats with good success. It goes without saying that any cat on any immune-system-suppressive drugs should be tested for general health before drug therapy starts, and frequently thereafter.

Yakov Williams

Yakov (a.k.a. Yaki) was a six-year-old neutered male Russian Blue when he first came to our clinic. Yaki lived in Southern California during those first years of his life. When he was five years old, he developed a mild coughing problem that was diagnosed by his original veterinarian as asthma after all other causes of cough were ruled out. Yaki only coughed during the spring and fall of the year, especially on windy days. When we first saw Yaki, he was on commercial dry cat food and was being treated for his asthma with antihistamines. We switched him to a canned hypoallergenic diet, and his owner reported much better control of his asthma signs after the diet change. For two years, Yaki did well on the new diet and antihistamines.

In the fall, when Yaki was eight years old, his owners had to move to a Southern U.S. state for several months for business. His owners and I discussed the potential problems that Yaki might have in his new environment. Because environmental inhaled allergens seemed to be a significant part of Yaki's allergic trigger, I was concerned that the move might cause him to have considerably more problems in his new residence. I prescribed cyclosporine for Yaki and sent this drug with his owner in case his asthma became more severe after the move. Yaki's owners promised to communicate with me frequently during their time away.

Two weeks after the move, Yaki began to cough more than he ever had before. The antihistamines and hypoallergenic diet were not controlling his disease. At my instruction, his owners began to give Yaki the cyclosporine on a daily basis. The improvement was dramatic. He stopped coughing almost immediately, and his owners reported that his condition became better than ever since his diagnosis of asthma. After a month on daily cyclosporine, I instructed his owners to begin dosing him every other day, and he continued to do well on this reduced dose. Once Yaki's owners returned to Southern California, we further reduced his dose of cyclosporine, and he continues to do very well on a very low dose of this drug.

Bernie Chambers

Bernie was a six-year-old, neutered male Egyptian Mau when we first saw him. During his early years, Bernie had had recurrent episodes of allergic skin disease that were treated with intermittent corticosteroids by mouth. This treatment seemed to control his problem for a time. Unfortunately, by the time we saw him after his owner had moved to California from another state, Bernie had severe stomatitis and asthma along with his skin allergies, which had become year-round. He had several areas of hair loss on his belly and thighs. He had chronic diarrhea typical of inflammatory bowel disease. He even had severe allergic otitis, with a polyp in one ear. Bernie was the most allergic cat I have ever seen. Because of his stomatitis, he was not eating his commercial dry and canned foods well, and had lost several pounds over the past six months. He coughed constantly, and hardly moved without emitting a deep, dry, hacking cough, with his head down and extended as though he were choking on something.

When we evaluated Bernie, he had an elevated white blood cell count, indicating both an allergic reaction and infection. He was negative for both feline leukemia virus and feline immunodeficiency virus. His liver and kidneys appeared to be functioning well. Bernie's workup showed no other cause for his cough but asthma. His ears were secondarily infected with both bacteria and yeast, and the polyp in his right ear made managing these infections very difficult. His diarrhea was not due to any parasitic disease that we could find, and there was no evidence of tumor in his GI tract.

We began to treat Bernie aggressively for his overwhelming allergic problems. We first changed his diet to raw rabbit with a multivitamin/mineral/amino acid supplement (see www.platinumperformance.com). We treated Bernie's allergic ears by removing his polyp with a laser and administering antibiotic/corticosteroid ear drops twice daily for a month. We used the laser to remove all of the extensive inflammatory tissue in his mouth. We performed a thorough cleaning of his teeth and gums but did not remove any teeth. I prescribed daily cyclosporine capsules. We sent Bernie home and held our breath.

Bernie did extremely well on this protocol. In four weeks, his sore, inflamed mouth was dramatically improved, and he was eating his raw meat diet well. Bernie's stools were completely normal, and had become normal within forty-eight hours of the diet change. His ears were normal in appearance with no discharge for the first time in months. Bernie coughed briefly about once daily, and his owner reported that he had ceased having his very frightening, "choking" attacks. In the following months, Bernie's signs continued to be well controlled on our protocol.

Because Bernie was doing so well three months after we first started treatment, I suggested we try to reduce his dose of cyclosporine to an every-other-day schedule. Unfortunately Bernie's asthma became worse when we did this. His coughing increased, although his other signs of allergy remained well controlled. We put him back on his original dose, and his asthma signs diminished once again. His owner treats his ears with steroid drops every other day. Two years later, Bernie continues to enjoy good quality of life and his owner is pleased. We check him regularly for any side effects of this treatment, and he seems to be handling therapy well.

27

Cancer in Cats—An Ounce of Prevention Is a Pound of Cure

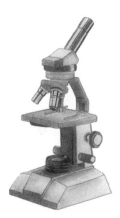

Cancer is a scourge in all species, including cats (www.fabcats.org/cancer.html). It often strikes without warning and may rapidly devastate the host, whether human or animal. Perhaps the most terrifying aspect of cancer is its mysterious origins. For most types of cancers, we have almost no understanding about what causes the malignancy in the first place. Only a few feline cancers have any presently known cause. Because of this, and because of the speed with which cancer can become unmanageable if it goes undetected and untreated, regular veterinary exams and close observation of the cat at home are the first line of defense against these potential killers.

Even Young Adult Cats Can Get Cancer

Many pet owners believe that only old cats are likely to develop malignant tumors (another name for cancer). The truth is, cancer has no real age boundaries, although cats, like other animals and humans, do have an increasing likelihood of getting cancer as they age. Some common types of feline cancers, such as leukemia associated with the feline leukemia virus (FELV), and some types of lymph system cancers such as lymphosarcoma, occur in young adult cats with some frequency. Even other, less common types will occur occasionally in younger felines.

Whatever the age of your cat, be vigilant for any signs of swelling or discomfort in your pet. Feline cancers occur in virtually every organ system and every area of the body. Although long-haired cats may mask a lump on the outside of the body better than will short-haired ones, the conscientious owner will pet and groom every part of the cat's body on a regular basis. When the cat is young and healthy, this habit of regular grooming and examining the body provides a good baseline of information about what is normal anatomy for your particular cat. Watch for any abnormal feel to your cat's body, including the head, legs, and tail. In female cats, make sure to pay close attention to the mammary glands (breasts), as this is a common location for tumors to develop, especially if your cat was altered after twelve to eighteen months of age, or isn't altered at present (see chapter 12).

Of course, tumors can arise inside your cat as well. Thorough examination of your cat's mouth, chest cavity, and abdominal cavity must be done by your veterinarian at every visit, or any time your cat begins to act sick. Any abnormalities that show up on the regular physical exam will be thoroughly evaluated to rule out cancer, so early detection can give a cure or good control of disease. As much as we all hate the thought of a pet having cancer, it is far better to know, and to know *early*, than to delay diagnosis and treatment. Some cancers in cats are entirely curable if detected and treated in the early stages.

What Can Cat Owners Do to
Safeguard Their Cats?

Cancers in cats, like cancers in other animals and people, are impossible to prevent entirely. We do know that there are some important precautions that owners can take to reduce the likelihood that their own cats will develop this difficult group of diseases:

1. As discussed above, be vigilant about your cat's physical condition. Never ignore any bump, sore, or blemish that comes up mysteriously or fails to heal quickly within a few days. Cancer often shows up as a nonhealing or rapidly growing lump or woundlike area on any part of the body. Your veterinarian can evaluate such an area and make a determination about whether a biopsy with surgical removal is necessary.

2. Never ignore vomiting, diarrhea, or lack of appetite that last more than a day or two at most. While these signs are most often not associated with cancer in the cat, especially the young cat, they are signs of a problem that must be treated, and your veterinarian will try to rule out the possibility of gastrointestinal or other abdominal cancers during the process of managing these signs.

3. Keep your cat's home environment as free of pollution as possible. If you smoke cigarettes or cigars, do not smoke in any place where your cat will inhale secondhand smoke! Research shows that cats accumulate molecules called *coat-associated carcinogens* (cancer-causing substances) on their skin and hair when they are exposed to tobacco smoke. The cat then grooms these toxic substances off the skin and hair, and swallows them. In the GI tract, these carcinogens can, over time, cause very serious forms of GI irritation (such as inflammatory bowel disease) and cancer to arise. I cannot emphasize strongly enough this point about not exposing your cat to secondhand tobacco smoke!

4. If you have a white cat, or a cat with a white face or ears, limit your pet's exposure to direct sunlight. Sun exposure is causative of a potentially very serious form of skin cancer in cats called *squamous cell carcinoma* (see www .fabcats.org/squamous.html). The best preventive measure against this cancer is not to let your white-faced cat sun itself during the middle of the day. For-

tunately, if caught early and treated aggressively, it may be possible to cure facial squamous cell carcinoma. Never ignore even small areas of rash or scabbing on the face or ears of any cat.

5. If your cat shows any signs of swelling in its lips, jaws, or neck, or if you notice a foul odor from the mouth, or unusual salivation, see your veterinarian immediately. There may be a tumor growing in the mouth, and early detection will be vital to saving your cat's life.

6. If your cat has difficulty breathing, or coughs repeatedly, see your veterinarian. While there are many causes of respiratory problems and cough in the cat, it is imperative that your veterinarian make sure that lung or chest cavity cancer is not present. Never smoke in your cat's living areas!

7. Have your pet spayed or neutered within the first six to eight months of its life. Early neutering is the best way to greatly reduce the risk of reproductive tract cancers, including breast cancers, in your pet later in life.

8. Chronic inflammation of the gastrointestinal tract, as we see in IBD (chapter 24), may actually transform into gastrointestinal cancer over time. Effective treatment of IBD-like disease is key to halting this transformation process. Again, never ignore persistent vomiting or diarrhea in your pet.

9. Remember that cancer is an enemy, but it is not necessarily an undefeatable enemy. You and your veterinarian have the best chance to win any battle with cancer if that battle starts early in the course of the disease.

If your cat is diagnosed with cancer, there are many therapeutic approaches that your veterinarian may recommend for curing or managing this problem. Surgery, chemotherapy, and radiation therapies have been used successfully alone or in combination to deal effectively with most of the cancers we see in cats. Your veterinarian may refer you and your pet to a veterinary oncologist, a specialist in cancer treatment in animals, for the most sophisticated treatments.

Recently, a new immune-system-stimulating substance derived from Agaricus blazei mushrooms has shown considerable promise as an adjunct in the management of cancer in humans (see www.atlasworldusa.com). I believe this extract has a role to play in the treatment of animal cancers as well. This drug is essentially nontoxic in animals (unlike many other drugs we use) and should be considered as part of the overall treatment protocol whenever we are faced with malignancies in our pets.

PART

4

The Truly Golden
Senior Years

28

The Older Cat and Preventive Nutrition

One of the things that trouble me most as a cat veterinarian is my clients' belief that their cats are "old" once they reach ten years of age or so. I am just amazed at how many of them believe their cats will automatically start experiencing the most serious of old-age medical maladies at the start of their second decades. I have even had my clients ask me if it is really humane to treat relatively minor problems in such "old" cats, since they will be at death's door soon. Nothing could be further from the truth.

The average cat can and should live well into the teens and beyond. While the *Guinness Book of World Records* tells us that rare individuals may live into their thirties, this is clearly not the norm. However, we should expect cats with good genes and conscientious care to live two decades, maybe more. The ten-year-old cat is only middle-aged, with many more wonderful, healthy years to go.

One of the reasons so many of my clients fear they will lose their cats long before they reach twenty is that in their recent experience, their cats *have* died prematurely. When they describe pets they have loved and lost in the last ten to fifteen years, many of those pets have died of conditions related to environmental factors, not a lack of natural ability to survive much longer. These factors include trauma, such as automobile accidents, to be sure. They also include exposure to fatal infectious diseases, and probably even breathing of passive smoke. An alarming number of these cats, however, have died at a young age of nutritional diseases, such as obesity-related problems (chapter 20), diabetes (chapter 21), recurrent bladder problems (chapter 23), inflammatory bowel disease (chapter 24), and kidney disease (chapter 29).

How to Feed Your Older Cat

Today, the pet food companies spend millions of dollars in marketing each year to convince cat owners that every life-stage of the cat requires a change to a different formula of their pet foods. There are kitten formulas, adult formulas, senior formulas (for cats seven years and over; no wonder cat owners think their cat is old at this age), and the like. Interestingly, the difference in these various formulas is little more than increased carbohydrate and fiber levels in the adult and older-cat products.

When I discuss life-stage feeding with my clients, I explain to them how cats in the natural setting deal with their nutritional needs as they become adult and geriatric. There is no such thing as a mouse, or bird, or lizard, or wildebeest (if you are a big cat) that is especially designed for the "older cat." All prey animals the cat hunts and eats as a juvenile, an adult, or a senior are the same in their nutrient composition. Adult and older cats do not acquire a taste or a need for more and more processed carbohydrate as the years go by, as the pet food companies seem to believe. The cat that is providing food for itself merely eats different amounts of the very same food, no matter what its age.

We have discussed at length the unique metabolic characteristics of the cat (see chapter 1). These characteristics do not change over the life of the animal. Adult and senior cats retain the same requirement for high protein, moderate fat, and low carbohydrate of the young cat. Although their calorie requirements may change over time, older cats accommodate this change by consuming smaller amounts of food, not by consuming a different kind of food. When "adult" and "senior" cat foods replace protein and fat in the "kitten" versions of their products, they create foods with poorer nutritional quality at times when a cat needs higher quality. The pet food companies' mistaken beliefs that ample protein somehow harms the cat's kidneys over time (see chapter 29) and that dietary fat causes cats to become fat (see chapter 20) cause faulty formulations for the older cat.

As a cat becomes older, its ability to digest and assimilate all of the dietary nutrients in its food decreases gradually. Yet, the older cat that eats a commercial adult or senior cat formula actually receives less nutritional value in its diet, creating significant potential for deficiencies. Lowered protein causes the high-protein requirements of the cat to go unsatisfied, and lowered calories from fat shortchange the skin and coat, and force the cat to eat yet more carbohydrate to get enough calories for energy. In short, the feline nutritional principles behind life-stage formulas are upside down.

When adult and senior cats eat the same diet high-protein/moderate-fat/low-carbohydrate diet that kittens thrive on, they also thrive. They eat less relative to their body weight, to be sure. I have seen this with hundreds of cats as they move through the stages of their lives. Older cats that stay on their kitten diet maintain their hard, lean body condition; their healthy, glossy coat; and their natural activity level. They are less likely to become overweight and sluggish, and they exercise more, naturally: they feel like exercising because their engines are running on the best fuel for their metabolic machinery.

Therefore, I tell all of my clients *not* to switch their kittens to older-cat formulas as they grow up. I know that this is the foundation for long life and vital good health throughout all of those years. I also tell my clients to expect their cats to live far beyond ten years of age. With proper diet and regular preventive care, this is not only a reasonable hope for these cats, it can be every owner's *expectation*.

29

Kidney Disease—A Modern Approach to an Old Enemy

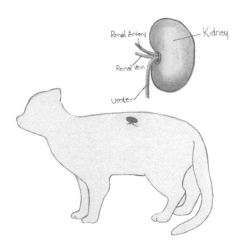

Renal Artery
Kidney
Renal Vein
Ureter

Scarcely anyone who has shared a life with cats is unacquainted with the medical condition known as *chronic renal disease* (CRD). In fact, some experts believe that CRD affects 8 percent or more of cats ten years of age and older. This is an often very frustrating and potentially life-threatening kidney dysfunction that can affect cats of any age, although we see it most commonly in middle-aged and older cats. Now is a very exciting time in the evolution of good management techniques for cats with CRF, after decades that might be considered the Dark Ages of treatment for this malady.

What Is CRD?

(see www.felinecrf.com/managd.htm)

Chronic renal disease is a term that is applied to the progressive loss of normal kidney function in cats with a variety of kidney diseases. This loss of normal function, which is essentially permanent in CRD, may arise in young cats with congenital or genetic kidney abnormalities, or older cats as a result of urinary tract obstruction, trauma, infections, poisons, diabetes, and other sources of damage to the cat's kidneys. In many older cats with progressive CRD, it may never be possible to determine the exact initiating cause of this loss of function. This kind of CRD is usually considered to be just an old-age change, although many cats live long lives without ever experiencing CRD. Thus, CRD is not inevitable except in those cats born with abnormal function. In the future, we may come to understand all of the subtle causes of the type of CRD that is associated with the aging process, and become better able to prevent it.

Regardless of the initial cause of CRD, management of this underlying cause is the first line of treatment. Poisoning, infection, injury to the kidneys, obstruction of the urinary tract, or congenital kidney defects must be identified so that early treatment to halt and even reverse some of the damage can be started. Once this initiating problem is under control or cured, management of the residual loss of function becomes key for both the veterinarian and the pet owner.

The cat with CRD often declines very gradually, and even the most conscientious owner may not notice the signs of this problem until it is well advanced. By the time the problem becomes apparent, the cat is usually losing weight, has a very unkempt appearance to the coat, may be very lethargic, has little appetite, may be drinking more water than usual, and also may begin to vomit food or just small amounts of yellowish fluid. Any or all of these signs are an urgent signal to see your veterinarian right away. Blood and urine tests can be performed to make the diagnosis and start treatment to reverse these signs.

There are a number of approaches to managing the lasting effects of CRD. Traditionally, veterinarians have relied on a change of diet as the central treatment for kidney dysfunction. Protein-restricted diets have gained great popularity over the past several decades as *the* central control measure in the cat with chronic kidney disease. Ironically, this switch to a low-protein diet is misguided, and may cause a great deal more harm than good in patients with CRD.

The History of Protein-Restricted Diets in CRD

In the 1940s, Dr. Mark Morris Sr., a very forward-thinking veterinarian, discovered that his canine patients with CRD seemed to feel better when he treated their disease with a new kind of diet. In those days, most pet dogs ate meat-based diets from their owner's table, or were fed largely all-meat by-product commercial foods available at the time for dogs. When Dr. Morris devised a diet with less meat and more cereal, these patients seemed to improve. Over the succeeding years, many pet food companies, including the very successful one that Dr. Morris founded, developed and marketed diets with lower amounts of meat and certain nutrients, including protein and phosphorus. For the dog, these diets seemed helpful in slowing the progressive signs of CRD. It was understandable that the idea of limiting protein in CRD patients would gain acceptance.

In the 1980s, research into canine kidney function and the effects of various environmental and nutritional factors showed that dietary phosphorus was an extremely important part of the problem in canine CRD. It was well known that phosphorus levels elevate in the bloodstream of dogs with uncontrolled CRD. This phosphorus elevation was shown to cause further damage to the kidneys, and contribute to the progression of the failure, leading to death if untreated. Diets high in meat have high phosphorus levels, since meat naturally has plenty of this mineral. Higher-protein diets also cause the blood urea nitrogen (BUN) levels to rise, and some experts believed that rising BUN levels might also contribute to the decline and death of CRD patients.

Research into the role of phosphorus in CRD suggested that perhaps it was the phosphorus in high-meat diets more than the protein in such diets that was harmful to the canine patient. Perhaps it was the reduction of phosphorus content in protein-restricted diets, not the protein restriction itself, which was helping the CRD patients on these diets. Were elevations in blood urea concentrations really harmful? Urea in the bloodstream has no known harmful effects on the body as compared to elevated phosphorus.

At the time, most experts considered these questions to be unimportant, because canine patients seemed to suffer no ill effects from eating cereal-based diets. The dog is an omnivore, and has a naturally lower protein requirement than the protein requirement in cats, at all life stages. The dog finds cereal-based diets appetizing and will usually eat them readily. There seemed no reason to worry about any potential ill effects of this kind of low-protein diets in the dog.

Once cats became popular as pets kept in the home and close to the hearts of their owners, management of CRD in felines was a problem that veterinarians faced with increasing frequency. Experts and practitioners merely transferred the principles of dietary management of canine kidney disease to management of this problem in cats. All of the pet food companies developed protein-restricted diets for cats, modeled after the same diets for dogs with minor modifications. Unfortunately, nothing seemed to help the feline CRD patient very much. Once a cat became sick from kidney failure, the course of the disease was usually hard to change, with a deteriorating quality of life, and death almost a certainty.

The fact that protein-restricted diets were not helping feline patients was obscured by their disease. Because CRD is a progressive and ultimately fatal condition, most veterinarians were hardly surprised when a patient on a low-protein diet failed to improve and wasted away. It was natural to blame the kidney disease for making the cat sick, for stealing its appetite, for weight loss, as well as all of the deterioration that seemed to follow the diagnosis in every case. No one thought to question whether dietary protein-restriction in an animal adapted to high protein intake had a negative effect on the outcome for the cat with CRD.

The truth is, it is possible to manage chronic renal insufficiency in the cat far more successfully than we have in the past under the old belief systems. Ironically, the centerpiece of this improved management regime for cats with renal disease is to avoid protein restriction! I now have no doubt that the practice of limiting the diet of CRD cats to an unpalatable, relatively indigestible, protein-poor formula, often a dry kibble with the limitations of that form of food for all cats, can actually contribute to the decline of cats with CRD. Today, we can do better for such patients. We can do *much* better.

What's Wrong with Protein-Restricted Diets for Cats?

It has become very apparent to me that a significant part of the deterioration of our CRD patients in years past was due to the protein starvation that was imposed upon them by those of us who followed the dogma of the day. My research into the nutritional aspects of feline diabetes caused me to rethink not only my views about dietary management of the diabetic cat, but also nutritional management of cats with many different chronic diseases, including CRD.

As we have discussed in earlier chapters, it is a serious mistake to treat any cat as though it were a small dog. Cats and dogs are so very different when it comes to their metabolic characteristics and nutritional requirements, that the widespread use of protein-restricted diets adapted for the dog has created more problems than it has solved in the cat. One of the most obvious problems with low-protein diets is that cats do not find them appetizing. Because the cat is an obligatory carnivore, diets with low amounts of protein from meat are not naturally palatable to members of this species. Pet food manufacturers have spent millions of dollars over the years in attempts to find low-protein formulas that would be appealing to cats, with extremely limited success.

While some of the more modern foods are a little more acceptable to cats than products of years past, there is still no protein-restricted "kidney-diet" for cats that the CRD patient will eat eagerly in sufficient amounts to avoid protein deprivation. When a cat will not eat the only food it is offered, the owner becomes frustrated and loses hope. The starving cat declines and dies.

Even when they are ill, cats continue to have very high protein requirements compared to most other animals. In fact, the debilitated cat may well have a higher protein requirement than its healthy counterpart. Yet the protein-restricted diet offers the CRD patient lower protein levels than the commercial foods of its younger, healthier years. Add to this the fact that the CRD patient finds this already protein-restricted diet unappetizing, and some degree of protein deficiency becomes certain. The pet food companies argue that as long as the quality of the protein in the diet is high, restricting the quantity of protein holds no danger of protein deficiency for the cat with kidney problems. This claim is not supported by science or clinical observations.

The quality of a protein is a measure of its digestibility and essential amino acid components. The cat requires *both* quality and quantity in its protein intake for health maintenance and recovery from disease. This is because it uses protein not only for tissue construction and repair, but also for energy production (see chapter 1). The cat on a protein-restricted diet cannot repair its own ailing body *or* produce enough energy to meet its needs. As a result, it wastes away and dies, and CRD gets all the blame. There have never been any scientific studies showing long-term benefits from a reduction in dietary protein that justify this restriction, compared to low-carbohydrate diets with higher protein, in the cat with CRD.

Recently, a study published by researchers at the University of Minnesota attempted to show that a certain protein-restricted, phosphorus-restricted feline diet provides benefits in the management of CRD.* This study looked at how cats with naturally occurring

*It is noteworthy that this study attempted to validate claims the sponsoring company had *already* been making for decades (see www.leda.law.harvard.edu/leda/data.784/Patrick06.pdf).

kidney failure responded to this low-protein diet as compared with similar cats being fed a commercial adult maintenance feline diet. Now, we must remember that the adult maintenance diet that was compared to the low-protein diet was the very kind of food that these cats were eating when they developed their CRD. This is an important consideration when we evaluate what this study does and does not prove about protein and phosphorus-restricted diets for cats with CRD. This study showed that in a small group of test cats, the cats on the protein-restricted diet responded better in some ways than did cats that continued to consume their regular adult commercial diet. Unfortunately, this study examined absolutely no other dietary approaches to the management of CRD. No diets of higher nutritional quality than the adult maintenance diet were compared with the protein-restricted diet.

This study provides absolutely no information about how a diet with *better* quality and quantity of protein and other nutrients than the commercial adult maintenance diet would have compared with the protein-restricted diet. This study entirely fails to fully evaluate the effects of a variety of diets with differing protein qualities and quantities in the management of CRD. Despite this failing, the sponsor of the study, a large pet food company that produces the largest selling protein-restricted diet on the market, has announced to the veterinary community that this study proves that its product is essentially the diet of choice in this disease. Unfortunately, this study may well be accepted by the veterinary community as the final scientific proof for this diet's superiority, even though it proves no such superiority of protein-restricted diets over other diets that better meet all of the needs of obligatory carnivores.

We have seen this kind of short-sighted research in feline nutrition before. In the 1970s, veterinary researchers conducted a study to compare the effects in diabetic cats of high-carbohydrate commercial foods versus high-carbohydrate commercial foods with significant amounts of indigestible fiber added. Both products were already on the market. From this relatively small and limited-design study, the authors concluded not only that high-carbohydrate diets with high fiber were superior to high-carbohydrate diets without fiber, but that such high-fiber foods were the *definitive* diet for the feline diabetic. We now know this is not at all true. Had this study included other diets with significantly lower amounts of highly-processed carbohydrate, the latter would have greatly outperformed both of the high-carbohydrate foods. Decades passed before veterinary researchers, including myself, reexamined the false dogma of high-fiber foods in diabetic felines. In the meantime, millions of sick cats were deprived of better approaches to their illness.

Similarly here, if the veterinary profession accepts this flawed and incomplete bit of research as the end-all and be-all of the question about dietary management of the cat with CRD, decades may pass before any real progress is made in truly unerstanding this terrible problem. We desperately need better science, conducted outside the influence of the pet food industry, in investigations that are broad enough in scope and design as to be genuinely instructive about how to use nutrition, as well as traditional medicine, to manage feline diseases such as CRD as effectively as possible.

What Nutrient Restrictions *Are* Indicated for the Cat with CRD?

What benefit there may be in protein-restricted diets comes from the phosphorus restriction these diets provide. In the cat with insufficient kidney function, high dietary phosphorus intake may promote further decline in that function. Limiting the intake of phosphorus in the diet is a very logical and constructive step to take with these patients, but accomplishing this by limiting a vital nutrient like protein is like the proverbial "throwing the baby out with the bathwater."

Phosphate binders that can be added to the cat's regular, palatable, high-protein diet (wet form only) are readily available and effectively remove substantial amounts of the dietary phosphorus from the food. Another strategy that works well is the addition of chopped, cooked egg white to the patient's wet diet. Egg white is high in top-quality protein but contains no phosphate, so it effectively "dilutes" the phosphorus in the food. This strategy allows the cat to have the protein building blocks of repair and energy production available in abundance, while reducing the intake of a nutrient that may be harmful to the patient. This is truly the best of both worlds.

BUN Levels Are Higher in Cats on Higher-Protein Diets. Is This a Problem?

Of note is the fact that cats on diets with naturally high levels of protein can have BUN levels that are somewhat higher than the so-called normal ranges that most laboratories report to veterinarians. This is true in even perfectly healthy cats. This is because urea is a nontoxic by-product of protein metabolism. It does not cause a cat to feel sick or become debilitated, but has been used as a signal flag for insufficient kidney function in dogs and cats for decades.

Unfortunately, the studies that were used to determine what "normal" levels of BUN were in the cat did not take into account what these levels would be if the cat ate a diet with natural levels of protein. They were studies of cats on the relatively lower amounts of dietary protein in commercial foods. Veterinarians whose patients are on higher-protein diets need to be aware of this difference. They also need to be aware that some degree of elevation is normal in such patients and is not harmful. This will be less a problem when reporting laboratories adjust their normal BUN ranges upward, to more accurately reflect what happens in cats on higher-protein diets.

Recently, a product called Azodyl was introduced to the veterinary market for reducing the level of BUN (blood urea nitrogen) in cats with CRD. This drug purports to interfere with the absorption of urea from the cat's intestines, thus lowering the level of this molecule in the patient's circulation. There are two very large problems with the use of Azodyl in cats, however. First, long-term-safety studies have not been done to prove that chronic use of Azodyl is safe in felines. Second, Azodyl has not been shown to improve the actual functioning of the cat's kidneys. Because BUN is not a source of the clinical signs in the CRD patient but is merely a useful diagnostic "marker," reducing only the amount of circulating urea nitrogen in the CRD patient provides no benefit. In fact, removing one of the diagnostic markers from the patient without improving function might well lead to greater difficulties in assessing the actual status of the patient over time. Azodyl appears to provide no benefit to the patient, and may even present a safety threat and complicate diagnostic evaluations of the cat with CRD.

Some experts insist that salt (sodium) must be restricted in the CRD patient. In my clinical experience and in review of the available scientific data, salt restriction is generally irrelevant to the patient's well-being, unless the patient has cardiac disease as well as CRD. Most good-quality, higher-protein canned cat foods, as well as homemade meat meals, have levels of sodium that are well tolerated by the cat with CRD.

What About Dry Cat Foods for Cats with CRD?

We have discussed in prior chapters how dry kibbled cat foods are inadequate and inappropriate diets for the cat. One of their many shortcomings is their very low moisture content. The urine of normal cats eating wet foods is less concentrated than those eating dry kibble, even when plenty of free water is available to both. As a result, the cat on dry kibble is relatively more dehydrated than those on high-moisture diets. This dehydrating effect of dry kibbled cat diets has especially serious implications for the cat with CRD.

The normal cat kidney is a very efficient water-saving organ. This capability is extremely important to an animal that evolved in arid and semiarid environments as the cat did. In the cat with CRD, the kidneys become increasingly unable to save water for reuse in the body. When this patient receives almost no moisture in its diet, this problem can become life-threatening. In fact, it is possible that years of consumption of dry cat foods contributes to the development of CRD in healthy cats by setting up a chronic state of dehydration. Chronic dehydration is as unhealthful for cats as it is for humans, and perhaps even more so.

New, Improved Methods for Managing CRD Cats

Today, although we still do not understand all of the factors that cause CRD to arise in the healthy cat, we do understand much more about how to manage it so that the patient can live years after diagnosis with good-quality life. First, the CRD cat must not eat a dry kibbled cat food. Certainly, the cat with kidney insufficiency should not be forced to consume a protein-restricted diet in dry or wet form. This is not required in any patient, and may make matters worse. Patients with an elevated blood phosphorus level should have phosphate binders or cooked egg white added to their food, to reduce the absorption of this mineral from the diet.

Cats with CRD typically develop a condition known as renal *secondary hyperparathyroidism*. This means that when the kidneys become unable to do their normal work of controlling the levels of phosphorus and calcium in the bloodstream, the parathyroid glands, located right next to the thyroid glands in the neck, begin to work harder to keep the level of blood calcium in balance with rising blood phosphorus by secreting *parathyroid hormone* (PTH). Balance between the calcium and phosphorus in the blood is critical for health of all animals. This balance requires activation of vitamin D (a hormone as well as a vitamin) by the kidneys. When the cat's kidneys begin to fail, they lose the ability to activate vitamin D normally. They also lose the ability to excrete excess phosphorus. As active vitamin D levels drop, blood calcium also drops and blood phosphate levels start to climb. In response, the parathyroid gland secretes PTH.

But ailing kidneys may not have the ability to activate vitamin D no matter how much PTH is put out by the parathyroid glands. Even though more and more PTH is secreted, in CRD the kidney simply cannot respond. Soon there is so much circulating phosphate that it begins to combine with the blood calcium, and calcium phosphate crystals begin to form deposits in the body's soft tissues. This removal of calcium from the circulation causes the bones to release calcium to maintain the blood calcium level. As mineral leaves the bones, they become soft. The bone crystals deposited in the soft tissues, including the kidneys themselves, interfere with normal functioning of those tissues.

To control this vicious cycle of imbalance and renal failure, veterinarians try to limit the normally high dietary phosphorus intake of the meat-eating carnivore by feeding protein and phosphorus-restricted diets or by adding a phosphorus binder to higher protein and phosphorus containing foods. This latter approach is by the far the better one, because limiting protein intake in the cat creates additional problems.

Recently, scientists studying cats with CRD have also begun to recommend supplemental *calcitriol* to control renal secondary hyperparathyroidism (see http://pets .groups.yahoo.com/group/calcitriol/). Calcitriol is the active form of vitamin D. Daily or intermittent supplementation with very small doses of calcitriol in mild to moderate CRD may be able to stop or greatly slow this overproduction of PTH, with its very serious consequences (see http://members.bellatlantic.net/~vze2r6qt/calcitriol/calcitriol3 .htm). Used properly by the veterinarian prescribing appropriately low doses and sufficient patient monitoring to avoid excessive blood calcium levels, calcitriol supplementation promises to be one of the most effective new CRD management tools in cats with this life-threatening disease.

In the past few years, a class of drugs known as *ACE inhibitors* (see www.felinegood .co.uk/treatments/en/ace_inhibitors.shtml) have been shown to have remarkable value in stabilizing the CRD patient. Although all of the ways in which these drugs provide this benefit are poorly understood, there is no doubt that they are helpful. The ACE inhibitor drug I like to use, benazepril, is a blood-pressure-lowering human pharmaceutical. Because a substantial number of CRD cats have high blood pressure (hypertension) as a consequence of their kidney disease, controlling high blood pressure may be one of the ways benazepril helps the feline CRD patient. ACE inhibitors may also increase blood flow to the kidneys, allowing these organs to better filter toxins from the blood. In some cats, benazepril alone does not control high blood pressure enough, and another drug called amlodipine (a different class of drug called *calcium channel blockers*) may be needed. Even when my patients do not have hypertension, I use benazepril in their management as I see a benefit in every patient, regardless of their blood pressure level.

When my CRD patients have poor appetites, I will use a drug such as cyproheptadine for a short time, to stimulate food consumption. In my experience with many CRD patients managed aggressively, the period of poor appetite lasts a very short time. The CRD cat that is receiving the right treatment will quickly feel better and regain its natural eagerness to eat. Of course, offering higher-protein foods that are naturally appetizing to the patient is an important part of getting the patient back on track and eating the food it needs to recover and become healthy again.

What About Fluids for the CRD Cat?

Without question, it is extremely important that the cat with CRD get enough fluid to support improved kidney function. I have found that if a patient has only mild to moderate dysfunction, a change to wet food (canned or homemade) coupled with ACE inhibitor drug therapy will stabilize or even improve dramatically the patient's kidney function. In these patients, it may not always be necessary to administer additional fluids by intravenous or subcutaneous injection. Those patients with more severe insufficiency at diagnosis will require fluids to maintain their kidney function.

One of the misconceptions in veterinary medicine at present is that intravenous fluids (also called IV fluids) are the best way to correct dehydration in the CRD patient. In truth, giving of fluids under the skin, or subcutaneously, is often the better approach, even in patients with rather substantial dysfunction. This is because it is extremely easy to overhydrate a cat with IV fluids, especially if the patient has heart or lung problems, and because the subcutaneous route of administration is quite efficient in providing fluids to the rest of the body in feline patients with little risk of overhydration.

Subcutaneous fluid therapy is also very easy for the cat owner to do at home on a regular basis (see www.marvistavet.com/html/body_subcutaneous_fluids.html). This is an important advantage for subcutaneous fluids, because some patients require fluid administration several times weekly. In all cases, conscientious home care will be critical to the quality of the CRD patient's life. The real cases included in this chapter illustrate the different strategies for successful fluid therapy for the feline patient with CRD.

Cats receiving fluid supplementation as part of their CRD treatment protocol should have potassium and B-vitamin supplementation as well. This is because the increased fluid flow through the kidneys in these patients can cause excessive loss of potassium and the water-soluble B vitamins from the body. Potassium and B vitamins can be added directly to the patient's fluid solution or can be provided to the patient through administration of oral supplements containing these vital nutrients. Your veterinarian can help you decide which of these methods is best for your cat.

What About Antibiotics?

Some patients with CRD have infections of the urinary tract that must be treated along with their kidney insufficiency. The treating veterinarian can determine whether a urinary tract infection is present as a cause or secondary complication of CRD and, if so, will prescribe an appropriate antibiotic for dealing with this part of the problem. Needless to say, if an infection *is* present, eliminating that source of disease is absolutely crucial to the success of all other management efforts.

What If Your Cat Has Anemia?

Many cats with CRD also have some degree of anemia. That is, they have fewer red blood cells in their bloodstream than they need to carry the oxygen to their body's cells. In health, the kidneys produce a hormone called *erythropoietin* that stimulates the bone marrow to produce those red cells. When kidney function decreases, this hormone may not be produced in sufficient amounts, and anemia can result. If your cat is anemic, your veterinarian may prescribe a blood transfusion or injections of erythropoietin, to restore the red blood cell numbers and make your cat feel better.

What About a Kidney Transplant?

Believe it or not, cats *can* receive a kidney transplant to replace the function of their own failing kidneys. The technology of feline kidney transplantation is several decades old, developed by surgeons at the University of California–Davis School of Veterinary Medicine and now performed at a number of centers around the United States. Unfortunately, kidney transplants in cats are very expensive and not always successful in restoring the cat to quality life. If medical management of your CRD cat is not successful and you are interested in finding out more about kidney transplants, talk with your veterinarian about whether your cat is a candidate for this procedure, and see the many Internet links, such as www.marvistavet.com/html/kidney_transplants_in_cats.html, for more information.

CRD Management

To summarize "twenty-first century" management of the feline patient with chronic renal disease:

1. Early diagnosis is critical. If your cat loses weight for no apparent reason, becomes lethargic or won't eat, vomits repeatedly, begins drinking lots of water, or shows any other signs of vague illness, see your veterinarian right away.
2. Avoid feeding protein-restricted diets. Many veterinarians are becoming aware that the traditional view of dietary management may be outdated. Discuss using higher protein, wet foods that your cat will enjoy eating, rather than the usual unpalatable "kidney diets." Protein does not "burn out" the cat's kidneys, as has been commonly believed. Your cat is a naturally "high-protein" machine, and protein deficiency will greatly decrease its ability to stabilize and recover.
3. If your cat has elevated blood phosphorus, your veterinarian will prescribe a phosphorus binder or cooked egg white to control this aspect of diet while allowing your cat to have the protein it needs from its diet. If your cat has normal phosphorus levels, your veterinarian may wish to start calcitriol supplementation.
4. Your veterinarian will measure your cat's blood pressure. If it is elevated, antihypertensive medications are indicated. I manage all of my CRD patients, even if they do not have high blood pressure, with the ACE inhibitor benazepril. This is because benazepril has benefits for the CRD patient that go beyond mere blood pressure control. My CRD patients take benazepril for the rest of their lives.

5. If your cat has a urinary tract infection, your veterinarian will prescribe a temporary course of antibiotics to control this problem.

6. If your cat is dehydrated, your veterinarian will prescribe IV or subcutaneous fluids to correct this problem. If necessary for long-term care of your cat, you will be taught to administer fluids at home. Giving subcutaneous fluids is easy for almost all pet owners, so don't be intimidated by this suggestion. Regular fluid therapy can be absolutely lifesaving for your cat. See www.vetmed.wsu .edu/ClientED/cat_fluids.asp and www.sniksnak.com/cathealth/subques.html.

7. If your cat has serious anemia, your veterinarian may prescribe erythropoietin to help the bone marrow produce more red cells to carry oxygen throughout your cat's body.

8. Have your veterinarian recheck your cat's progress regularly. Over time, your pet's treatment may change; perhaps some elements of treatment may be decreased or discontinued as your cat's health improves. Successful management of CRD is an ongoing team effort.

Chuck Robinson

Chuck was a thirteen-year-old neutered male cat who came to my clinic for a routine geriatric checkup. Chuck actually looked older than his age, his coat was dull and his skin was flaky, and he was slightly underweight. His appetite was normal, according to his owners, but they reported that he had been slowing down and becoming sluggish lately. They assumed this was just because he was getting old. Chuck needed a dental cleaning, but he seemed otherwise normal physically.

Chuck's geriatric blood work and urinalysis showed that he had moderately elevated BUN and creatinine levels (like BUN, creatinine is another molecule that accumulates in the bloodstream when the kidneys decline). He was not anemic and had no evidence of infection. His urine also reflected a mild degree of kidney insufficiency. His blood pressure was normal. I instructed Chuck's owners to feed him a good-quality canned cat food. I also prescribed benazepril for him. I asked Chuck's owners to bring him back in two weeks to recheck his blood work. If his kidney function tests continued to decline, we would add fluids to his treatment plan.

Two weeks later, Chuck's blood work and urine showed not only stability, but overall improvement. His creatinine levels were now normal and his BUN was only slightly elevated. Chuck's phosphorus was still normal. All other laboratory blood levels were normal, as they had been when we first examined him. As of the publication of this book, Chuck has been stable on benazepril alone for almost two years. He eats well and has gained a pound. His coat is glossy and sleek, and his owners say he is very active for his age. His appetite remains good.

Georgia Benson

Georgia was a fifteen-year-old spayed female cat that came to my clinic because she had refused to eat for two days. I had seen Georgia one year earlier, at which time she seemed very healthy for her age. Now, she was dehydrated and seemed listless. Her coat was dull and dry. Her kidneys were of normal size and contour, and the rest of her physical exam was normal. Georgia's blood work and urinalysis showed that she had significant renal insufficiency. Her BUN and blood creatinine were significantly elevated, and her serum phosphorus levels were also greatly elevated above normal. Georgia had no evidence of urinary tract infection, but she was slightly anemic. Her blood pressure was within the normal range.

Georgia's owner did not want to leave her in the hospital overnight for IV fluids, so we agreed to allow her to receive fluids daily by subcutaneous administration at home. We provided a detailed demonstration of how to do this, and Mrs. Benson felt confident that she would be able to give Georgia her fluids every day as I directed. Because Georgia's blood phosphorus level was increased, I prescribed a powdered phosphorus binder to be put into her high-protein canned food at each meal. I also prescribed benazepril for Georgia. Before she left the clinic, we gave subcutaneous fluids to her to get her started.

We rechecked Georgia four days later. Her owner reported that she had started eating well by the day after her visit to the clinic. The administration of fluids had proved very easy for the family. She had received all of her prescribed medication every day, and accepted the powdered phosphorus binder in her food without complaint. Georgia's blood work at four days post diagnosis was nothing short of spectacular. Her BUN and creatinine levels had been cut to barely above normal, and her phosphorus level was within the normal range! She was eating normally and had begun to gain weight. We sent Georgia home with instructions to continue her subcutaneous fluids on an every-other-day basis, and to continue all other medications as before.

We rechecked Georgia one month later. Her owner reported that she seemed back to normal in all ways. Georgia's blood creatinine was in the high normal level and her BUN was slightly above normal (as expected in a cat on a high-protein diet). Her phosphorus level was normal. Georgia's owners were very encouraged by her improvement and stability, and were committed to continuing her management with fluids and medication for the rest of her life.

Eighteen months later, Georgia continues to do extremely well at home on fluids, benazepril, a phosphate binder, and a commercial high-protein diet. Her owners believe the quality of her life is very good, and they hope for several more years with their beloved feline family member.

Dusty Rhoades

Dusty was an eighteen-year-old neutered male cat who visited our clinic for the first time several months after his diagnosis with CRD at another clinic. He had been prescribed a protein-restricted diet by his referring veterinarian, but had been in and out of the diagnosing veterinarian's hospital during those months because his CRD was extremely unstable. During his hospitalizations he received IV fluids, which seemed to make him feel better for a week or so, but he would slowly decline after discharge and require rehospitalization within seven to ten days. Dusty's owners were desperate. Dusty did not like the protein-restricted diet that had been prescribed for him, and he had lost three of his original ten pounds during the past six months.

When we first saw Dusty, he was visibly weak and uncoordinated. His gums were pale. He was markedly dehydrated and his heart rate was very rapid. Dusty's kidneys were small and irregular. He appeared to have impairment of his vision. He was in very serious condition. We took blood and urine, and performed a blood pressure measurement. Dusty's BUN, creatinine, and phosphorus levels were severely elevated, and he was markedly anemic. He had dangerously high blood pressure, and this high pressure had caused the retinas of his eyes to detach partially, resulting in partial blindness. Dusty's urine was very dilute, because his kidney's had lost much of their ability to recapture water as they filtered his blood. He was also losing considerable amounts of protein in his urine. Dusty's heart function appeared normal.

We placed an IV line and started to rehydrate the patient carefully. We started oral benazepril and amlodipine to control his high blood pressure, and also began to give Dusty injections of erythropoietin every other day to stimulate red blood cell production if possible. With the help of cyproheptadine to stimulate his appetite, we were able to coax Dusty to eat small meals of canned cat food with powdered phosphorus binders added. We also gave him injections of metoclopramide, an antinausea drug, during the first day to prevent vomiting, and a broad-spectrum antibiotic to prevent infection during treatment.

By the third day of this therapy, Dusty was much improved. He could stand and walk much better than before, and his appetite was increasing. We removed his IV line and began to administer his fluids subcutaneously. By Dusty's fifth day, he was ready to go home. His BUN and creatinine levels were still elevated, but improved over his original levels. His blood pressure was almost within the normal range. He was still partially blind, and I advised his owners that if his vision was going to improve, that might take weeks or months for that change to occur. We discharged Dusty on his subcutaneous fluids to be given at home by his owners. They were to give his phosphorus binder in his canned, high-protein food at each meal, and to administer his benazepril and amlodipine daily. We sent erythropoietin home to be given twice weekly by subcutaneous injection, as well as oral antibiotics. Dusty was to return in two weeks for a recheck.

When we saw Dusty two weeks later, we were pleased with his progress. His blood pressure was almost normal, and his retinas had begun to reattach. He seemed to have better vision than before. His BUN and creatinine levels were only mildly elevated out of the normal range. His urine was still very dilute, but he was losing far less protein in his urine than before. Dusty had gained a half pound and seemed much stronger. His anemia was resolving as well.

Today, over a year later, Dusty receives subcutaneous fluid therapy at home every other day. His owners also give him benazepril and amlodipine every day, by mouth. His renal function tests are still somewhat elevated but have stabilized. Dusty readily eats a canned, high-protein cat food with phosphorus binder added to each meal. He has not needed injection of erythropoietin for many months, and his red cell numbers are stable in the low normal range. Dusty's owners believe he leads a good-quality life. He is interactive with the family, and eats well. His vision is not perfect, but he gets around very well. For now, his CRD is not progressing and we are optimistic that he will remain happy for some time into the future.

Today, all of my CRD cats that are candidates for daily low-dose calcitriol supplementation receive this additional therapy as part of their CRD management. I am encouraged that this addition to my CRD protocol will provide even better long-term results for these patients. Talk with your veterinarian about adding calcitriol to your cat's treatment regimen.

30

Hyperthyroidism—Keys to Early Diagnosis and Treatment

Feline hyperthyroidism is one of the most common chronic diseases we see in the middle-aged and older cat (see www.avmi.net/NewFiles/Hyperthyroidism/Hyperthyroidism.html and www.marvistavet.com/html/thyroid__signs__symptoms_and _d.html).

Although veterinarians did not commonly recognize this condition in cats prior to the early 1980s, it is now virtually an epidemic in cats over ten years of age. In my practice, I diagnose hyperthyroidism more than any other single chronic disease in my older patients. Hyperthyroidism is the condition caused by excessive thyroid hormone production by the two small thyroid glands located in the front of the cat's neck.

Because of its relatively recent and dramatically increasing occurrence, many veterinarians suspect that hyperthyroidism is caused by one or more environmental factors. In other words, we believe that some aspect of the indoor, highly controlled life of the well-cared-for feline is leading the older cat to develop this disease. Researchers are looking for these factors, but so far, we know little about what may be causing this very common, and serious, hormonal imbalance.

One small study done recently *appears* to implicate the lining of the cans in which commercial canned foods are packaged, but this finding is very inconsistent with my own observations. While I see dozens of hyperthyroid cases each year, a great many of these cats have diet histories of exclusive dry food consumption. If the cans used to produce commercial wet cat foods are, in fact, a causative factor, they certainly cannot be the only factor. This initial study has not been repeated by other researchers. Until more work is done showing this effect and explaining how dry-fed cats get hyperthyroidism, I remain very skeptical about this finding.

On the other hand, common pet food ingredients such as soy deserve suspicion in the hunt for the cause of hyperthyroidism in cats. Soy is known to have considerable effect on the human thyroid gland, and its addition to cat foods to increase the protein content of those products inexpensively is on the rise today. It is altogether possible that this very unnatural ingredient in the feline diet is adversely affecting thyroid function in commercial-food-fed cats. Unfortunately, it is unlikely that the pet food companies will sponsor such investigations into potential harmfulness of any of their ingredients, so the funding for genuinely objective research will have to come from some other source.

What Are the Signs of Feline Hyperthyroidism?

The thyroid gland is one of the "master" glands in the body. Thyroid hormone drives the metabolism of the cat, and when excessive amounts of this hormone are produced, the metabolism of the patient speeds out of control. Cats with this condition often lose weight gradually for no apparent reason. Many patients have big appetites, but can't seem to maintain their body weight. Some cats with hyperthyroidism do not have ravenous appetites, but gradual weight loss is still a consistent feature. Some patients develop gastrointestinal signs like vomiting and diarrhea, and some cats become restless. Excessive water drinking and larger-than-normal urine production are also common in hyperthyroid cats. In severe cases, high blood pressure and early heart failure become a problem. A veterinarian may be able to feel the enlarged thyroid glands at the front of the patient's neck, although this is not a consistent finding in the exam of the hyperthyroid patient.

In fact, feline hyperthyroidism can cause almost any of the common symptoms of illness in the cat. Because this is a disease so often seen in cats over ten years old, your veterinarian will want to do a special blood test on your older cat as part of the complete evaluation of any abnormal signs. A number of other diseases share the signs typical of hyperthyroidism so a thorough medical workup is very important for the cat suspected of having hyperthyroidism.

How Is Feline Hyperthyroidism Diagnosed?

In theory at least, feline hyperthyroidism is relatively easy to diagnose. A blood test, known as a thyroxine, or T4 level, is performed on a blood sample from the patient with other signs that suggest the patient has hyperthyroidism or as part of a routine geriatric workup. Reference laboratories that perform this test have established ranges for levels of this hormone that allow the veterinarian to distinguish normal levels of T4 from abnormal levels. If the patient's T4 level is out of the normal range on the high end, a diagnosis of hyperthyroidism is essentially certain. By this reasoning, if the patient's T4 level is within the normal range, the cat does not have hyperthyroidism. Unfortunately, it's just not that simple.

The reference ranges that most commercial laboratories use result in a large number of false negatives. That is, a cat with actual hyperthyroidism may have a T4 well within the normal range, causing the veterinarian to conclude erroneously that the patient does not have this disease. These errors are possible because the reference ranges that the various labs use are far too wide and are not age-adjusted. As the healthy cat becomes older, its thyroid produces a smaller and smaller amount of hormone. Thus, older cats naturally have much lower levels of circulating hormone than young cats.

In my practice, I perform T4 tests as part of a routine comprehensive blood screen on a large number of cats every year. These patients may be old or young, healthy or sick. Although most laboratories place "normal" T4 levels in the range between 0.8–5.0 micrograms/deciliter (a measure of the amount of thyroid hormone per unit of blood volume), I have never seen a total T4 test result in a healthy cat, even a young one, above 3.5 micrograms/deciliter. On the other hand, the normal, healthy older cats I have tested always test below 2.0 micrograms/deciliter. This suggests that the laboratory ranges are too wide to allow veterinarians to accurately detect all of the hyperthyroid cats in their practices.

Several years ago, I began to notice that many of my patients with classic clinical signs of hyperthyroid disease had T4 levels at or even *below* the mid-range of normal for the laboratory I use. I was certain these cats had hyperthyroidism, and in some I could even feel enlarged glands. I am lucky enough to be relatively close to a center where thyroid imaging, a method of taking special "radiographs" of the thyroid glands, is available and affordable for my clients. I decided I would send all of these atypical cases to the center to have this test done. In every case, this special test showed these sick cats with low normal T4 levels did have hyperthyroidism. Clearly, the T4 test is very unreliable as a test for hyperthyroidism unless the T4 value is elevated above the normal range.

I have seen several hyperthyroid cases over the years where the referring veterinarian had, understandably, discounted the presence of this condition on the basis of a very normal T4 test. There are additional blood tests that can be done to follow up on a T4 test (these additional tests are called a T3 suppression test or a T4 by dialysis test), and in areas where thyroid imaging is not available, one or both should be done in the suspected hyperthyroid. An easy way to detect this condition in cats that have seemingly normal T4 levels but have only subtle signs of hyperthyroidism is to repeat the T4 test about 90–120 days after the first test. No matter what the original T4 level, if the cat's thyroid hormone is increasing over this time, then the veterinarian should be very suspicious that hyperthyroidism is present, because thyroid hormone levels in normal animals fall as the patient ages.

Clearly, some older cats develop the clinical disease of hyperthyroidism at hormone levels previously believed to be normal. I always suggest to my colleagues that when their clinical diagnostic skills tell them they have a hyperthyroid patient, they should never give up that diagnosis on the basis of a "normal" T4 lab result.

Of course, the best solution would be for reference laboratories to revise their normal ranges for T4 in the cat. To do this, these laboratories will need more feedback from veterinarians to alert them to how misleading their ranges really are. In the meantime, veterinarians and pet owners must view the T4 results they receive in light of the patient's clinical signs and the absence of other diseases to explain those signs.

How Do We Treat Hyperthyroidism in the Cat?

The cat with hyperthyroidism has an excess of thyroid hormone produced by thyroid glands which have become overactive and enlarged (hyperplastic). Left untreated, the hyperthyroid cat will die of complications of its disease. Today, there are three options for managing the clinical signs of this condition in the cat. These include medical (drug) treatment, surgical treatment, and radioactive iodine treatment. All of these approaches reduce the amount of hormone that is produced in the patient's body.

Medical management of the hyperthyroid cat requires daily oral medication with a drug called methimazole (Tapazole). Methimazole interferes with the assembly of the thyroid hormone molecule in the overactive glands, but does not reduce the size or hyperactivity of the glands. Most veterinarians place their newly diagnosed hyperthyroid patients on this kind of treatment at least initially. Methimazole treatment will generally improve the clinical signs the patient is experiencing, sometimes very dramatically. Because the drug only interferes with production of the excess hormone, but does not reduce the size of the glands or change their hyperactive state, the owner must give it every day without fail. Periodic blood tests are necessary to monitor the progress of the patient on methimazole.

Surgical treatment of hyperthyroidism involves the physical removal of the thyroid glands. Although this method of treatment does completely eliminate the production of hormone in most cases, it is falling from favor as the gold standard for dealing with this condition. This is because of the possibility of surgical complications, the rare but possible recurrence of the disease if some thyroid tissue is left behind, and because a better, less invasive option is available through radioactive iodine therapy.

Treatment of hyperthyroidism with I^{131}, or radioactive iodine isotope, is the preferred method of treating and curing cats with this disease. This method of dealing with hyperactive thyroid glands has been used in humans for many decades. Within the past ten years it has been adapted for use in feline patients, with good success. The patient must have access to a specialized facility that is licensed to administer the iodine, but fortunately, these centers are becoming more and more numerous throughout the United States. Treatment involves a simple subcutaneous (under the skin) injection of the radioactive isotope.

The patient must be hospitalized for four to five days after the injection while the radioactivity in the cat's body diminishes to safe levels for discharge. At home after the treatment, the cat gradually returns to normal as its overactive thyroid gland tissue continues to be eliminated by the radioactivity of the isotope. Some veterinarians consider the I^{131} method to be the most expensive of the three methods of managing hyperthyroidism. Actually, this is not the case. I explain to my clients that although medical management may seem less costly in the short run, over the course of two to three years of such drug therapy and careful veterinary monitoring, it is quite possible to spend at least as much for methimazole therapy as for radioactive iodine treatment.

Because methimazole does not cure this disease, but only restrains it on a day-to-day basis, this drug must be given for the rest of the cat's life. Radioactive iodine treatment, however, permanently eliminates the overactive thyroid tissue. Many patients can become entirely normal within a few months of I^{131} treatment. If your cat is diagnosed with hyperthyroidism, ask your veterinarian to explain all of the options.

My clients often ask me if it "makes sense" to treat the geriatric patient with I^{131}, given the more advanced age of these cats. I explain that hyperthyroidism is a disease of only older cats. Therefore, virtually all of the patients that need I^{131} are geriatric. The owner of a fifteen-year-old cat with simple hyperthyroidism can expect their pet to live several more years with treatment. For me, this is definitely worth the effort to cure this disease.

Complications in the Hyperthyroid Patient

Some hyperthyroid cats have other complicating diseases along with their excessive hormone production. The two most common complications are renal disease (see chapter 29) and hyperthyroidism-related heart disease (see chapter 31).

If your cat is diagnosed with hyperthyroidism, your veterinarian will already have checked to make sure your pet's kidneys are working properly. In a percentage of cats, kidney function will be abnormal at the time the hyperthyroidism becomes apparent. If this is the case, your veterinarian will recommend treatment for this problem, along with treatment of your pet's hyperthyroidism, using some or all of the approaches described in chapter 29. Kidney disease associated with hyperthyroidism should be treated as any other kidney dysfunction would be.

One problem that veterinarians anticipate when treating cats with hyperthyroidism is the appearance or worsening of kidney insufficiency. The hyperthyroid state can mask the presence of kidney problems in some cats. When such a hyperthyroid patient is treated by any of the methods discussed above, this hidden kidney insufficiency may suddenly become apparent. If kidney problems already exist at the time treatment is started, it may become worse. As long as your veterinarian is alert to this possibility and ready to treat this complication if it arises, the situation can be controlled.

I have heard some experts say that the hyperthyroid cat with kidney disease may not be a candidate for treatment of its hyperthyroidism at all. Their view is that if treatment of the patient's excess thyroid hormone level causes its kidney problems to worsen, then it may be better to leave the patient with its hyperthyroidism untreated. I disagree with this view.

The cat with hyperthyroidism and kidney disease has two serious, life-threatening problems. Because we can manage or even cure one of those diseases, the hyperthyroidism, I believe it is far better to eliminate the effects of that condition, leaving the cat with one fewer life-threatening diseases to deal with. Even if the renal dysfunction worsens after this treatment, there are good management techniques for dealing with this problem as described in chapter 29.

Eliminating the patient's hyperthyroidism lessens the likelihood of at least two other life-threatening complications of excess thyroid hormone levels, high blood pressure and heart failure (see chapter 31). The heart problems associated with hyperthyroidism are the result of the elevated blood pressure and rapid heart rate we see when thyroid hormone levels are too high in the patient. The hyperthyroid cat has its internal "accelerator" pressed down at all times, causing the heart to work harder and harder, and eventually fail. Preventing this failure is one of the best reasons for prompt diagnosis and treatment of the hyperthyroid cat. If these problems are present in your cat at the time its hyperthyroidism is diagnosed, your veterinarian will prescribe medications to control them.

As a treating veterinarian, I much prefer to deal with a simple kidney dysfunction, rather than hyperthyroidism and heart disease as well. In all cases, however, your veterinarian will always be in the best position to advise you about the right treatment choices for your particular pet.

Sandy Thomas

Sandy was a fourteen-year-old neutered male when we first saw him for vaccines and a general geriatric examination. On his physical exam, Sandy weighed nine pounds, his coat was somewhat dull, and his owners told me that he "shed a lot." His owner reported that he had been ten pounds a year earlier at his last exam at another practice. There was no explanation for his weight loss as his appetite for his dry kibble diet was unchanged over that year and he had had no health problems of any kind that the owners knew of. Sandy had been vaccinated just the year before. I explained that I did not give vaccinations annually to indoor cats of this age. Sandy most likely had good immunity from his years of annual vaccinations, and his risk of exposure to these diseases was very slight given his indoor lifestyle.

Sandy's heart rate was about 175, and his blood pressure was normal. He had no evidence of heart disease. He had no thyroid enlargements that I could feel. All of his urine and blood examinations were within the normal range. His T4 level was 2.5 micrograms/deciliter, right in the middle of our lab's normal range. He had moderate calculus on some of his teeth and mild gingivitis. He appeared to be a healthy middle-aged cat except for his unexplained weight loss and his dental disease. I recommended that Sandy switch to a good-quality canned cat food and have a dental cleaning as soon as possible.

I also told the Thomases that I was somewhat suspicious that Sandy was becoming hyperthyroid. In my experience, a T4 of 2.5 was excessive for a fourteen-year-old cat, even though it was not elevated out of the lab's normal range. Because I could find no other explanation for Sandy's gradual weight loss over the past year, I wanted to follow up on this hunch with another T4 test in three months, as long as he seemed to be feeling well during that time. Three months later, we repeated Sandy's T4 test. His level at this second test was 2.9! He had lost another four ounces, despite a good appetite for his canned food diet. I was now convinced that this cat was hyperthyroid. Cats, like other animals, have falling thyroid hormone levels as they age. When an older cat's T4 levels rise over time, hyperthyroidism must be suspected, even if many of the classic signs of this condition are absent. We started Sandy on methimazole for thirty days, and then sent him to have I[131] therapy.

Two years later, Sandy's T4 is 0.9 and slowly falling as he gets older. His kidney function is normal. Sandy escaped the devastating effects of undiagnosed hyperthyroidism and because his disease was treated early, he can live many more years as a healthy, happy kitty.

Rusty Manville

Rusty was a fifteen-year-old neutered male cat that first came to my clinic because of weight loss over several months complicated by vomiting two to three times daily for about three days. Prior to the onset of his vomiting, Rusty had a ravenous appetite, according to his owners. Rusty weighed eight pounds at his first exam, down from twelve pounds a year earlier when he was examined by another veterinarian. At eight pounds, Rusty was about two pounds underweight. He had been about two pounds overweight at twelve pounds. Rusty's coat was dry and he had seriously flaky skin. He was slightly dehydrated, his heart rate was over 200 beats per minute, and he had a very faint heart murmur. When I palpated the front of Rusty's neck where his thyroid glands were, I could feel small enlargements of these glands.

Rusty's blood work showed slight elevations in his liver enzymes, but was otherwise normal, except for his T4 level, which was 6.0 micrograms/deciliter. His urinalysis was normal. His blood pressure was slightly elevated above the normal range but his EKG was within normal limits except for his rapid heart rate. Chest X-rays showed a normal heart and lungs for a cat of this age. Rusty was clearly hyperthyroid with early heart disease, likely secondary to his hyperthyroidism. We gave Rusty some fluids subcutaneously and started him on methimazole, to decrease the level of thyroid hormone in his system, and benazepril for his elevated blood pressure. We also sent metoclopramide home to control any vomiting during the next few days. We also discussed with the Manvilles the option of sending Rusty to the nearby center for I[131] therapy of his disease once he had been on methimazole for at least thirty days. We would evaluate his kidney function again before making this decision. They agreed to think about it.

We rechecked Rusty at two weeks post initiation of therapy. The Manvilles reported that his appetite was less ravenous now, although still greater than normal for him. He had gained four ounces since his last exam. Rusty's excessive water consumption and urination seemed improved to his owners and he was well hydrated now. Rusty's murmur was still present but his heart rate was 170 beats per minute. His blood pressure was now normal. Overall, Rusty's condition was improved on medication. We scheduled another recheck for two weeks later.

At one month after diagnosis, we rechecked Rusty again. He had gained another four ounces and his general condition was much improved. The Manvilles told us that his appetite was nearly normal and his water consumption was as well. Rusty's blood work was also improved. His liver enzyme levels were normal now, his kidney function tests were still normal, and his T4 was 3.0. Rusty's heart rate was normal and his murmur was barely perceptible. Once again, I discussed having Rusty go for I[131] therapy. The Manvilles agreed to do so if Rusty was still improving in another month. We refilled Rusty's methimazole and benazepril.

We rechecked Rusty again at sixty days post diagnosis and he had gained another five ounces. His kidney's were functioning well, as was his heart. His blood pressure was normal. We scheduled I[131] treatment for him as planned. He was taken off the methimazole a few days before his treatment, but we continued his benazepril as before. Rusty's I[131] treatment was uneventful. When we rechecked Rusty thirty days after he completed his I[131] treatment, he was nearly a new cat. His T4 level was 1.0 and even his murmur had disappeared! His kidney function tests were again normal, as was his blood pressure, so we discontinued his benazepril.

Eighteen months post I[131], Rusty is a healthy seventeen-year-old cat. His owners love him dearly and are delighted to have this quality time with him. He has a truly normal T4 for his age. We recheck him every six months, just to make sure he stays healthy.

Kitty Boswell

Kitty was a seventeen-year-old spayed female when we first examined her. She was emaciated at six pounds, and her owners had only recently realized how much weight she had lost because she was a long-haired cat and her coat had masked the drastic deterioration in her condition over the past few months. Kitty had been eating less and less of her dry kibble over the past two months, but her owners just thought that she was "slowing down" due to her age. Her heart rate was 190 beats per minute but she did not have a murmur. Kitty was moderately dehydrated and her demeanor was depressed. Her blood pressure was normal. I believed I could feel a slightly enlarged right thyroid gland in the front of her neck.

When the Boswells brought Kitty in, they admitted they expected me to recommend euthanasia. They knew she was in poor condition and imagined that she had something so seriously wrong with her that there would be no helping her. I was determined to save this cat if I possibly could. Kitty had no tumors in her abdomen that I could detect by palpation, and her chest X-rays were within normal limits for a cat her age. There was no evidence of tumors in her lungs or abdomen. Her liver was normal in size on her X-rays and her kidneys appeared only slightly small as well. Ultrasound of her abdomen showed some scarring of her kidney tissue, but nothing extraordinary for an seventeen-year-old cat.

We drew blood and urine for testing. Kitty's liver enzyme levels were moderately elevated as were her kidney function tests (BUN of 60 and creatinine of 4.5). Her urine was very dilute with a small amount of protein. Her urine protein:creatinine ratio was 0.6, consistent with her other kidney function values. There were no bacteria or crystals in her urine. We were surprised to see that her T4 was only 2.4 micrograms/deciliter, a number right in the middle of the "normal" range for our laboratory. From all of this, I concluded that Kitty had moderate chronic kidney disease. I was uncomfortable about her

T4 level, however. Even though it was not even close to being out of the normal range for our lab, I believed that a 2.4 T4 level was too high for a seventeen-year old cat.

Kitty's owners agreed to have her thyroid glands imaged at the nearby center. Sure enough, Kitty's right thyroid gland was larger than normal, and the radiologist determined that this gland was likely producing excess thyroid hormone for her age. After a thirty-day course of methimazole to assess Kitty's response to thyroid suppression with this drug, her T4 level was 1.0 micrograms/deciliter (down from 2.4) and her kidney function tests were stable on benazepril at the level she had before diagnosis. I believed Kitty was a good candidate for I[131] so she went to the center for this procedure.

One year later, Kitty continues on daily benazepril to help her kidneys continue to function, and her CRD is stable. Her owners give her subcutaneous fluids at home three times per week as well. Her T4 level is 0.8 micrograms/deciliter. She has gained two pounds and looks well. We will continue to monitor her progress every six months but expect her to have good quality of life for some time to come.

31

Heart Disease and the Cat— Know It When You See It

Fortunately for cats and cat owners, heart disease occurs less frequently in this species than in some others, including humans and dogs. Nevertheless, cats can develop a number of serious heart (also called *cardiac*) problems in youth and old age and it is important that their caregivers understand how these conditions appear in the sick feline.

Like other animals, kittens can be born with heart defects. Such kittens usually fail to grow and thrive. When they are examined by a veterinarian, murmurs and abnormal rhythms in the heartbeat may be detected. X-rays and ultrasound techniques will show the source of the problem. Some of these defects in youngsters can be managed with medications, others may prove to be fatal as the kitten develops and outgrows the limitations of its heart. Any weakness or failure to thrive in a young kitten is a signal to have that baby checked out, including a good heart exam, immediately.

Feline Cardiomyopathy

Some congenital problems in cats are not apparent until the cat becomes a young adult. *Cardiomyopathy* (see www.fabcats.org/cardiomypathy.html and www.homevet.com/petcare/felcardi.html) is a group of diseases that occur when the cat's heart muscle is abnormal, interfering with its ability to pump blood throughout the body. The cat with any of the types of advanced cardiomyopathy will often have difficulty breathing and become reluctant to exercise. Fluid may accumulate in the chest cavity or abdomen. Some cats may cough and produce clear or in severe cases, bloody fluid. Cardiomyopathy is a condition that is diagnosed during a thorough exam of the heart. Your veterinarian will use EKG and ultrasound imaging to diagnose this problem, or may refer you to a veterinary cardiologist for this very expert workup. Patients with mild to moderate disease have the best chance to lead relatively normal lives with the help of certain drugs that can help the heart pump more efficiently. In all cases, early detection is very important to the survival of the cardiomyopathy patient. Severe cases have a poor prognosis, unfortunately.

Acquired Heart Disease

While cardiomyopathy is usually a disease of younger cats and considered an inherited problem, older cats can more rarely develop faulty heart function as well. Some geriatric cats may show signs of congestive heart failure when the heart valves do not open and close properly or when the heart muscle becomes weak with age.

Hyperthyroidism can also cause significant heart dysfunction in the feline patient (see chapter 30). These kinds of heart diseases are called "acquired" because they are not present at birth and develop only after many years of life and many stresses have been put upon the heart over those years.

The signs of acquired heart disease in the cat may be very similar to the signs of cardiomyopathy, because the underlying failure of heart function is basically the same in these diseases. Once again, your veterinarian will be able to diagnose the type and extent of the problem, or will refer you to a specialist for tests, including an echocardiogram, a type of ultrasound exam. When acquired heart disease is apparent, there are many very effective drug therapies, including digitalis, benazepril, atenolol, enalapril, and others, that can stabilize the cat with heart failure, often for years. If your cat has hyperthyroidism, treatment of that underlying condition will often resolve the heart disease. Your cat's ability to live good-quality life with heart disease depends on early and accurate diagnosis, so never delay having your cat examined immediately if you see signs of weight loss, reluctance to exercise, difficulty breathing, coughing, general weakness, or any other abnormal behavior.

Feline Heartworm

(www.heartwormsociety.org/FelineHeartwormInfo.htm)

Although it is far less common in the cat than in the dog, heartworm disease does occur in felines, especially in areas of the country where this parasite is common in dogs. As in dogs, heartworms are transmitted to the cat by the bite of a mosquito carrying the infective larvae of the worm. One of the most common signs of feline heartworm disease is coughing, although this parasite can cause much more severe lung and heart problems in the previously normal cat. Unfortunately, some patients die suddenly as the first and only evidence that they are infested with this worm. Veterinarians in areas where heartworm is a significant problem (e.g., the southeastern United States) will test the blood of any coughing cat for heartworm. Cats with heartworm disease may have abnormal chest X-rays as well. There are preventive medications suitable for protecting the cat against heartworms, just as there are such medications for dogs. Generally, these preventives are not prescribed for indoor cats in geographical areas where the incidence of heartworm is low.

Nutrition for the Cat with Heart Disease

As we have discussed in previous chapters, proper nutrition is the foundation of health and recovery from disease in the cat. Unfortunately, some of our present feeding practices leave a great deal to be desired, and a great deal to be improved upon for the healthy and diseased pet cat. Dry cat foods are never indicated for the cat with heart disease, even though many such foods are labeled and sold for "heart disease in the cat." Even though the canned foods designed for the cat with heart disease avoid the high-carbohydrate faults of the dry version of such diets, they may not be optimum for the feline cardiac patient, either.

Foods for the cat with heart disease usually restrict protein and salt, presumably to help the heart function better and keep the kidneys healthy. Protein restriction is not needed for the heart patient, just as it is not needed, or even healthy, for normal cats and cats with other medical problems. Sodium, or salt, restriction may or may not be necessary for a heart patient, depending on many factors. If your veterinarian decides that regular canned cat foods are too high in salt for stabilizing your cat's heart problems, you may wish to mix a regular wet food with a low-salt diet, or add salt-less protein sources to one of the canned "heart" diets.

An excellent protein that contains no phosphorus (for kidney health), and no salt, is cooked egg white. Egg white is the highest-quality protein available and it can be mixed into a lower-protein diet to increase the protein level of such a food. Of course, your cat must be willing to eat a low-salt diet if it is to be effective. If your pet finds prescription-type, low-salt diets unpalatable, you and your veterinarian will have to find alternatives that appeal to the patient. Weight loss is a common problem in the feline with heart disease, so diets must be appetizing to the patient.

For many feline patients with heart disease, the prognosis is good with proper home and veterinary care.

32

Vaccines for the Senior— A New Perspective

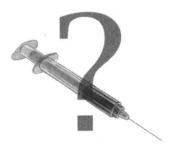

As we have discussed in chapter 10, veterinarians today think differently about vaccinating pets, especially cats, than they did in decades past (see www .petcaretips.net/should_vaccinate_pets.html). In my practice, I do not provide annual vaccinations for my older patients. The vast majority of my patients of all ages live entirely indoors. The outdoor environment in the neighborhoods around my clinic has high automobile traffic and a substantial population of predators of the cat, including coyotes. My clients understand that they cannot safely keep their cats outdoors. Because of this, the risk of most infectious diseases for my patients is substantially less than it would be if they roamed free outside.

The risk of vaccine-associated reactions, including a very aggressive type of cancer, is very real. Every year, I treat cats for these reactions, and I know from this experience that these adverse consequences of repetitive annual vaccination occur with enough frequency to be taken seriously. By the time one of my patients is ten years old, I vaccinate for fewer diseases and vaccinate far less frequently; in fact, I may discontinue vaccination altogether. There are guidelines available to veterinarians for making good decisions about how to design a vaccination protocol for every patient (see www .winnfelinehealth.org/health/vaccination-guidelines.html). This decision must take into consideration a cat's particular risk factors in light of the often greater risk of serious diseases that can be caused by overvaccination.

My advice to all cat owners is to take the time to discuss with their veterinarian, at length, whether to vaccinate their pets for the many different diseases for which vaccines are available, and how often to administer those vaccines that *are* needed. Older cats that have received regular vaccination against the major infectious diseases can be reasonably presumed to have high levels of immunity by the time they reach ten years and beyond. Any additional vaccinations should be well thought-out and thoroughly discussed with the cat owner before they are administered. This additional care and discussion takes time, but may prevent serious vaccination-associated consequences for the patient.

33

Arthritis in Cats—
Making the Pain Go Away

While cats seem somewhat less likely to develop arthritis than dogs are, I see many geriatric cats with painful joints in my practice. Usually, these patients are ten years of age or older, although arthritis can occur as a result of injury in patients of any age. Because cats are so good at masking pain from any cause until the problem is advanced, the cat with lameness caused by arthritis usually has significant changes in the affected joint by the time the owner notices the problem. Obesity, so much a problem in cats today, often complicates the medical condition. Fortunately, my patients need not suffer their arthritis in silence. Today, we have better methods for helping the arthritic cat than ever before.

The Limping or Painful Cat

(see www.sniksnak.com/cathealth/arthritis.html)

The first sign of arthritis (also known as *degenerative joint disease*, or *osteoarthritis*) in most cats is lameness in one or more joints. The patient may merely favor any of the four limbs, or may be unwilling to put any weight at all on a foreleg or hind leg. Back pain, which may signal arthritis in the vertebrae, may make the patient irritable or unwilling to be handled. Sometimes arthritis is accompanied by a swelling in the affected joint, but usually the joint damage is so long-standing that there is no outward sign of the pain within.

Pain in or near a joint can arise from medical conditions other than arthritis. For example, the older limping cat may have a type of bone or cartilage tumor developing in the painful leg, or an infection in the soft tissues around the joint and bone. Diagnosing each of these very different types of problems requires a veterinary examination, usually with X-rays of the affected joints. Any cause of joint or bone pain in the cat can be treated, usually with very good results, but early diagnosis is key in all cases. Never ignore evidence of pain in your cat. Not only is it inhumane to wait and see in such situations, but delay in treating cancers, infections, or other serious acute conditions may cost your pet its life.

What If My Cat Has Arthritis?

If your veterinarian finds that your cat has arthritis, there are steps you can take to relieve the pain and improve the quality of your pet's life. First, if your cat is overweight, a weight-loss program is a must, to reduce the weight-bearing on the affected joint. We have discussed in chapter 20 the problem of feline obesity and its cause in high-carbohydrate dry cat foods. If your cat is eating this kind of food, I recommend that you make a switch to wet form food (canned low-carbohydrate commercial cat food) immediately. Your pet's excess weight is the result of an upside-down diet. Correcting that diet will allow your cat to lose the weight gradually and safely. In addition, I always recommend that my arthritis patients receive a multiple vitamin/mineral/essential fatty acid supplement (see www.platinumperformance.com) with their food, to ensure adequate intake of anti-inflammatory nutrients.

Along with the obvious benefit of weight loss, patients with arthritis that are on a low-carbohydrate diet become more naturally active than those on a high-carbohydrate dry diet. Moderate exercise actually helps the cat with arthritis. When the cat becomes more active on its own, weight loss accelerates and the muscles become toned. Better muscle tone provides better support for painful joints.

Some experts recommend supplements such as glucosamine for pets with arthritis. Although we do not understand exactly how glucosamine reduces pain and inflammation in the arthritic joint, a number of good studies have shown that it does just that. In my experience, I have seen some patients improve on this supplement alone. Others seem to get little benefit and require more potent pain relieving medications.

Recently, a new and very exciting anti-inflammatory drug has become available for use in cats and dogs. This drug is meloxicam, known by the trade name, Metacam. Up to now, most veterinarians have used corticosteroids to relieve arthritis pain, but corticosteroids have some serious side effects in animals and people. Although meloxicam should not be used, or used very carefully, in cats with kidney disease, I have found it extremely helpful in cats with normal kidney function for a variety of painful conditions, including arthritis. Your veterinarian will perform a blood test and urinalysis before prescribing this medication for your cat. If your cat is a candidate for meloxicam, you will use a few drops daily at first and will eventually space the doses of drug so that you are giving medication every other day or even less often.

In some cases, your veterinarian may recommend surgical correction of the problem, but this is less common in the cat than in the dog. In most cases, weight loss, regular moderate exercise, glucosamine and anti-inflammatory vitamin supplements, plus meloxicam if your cat has normal kidney function, all promise that your cat can live pain-free with its arthritis for many years.

PART

5

Ten Myths of Cat Care

MYTH #1: Pets Are Living Longer Today Because of Commercial Pet Food

I have heard cat lovers, some of them experts in feline health, say that cats are living longer today than ever before. Truth is, we don't really know that for a fact, unfortunately. Evidence about changes in the life span of cats over the past several decades is sparse, and we cannot draw the conclusion that cats today live longer on average than cats thirty to forty years ago, for example. What does seem clear is that today's *indoor* cats live much longer than do cats that live outdoors. The evidence for this conclusion is strong.

Those who would give commercial pet food even partial credit for this increase in life expectancy in the indoor pet cat, however, have absolutely no evidence to back up this conclusion. There are many factors that affect the life span of cats under indoor and outdoor circumstances. Indoor cats are more protected from death due to automobiles and predators, they are more protected from exposure to infectious disease, and often they receive more medical care than do outdoor cats, to name just a few of the important differences between these two groups. It is easy to sweep commercial food consumption right along with all of these other factors as contributing to longer life in today's cats. Unfortunately for this particular factor, there is no reason to believe it has anything to do with the longer life of the house cat. Let's look at an analogy to understand how this might be so.

Humans in the United States enjoy longer life expectancy today than they did fifty years ago. During those decades of improving average life span, those same people have consumed ever-increasing amounts of fat-laden, sugary, carbohydrate-rich fast food and other types of overprocessed convenience foods. We are far more obese today than in decades past, and human nutritionists nag us endlessly about changing our diet to include better-quality, fresh, whole foods. Imagine anyone believing that this increasing consumption of highly processed fast foods and increasing obesity actually contribute to our increasing life span! We are living longer *in spite* of our diet, not because of it. Many other factors, such as less tobacco smoking, the use of seat belts, better prenatal and postnatal care, and astonishing high-tech medical advancements for defeating disease and injury, account for our increasing longevity. Our convenience-oriented diet is actually working against longer life, but cannot defeat all of these other strong protective factors in our lives.

So it is with our cats. When they live indoors, they may live longer than if they lived outdoors, but commercial foods, particularly dry kibble, have no part in adding those extra years. If anything, they are depriving our felines of even greater health and longevity.

MYTH #2: Dry Food Is the Best Form of Food for Cats

Some experts recommend feeding dry food because owners can leave it out during the day without concern about spoilage. The idea that cats must have constant access to food is illogical and unnatural, however. This belief in a house cat's need for food on demand is nothing more than a myth perpetuated by pet food companies to sell billions of tons of pet food. In the wild state, the cat eats when it has a successful hunt. This is certainly not a constant occurrence. Long periods of time may elapse between meals for cats, large or small, that must fend for themselves. Meal feeding simulates this natural cycle of feasting and fasting that is the cat's heritage. Free-choice dry food feeding creates unnatural and physiologically damaging imbalances within the cat's body. Dry cat foods deprive the cat of moisture needed for all bodily functions and create a nearly constant alkaline urine pH that can lead to disease.

Some manufacturers try to overcome this alkaline pH by adding acid to their dry diets, but this acidification can lead to other equally serious problems. Dry kibbled cat foods have substances called "digests" sprayed on the outside of the kibble. This digest is fermented by-products of meat-processing. While digest has no nutritional value, it is specifically designed to be highly palatable for the cat and can even cause actual addiction to dry foods. This explains why some cats refuse to switch from high-carbohydrate dry cat foods to more healthful wet foods.

Dry kibbled cat foods also dump unnatural amounts of sugar into the cat's bloodstream, completely upsetting its natural metabolic processes. This imbalance can, and often does, lead to obesity, diabetes, and other serious disease conditions. Ironically, some experts are beginning to recommend mealtime-only feeding of even dry cat foods, in response to the epidemic of obesity in pet cats. If the convenience factor of dry kibble is gone, what possible advantage can such foods possibly claim over more digestible, lower-carbohydrate canned foods? No convincing studies have been done to prove that dry kibbled cat foods are anything more than the nutritional equivalent of junk food for cats.

MYTH #3: Dry Cat Foods Are More Economical than Canned Foods

Some experts claim that dry kibble is a better value for the pet food purchaser. They point to the fact that kibble has less water, therefore the purchaser is buying less water with each pet food dollar. Because the cat evolved consuming prey with 78 percent or more water, however, feeding a dehydrated food simply forces the cat to try to consume more water to make up for this abnormal dietary moisture intake. While it may be true that a cereal-based food is cheaper than a meat-based food, pound for pound, who would consider feeding a child nothing but breakfast cereal just because breakfast cereal is cheaper than a more balanced diet of meat and fresh vegetables?

Such economy would clearly be false economy, even though most breakfast cereals have lots of added vitamins and minerals to make them seem to be good nutrition. Like children, cats should not be fed foods with the least expensive ingredients, just to save money! In humans and in animals, the costs of treating the chronic diseases that would result from such a "least-cost" diet far exceed the short-term savings.

MYTH #4: Dry Cat Food Cleans a Cat's Teeth

Pet food companies tell us that dry food has a cleansing abrasive effect on a pet's teeth. While this idea has a momentary intuitive appeal, the truth is that the evidence in practice refutes this idea. Today, most cats eat dry cat food, yet veterinarians continue to see tremendous numbers of patients with serious dental and periodontal disease. Clearly, these diets are not protective against these conditions. Many of the very serious conditions we see in cats' mouths, such as the gum-line cavities called resorptive neck lesions, occur in cats eating dry food. I have never heard of any human dentist telling a patient to eat potato chips, corn chips, or dry breakfast cereal to clean the teeth. Have you?

In fact, dry kibble, like those snack foods, becomes a very sticky paste when mixed with saliva in the mouth, and adheres to the teeth and gums to a greater extent than does wet food, which is swallowed more completely after chewing. The processed carbohydrates and sugar in the dry kibble paste can then support bacterial growth. Dry cat foods are also coated with very acidic substances to make them palatable to cats. When these foods are the main diet of the cat, the oral environment can become more acid than normal, and damage can result to the enamel, possibly even causing the resorptive lesions. If anything, dry foods may even promote plaque and tartar formation, with the resultant gum disease and enamel erosion.

MYTH #5: AAFCO Feeding Trials Prove Pet Foods Are Safe for Continual Feeding

The pet food companies' AAFCO feeding trials are incapable of proving the lifetime-feeding fitness of a pet food. The following true story shows why:

In around 1988, a young cardiology resident at the University of California–Davis noticed something rather interesting. One of his feline patients, a cat he was treating for a heart disease called congestive cardiomyopathy, had an extremely low serum taurine level. Taurine is an essential amino acid required for proper eye and heart function in this and many other species. The patient ate an exclusive diet of a "high-quality" premium commercial cat food, which should have supplied all of the taurine this cat required. After all, the food was "feeding trial tested," and supposedly shown to be complete and balanced for all life stages in these feeding trials. Surely this cat's heart disease was not due to consumption of a taurine-deficient diet?

Over the months following his initial observation, the veterinarian began to investigate other clinical cases of feline congestive cardiomyopathy. To his amazement, he discovered that virtually all of the cases of this disease that he studied had low taurine levels in their bloodstream, and many of them improved dramatically when they received taurine supplements. These cats had been eating "feeding-trial-tested" foods. How could such well-tested cat foods be responsible for a fatal heart disease in cats? How could such well-tested cat foods be the direct cause of a deadly dietary deficiency in cats?

The answer became clear over the course of this veterinarian's investigation. The processing of the products somehow "inactivated" the taurine contained in the foods. If this were the case, however, why didn't the feeding trials of these foods disclose this terrible flaw? Why? Because the feeding trials were of such limited duration, usually no longer than six months, that only *rapidly* damaging inadequacies and toxicities would ever be disclosed through them.

Most cats would not become sufficiently taurine deficient in just a few months to show obvious symptoms during the feeding trial. Thus, these products were produced, feeding-trial-tested, and marketed for many years, causing the death of many cats, before a lucky turn of events and the keen observations of a young veterinarian allowed the problem to be identified and corrected. The pet food companies and their "rigorous testing for safety and efficacy" had allowed the development of a fatal disease in thousands of cats, and that problem was only discovered by someone who wasn't even looking for a dietary deficiency.

MYTH #6: By-Products in Pet Foods Are Bad

You may read that meat by-products in cat foods are low-quality ingredients. This is an idea that is used by some companies to market their "no by-product" foods. The truth is, some by-products *are* inappropriate as part of pet foods, but this is certainly not true of *all* by-products. In the early days of commercial pet food production, ingredients such as the beaks, feathers, and feet and other poor-quality parts of food animals were used commonly in some pet foods. This practice is not a part of the production of better-quality foods, however, especially now that there is significant pressure from the public against the inclusion of such non-nutritious fillers.

The food category known as "meat by-products" can include ingredients that are excellent for cats. For example, any part of the beef that is not sold for human consumption, such as the spleen and lungs, is considered a by-product. Such organs from USDA-inspected animals are quite acceptable as part of the diet of the cat. A food that has no by-products may have large quantities of second- or third-grade processed cereals, vegetables, and fruits. With all of these useless, even harmful, ingredients in its foods, the manufacturer can make the seemingly important claim to using no meat by-products. Yet, its food can be much less nutritious than another product with excellent-quality meat by-products and no useless plant-material ingredients. In deciding which canned foods to choose and feed their cat, educated buyers must read pet food labels (see appendix I). Ingredients such as cornmeal, corn flour or grits, rice or rice flour, soy, carrots, potato, sweet potato, and fruit should raise a very big red flag. The best cat foods are made by reputable manufacturers *and* lack plant-based ingredients.

MYTH #7: Raw Meat Is Bad for Cats

I am often asked about why I feed raw meat to my own cats. Many people believe that feeding raw meat to their pets will lead inevitably to food poisoning. This is illogical, because cats evolved over hundreds of thousands of years in adaptation to this very raw meat diet. In over two decades of veterinary practice, I can honestly say that I have never seen a single case of food poisoning from feeding human-grade raw meat to a cat. In fact, feeding cats highly processed, cereal-based foods creates far more feline disease than raw meat ever has.

Of course, the feeding of raw meat requires care and common sense: feed fresh meat or freshly thawed meat, and add supplements according to good nutritional principles (see www.catnutrition.org). If you prefer to lightly cook your cat's meat diet, you may do so without harm to the nutritional benefit. Be sure to add vitamin supplements after you cook the meat, if you are feeding raw meat only.

MYTH #8: Cats Tolerate Corticosteroids Without Side Effects

In veterinary school, I was taught that cats, unlike dogs, seem to tolerate chronic administration of corticosteroids without serious side effects. As I practiced with both species, however, I began to realize that this was not necessarily true. I saw numerous cats with signs of liver dysfunction and even diabetes after they received even moderate doses of long-acting injectable steroids or long-term oral steroids. It appeared to me that cats *were* quite sensitive to the potential side effects seen in dogs and humans.

I also observed another strange thing: The cats that seemed most sensitive to side effects from steroid treatments were also the cats that ate dry cat food. After researching why this might be, I concluded that feeding of highly processed, high-carbohydrate foods was stressing the cat's liver and pancreas. As we have discussed in earlier chapters, this is because these organs in the cat are not suited to handling all of this sugar and processed carbohydrate. Constant flooding of the cat's system with unnatural levels of these substances stresses the two organs most involved in energy metabolism in this species.

We know that corticosteroids also stress these organs. When patients who are eating dry foods also receive corticosteroids as part of some disease-management protocol, the combined stresses are too much for the liver and pancreas of some cats to endure. These are the cats that start showing signs of liver dysfunction and diabetes. When I use corticosteroids in my patients eating wet diets without starchy, sugary ingredients, however, I do not see side effects. These cats actually do seem somewhat resistant to the undesirable side effects associated with long-term or high-dose corticosteroid use. I advise all of my clients with cats that need steroids to manage their disease, that they must never feed dry cat foods if they wish to minimize the risk of dangerous steroid side effects.

MYTH #9: All Cats Should Be Vaccinated Every Year

In the past decade, veterinary researchers have discovered that vaccinating pets every year of their lives may be unnecessary and even dangerous to their health. Years earlier, human researchers learned that people develop very long-lasting immunity from vaccination without frequent boosters. They also learned that some vaccines had the potential to cause serious, even fatal, reactions in people. Because of these discoveries, most of us receive very few regular vaccinations after we reach adulthood. Only when we are exposed to unusual risks (as when we are injured and exposed to tetanus-causing organisms, if we are members of at-risk age groups for flu, or when we travel to certain foreign countries) do we receive "special" vaccinations as adults.

The tendency to vaccinate pets every year was motivated by good intentions. Many epidemic diseases in pets have been eradicated, or nearly so, by widespread vaccination of dogs and cats. In the absence of epidemic situations, however, regular annual vaccination for all of the infectious diseases that affect pets is unwarranted. Be sure to talk at length with your veterinarian about your pet's risk of exposure before having your cat vaccinated.

MYTH #10: Female Cats Should Have a Litter of Kittens Before They Are Altered

This is one of the most common misconceptions. There is no evidence whatsoever that there is any benefit to allowing your female cat to become pregnant and have a litter before she is altered. In fact, cats that are altered before they reproduce have less risk of some serious diseases, and they do not contribute to the serious pet overpopulation problem. The personality of altered cats is just as affectionate, and far more home-loving, than that of the cat that is interested in breeding. While cats do tend to become overweight after altering, this problem is very easy to avoid by feeding canned or raw foods rather than dry kibble. The best time to alter (spay) your female is about three to six months of age. Your veterinarian can discuss all of the benefits of spaying with you, and will recommend the best time for performing this procedure.

APPENDIX I

How to Read a Pet Food Label

Although most pet food purchasers do not realize it, there is a science to reading the labels of the food they buy for their pets. There are rules set out by governmental regulators that dictate what information must be included and how it must be presented in print. Unfortunately, most pet food purchasers do not know these rules, allowing manufacturers to manipulate them to present their products to the consumer in the best possible light. It *is* possible, however, for the pet owner to learn a few of the most common tricks about pet food labeling, to allow the best possible choice of foods among the hundreds of choices. We will cover the most important of these bits of information here.

First, one definition is important in understanding how to read a pet food label. We will use the term "dry-matter basis" over and over again in the rest of this discussion.

"Dry-matter basis" means the amount of a particular ingredient or nutrient, expressed as a percent of the total in the can or bag, if the moisture in the food is removed. This is an important concept because it allows comparison of dry and canned foods, with their very different moisture content, in a fair way. It allows the pet food shopper to compare "apples to apples," so to speak.

Dry kibble has about 10 percent moisture. This means that the rest of the ingredients compose 90 percent of the food. If we want to remove the moisture to reduce the contents to only the "dry matter" that is in the food, we perform a simple calculation. If the protein listed on the label of the kibble is 25 percent, we divide that 25 percent by .9 (the mathematical equivalent of 90 percent), to get 27.8 percent. Try this on your calculator. So, a dry kibble with 10 percent moisture and 25 percent protein has 27.8 percent protein *on a dry-matter basis*. You can perform this calculation on all of the nutrients listed on the label.

Canned, pouched, and homemade wet foods have about 75 percent moisture, the rest of the ingredients compose 25 percent of the food. To remove the moisture and reduce the contents to only the dry matter that is in the food, we perform the same simple calculation. If a canned food has 10 percent protein and we divide the 10 percent by .25 (the mathematical equivalent of 25 percent), we get 40 percent protein on a dry-matter basis. You can perform this calculation on all of the nutrients listed on the label.

Notice that in the two hypothetical foods we've compared, it appears before we reduce the foods to their dry-matter basis that the dry food has a lot more protein in it than the canned food (25 percent compared to 10 percent). When we do the calculation to make these foods actually comparable, it is apparent that the canned food has much more protein than the dry kibble (40 percent compared to 27.8 percent). This illustrates how important this simple calculation is when you are comparing dry and wet food labels.

THE NAME OF THE FOOD

The name of a cat food tells a good deal about what's inside, if you know how to translate that name. If a food is called "Beef Cat Food," for example, the rules say that the food *must* have at least 95 percent beef on a dry-matter basis. If the food has the name "Beef Entrée" or "Beef Feast," etc., then it need only have 25 percent of the named meat. If the name includes the word "with," as in "Cat Food with Beef," the food only needs to have 3 percent of the named meat, in this case, beef. The meat specified in all these examples may not be the only meat in the food, however. Many foods with a meat named on the front of the label will have other meat proteins, usually from fish, not included in the product's name. This becomes very important if your cat is allergic to certain meats or fish. You will want to read labels closely, and not just choose a food based on the manufacturer's name for a flavor. You need also to read the ingredient list.

THE INGREDIENT LIST

The rules of pet food labeling require that ingredients be listed by decreasing weight, or predominance, in the food. For example, if a food has the following ingredients: "water, beef, liver, meat by-products, corn grits, corn flour, corn gluten meal, chicken fat, vitamins and minerals," we know that water is the most predominant ingredient in the food, with beef, liver, etc., following in decreasing amounts. This particular label illustrates one of the tricks employed by companies to disguise the actual amount of a certain class of ingredients. In this case, corn grits, corn flour, and corn gluten meal, although basically the same ingredient, have been separated into components by weight to allow corn to be listed behind the meat ingredients. In some foods of this type, corn may actually be the most predominant ingredient after water, but because it has been split out into three different corn-derived ingredients, these ingredients dropped to a lower place on the label. You will see this labeling practice applied to other cereals as well.

Sometimes you will see a dry food with something like "chicken" as the first ingredient. The ingredient known as "chicken" has high moisture content (75 percent or more), and has to be dehydrated, or reduced to "chicken meal," during the mixing and extrusion process. If it had been listed as "chicken meal" on the label, however, it would not have had its moist weight, and would have dropped lower on the list of ingredients. For example, a dry food with the ingredient list "chicken, corn flour, chicken fat, soy protein, and so on" probably doesn't have more chicken than corn flour by weight in the finished kibble, but listing the chicken *before* it reached its dry form in the kibble allowed it to be listed first, legally, on the label.

Because pet owners are now reading labels more closely than ever, pet food companies use these and other practices to make the lists more appealing to pet food buyers. Not surprisingly, bending the rules in such a manner is more misleading in dry kibble, in which cereals and other nonmeat fillers are such an important part of the formulas.

THE GUARANTEED ANALYSIS

The rules of pet food (and human food) labeling call for the manufacturer to list some basic nutrient percentages on the label for the prospective purchaser to see. A typical canned food label may have a guaranteed analysis that looks like this:

Crude protein	Min. 9.5%
Crude fat	Min. 5.0%
Crude fiber	Max. 0.8%
Moisture	Max. 75%
Ash (minerals)	Max. 2.0%

Notice that there is no listing for carbohydrate, a very important consideration when buying cat food. There is an easy way to find out approximately how much carbohydrate is in such a food. Simply add all of the listings from protein through ash (do not add any other listed nutrients, such as calcium, magnesium, and phosphorus, as they will simply be part of the ash or the other supplements that are too small to be needed for this calculation). In this case, we would add 9.5 percent plus 5.0 percent plus 0.8 percent plus 75 percent plus 2.0 percent (for a total of 92.3 percent) and then subtract from 100 percent to get the remainder, which is carbohydrate. Don't worry about the fact that these are maximums and minimums. This process of addition will get you very close to the true carbohydrate number, and will allow you to compare to other pet foods in a very fair way.

In the example above, the total of all noncarbohydrate nutrients, including moisture, is about 92.3 percent. When we subtract from 100 percent, we get 7.7 percent carbohydrate, on a wet basis. This may not seem like a lot, but it is actually far too much for a canned food. Many canned foods will have as little as 4 percent or even less carbohydrate on a wet basis. To convert this amount of carbohydrate to a dry-matter basis, remember we just take 7.7 percent and divide it by .25 (because this canned food is 25 percent dry matter). That 7.7 percent divided by .25 gives almost 31 percent carbohydrates on a dry matter basis!

A much better canned food guaranteed analysis would be:

Crude protein	Min. 11%
Crude fat	Min. 8.0%
Crude fiber	Max. 1.5%
Moisture	Max. 75%
Ash	Max. 2.5%

If you add all of these together, you get a total of 98 percent without carbohydrate; 100 percent minus 98 percent leaves 2 percent carbohydrate on a wet basis. When we divide 2 percent by .25, we get 8 percent carbohydrate on a dry-matter basis. This is a far more desirable carbohydrate level than that we calculated above at 31 percent.

Believe it or not, performing these calculations can become almost automatic when you are shopping for cat food for your pet. Similarly, you will become very skilled at reviewing ingredient lists to determine what is actually in that can or pouch. Not all commercial wet foods are low in carbohydrate, as we see in the above examples. Both the ingredient list and the carbohydrate calculation from the guaranteed analysis give you valuable tools in deciding which canned foods you should choose for your cat. Be sure to check the label of each flavor of the same brand, as ingredients can vary widely.

THE AAFCO STATEMENT

All pet food labels carry some kind of AAFCO statement. This statement seems to indicate that the food has been thoroughly tested as good food for the life of the cat or kitten. See chapter 3 for a discussion about why this statement does not actually guarantee that the food in the can or bag is good for your cat's lifetime.

APPENDIX II

Food Analyses

(All values are "dry-matter basis")

	PROTEIN	FAT	FIBER	CARBOHYDRATE	TAURINE
Premium "regular" dry food[1]	34%	22%	1.6%	38%	.17%
"Low-carb" dry food[1]	53%	23%	.6%	13%	.40%
Premium canned food #1[1]	42%	24%	4.6%	28%	.37%
Premium canned food #2 (from manufacturer's label)	54%	11%	7%	13%	.22%
Dehydrated powdered cat food (from manufacturer's label)	33%	29%	2.6%	31%	.15%

	PROTEIN	FAT	FIBER	CARBOHYDRATE	TAURINE
Raw rabbit w/supplement[2,3]	66%	4.5%	.7%	3.8%	.64%
Raw rabbit w/o supplement[3]	66%	4.5%	.7%	3.8%	.07%
Raw chicken w/supplement[2,3]	53%	27%	2%	>1%	1.1%
Turkey organ meat w/supplement[2,3]	66%	11%	<1%	16%	1%
Beef heart w/o supplement[2,3]	66%	14.4%	5.7%	9%	.20%
Felines Pride Raw Chicken[4]	55%	28%	.56%	5.5%	.20%
Rat carcass[5]	55%	38%	1.2%	2–3% (estimated)	NA

1. Analyses performed by Eurofins Scientific Inc., Des Moines, IA.
2. The supplement used here is my favorite, Platinum Performance Feline Wellness, an excellent, well-balanced, and very palatable amino acid/vitamin/mineral supplement that I use with all of my own cats. See www.platinum performance.com.
3. The meats analyzed are from Omas Pride (see www.omaspride.com), producers of human-grade raw frozen meats for cats and dogs. I feed Omas exclusively to my own cats and recommend it to my clients.
4. Analysis supplied by Felines Pride (www.felinespride.com) and conducted by New Jersey Feed Labs, Trenton, NJ.
5. From "The Carnivore Connection to Nutrition in Cats," Deborah L. Zoran DVM, PhD, DACVIM, in *JAVMA* 221, no. 11, December 1, 2002.

Comments about these analyses:

• As expected, the "regular" dry cat food has the highest level of carbohydrate of all the cat foods evaluated. This is not only typical of the dry foods you can buy for your cat, including premium brands; it is not even the highest level on the market! Not only is 38 percent carbohydrate a completely unacceptable amount of carbohydrate for the cat, this carbohydrate is highly processed cereal carbohydrate, with a very high glycemic index. This is the most diabetes-causing of all types of food available for cats. No cat should ever eat such a diet.

• Unfortunately, even the "low-carbohydrate" dry diet evaluated has relatively high carbohydrate content, especially because the carbohydrate in this diet is highly processed potato, with an extremely high glycemic index. This diet does not maintain normalcy in recovered diabetics, and should be avoided in all cats.

• Even some canned foods contain dangerously high levels of processed carbohydrate, as in premium canned food #1. If you read the label of this food, you will see several cereal ingredients within the first few ingredients listed. This is a red flag that this is a high-carbohydrate food, even though it may be canned. Canned and pouched foods do not need cereal for processing, as dry foods do. These ingredients are always inexpensive fillers with no nutritional purpose, and are potentially dangerous for the cat.

• Premium canned food #2 has a more desirable carbohydrate content than #1, but even this level, which is typical for canned foods that I recommend to my clients, is much higher than the natural diet of the cat. The way to dilute this high carbohydrate in wet commercial foods is to add raw or cooked meat to your cat's diet.

• All of the meats tested had much lower carbohydrate content, except for turkey organ meat (hearts, gizzards, and livers). This may well be due to glycogen, a natural sugar stored in the livers of all animals. Of course, no cat would survive on a diet of liver alone, so this level would not be the final amount of carbohydrate in the natural feline diet. Muscle meat of rabbits and chickens has almost no carbohydrate, as expected. A natural diet of muscle, bone, and organ meat of prey animals would have less than 10 percent unprocessed carbohydrate.

• *Commercially* available rabbit meat is lean compared to commercially available chicken. A combination of both types of meat provides a better dietary fat level than the rabbit alone. Further, adding organ meat, including heart, also increases dietary fat, a necessary nutrient for providing essential fatty acids and calories to the diet.

• The taurine levels of all foods tested were above the minimum level recommended by the National Research Council (NRC). While the commercial rabbit tested had the lowest level of natural taurine, this level should support health in the cat according to the NRC, especially because raw or lightly cooked meat does not undergo taurine-destroying processing, as commercial foods do. We see that the supplement increased the level of taurine dramatically (an eightfold increase) in the rabbit. For reasons that are not clear, raw commercial chicken has a high taurine level (.12 percent) even without supplement.

• Raw meat that is already fully supplemented and tested in both the laboratory and in cats is available from such companies as Felines Pride (www.felinespride.com). I have personally used this presupplemented, high-quality product, and feel that it represents an excellent option for cat owners who wish to avoid the work of purchasing meat and supplements separately and desire a very palatable, nutritious, raw-meat source to upgrade their pet's diet. Although this product is not the lowest-cost way to feed raw to your pet cat, it is very high-quality, from a company that provides excellent availability and customer service.

Taking all of this information into consideration, I believe that there are three options for nourishing the cat properly to avoid nutritional disease: Low-carbohydrate wet foods (canned or pouched), with no cereal, vegetables, or fruits, can support good health in the feline (see www.catinfo.org). So can raw or lightly cooked fresh meat, which is my personal preference for my own cats. A combination of good-quality canned and raw is also an alternative for good health in cats.

I feed Feline's Pride raw meats or a diet of equal parts raw rabbit with bone, raw chicken with bone (ground, never whole), and raw organ meat (turkey or beef). I also recommend this kind of diet or similar to my clients (see also www.catnutrition.org and felinespride.com). To unsupplemented raw meat I add Platinum Performance Feline Wellness at the manufacturer's recommended dose each day (see www.platinum performance.com). I have reared many generations of Ocicats with this formula, including young kittens and nursing females, with excellent results.

In many years, I have experienced no cases of food poisoning or any other adverse effect of a raw-meat diet. In fact, cats on a meat diet have better body condition, coat quality, and vitality than do cats fed any other kind of diet, in my considerable experience. I have many clients who feed some wet commercial foods and raw or cooked meat in combination. This is a fine alternative to one or the other alone.

APPENDIX III

Protocol for Success in Managing Feline Diabetes

(see www.yourdiabeticcat.com)

This protocol consists of three indispensable parts: proper diet for the diabetic cat, proper drug/hormone therapy (that is, the right insulin), and proper use of that drug therapy and that diet to restore the patient to normal pancreatic function.

DIET

Because improper diet is by far the most common cause of type 2 diabetes mellitus in the cat, diet must be the foundation of the management of this disease. Although the veterinary profession has been conditioned to believe that high-fiber dry diets are capable of assisting in the management of feline diabetes, the reality is that this disease has historically been extremely difficult to deal with *because* of this mistaken belief. The practice of feeding dry, high-fiber foods to our diabetic patients *is utterly in error.* In fact, these foods have two massive flaws. The first is the high amount of carbohydrate in them promotes high blood glucose, notwithstanding the fiber contained in them. These diets are usually "low fat" as well as high in fiber and, because of this, much of the usual fat in the formula has been replaced with even more digestible carbohydrate than is present in regular formulas (in the highly mistaken belief that it is dietary fat that makes cats fat).

The second serious flaw is the high fiber itself. As an obligatory carnivore, the cat has a GI tract that is short compared with that of the dog or humans. During evolution, the cat's gastrointestinal tract adapted to the intake of calorie-dense, vegetation-poor foods by reducing its length and thus its ability to undertake prolonged digestion of fibrous foods. High-fiber foods ignore this fact, providing an unnatural burden on the feline GI tract that results in excessive system bulk and reduced nutrient absorption.

Therefore, to manage feline type 2 diabetes, the patient *must* be provided a diet that is high in protein, moderate in fat, and ultralow in carbohydrate, especially carbohydrate from extruded cereals and plants with high glycemic indices, such as corn and potato. No feline diabetic should eat any type or brand of dry food. This includes all of the dry formulas labeled as "for the management of diabetes." Allowable foods include low-fiber canned foods designated "for the management of diabetes," and a number of other brands of canned or pouched foods with low carbohydrate content. Raw meat is also an excellent diet for cats, diabetic and nondiabetic alike.

To find a good wet commercial food for any cat, be sure to read the label on the can or pouch. If you see such ingredients as corn flour, corn grits, corn gluten, rice or rice four, potato, sweet potato, carrots, or any kind of fruit, don't feed your cat that food. Cats do not need cereals, vegetables, or fruit. These ingredients are included because they appeal to the pet food purchaser. They have nothing whatsoever to do with good feline nutrition. Not only will a low-carbohydrate canned food reduce the wide blood glucose swings seen in feline diabetics, it will also reduce the pathologic overeating seen in cats consuming dry foods that provide little or no sense of appetite satisfaction.

PROPER INSULIN

Animal-source protamine zinc insulin (PZI) is, by far, the most effective form of insulin available for use in the diabetic cat today. Beef and pork insulin molecules more closely resemble natural feline insulin and give the greatest response for the lowest dosages in the vast majority of feline diabetics. It can be dosed at six- to twelve-hour intervals and, because many canned or pouched cat foods are supportive of low blood glucose, PZI allows good control of the diabetic cat, far superior to that from NPH, Humulin insulin, or the newer human products called Lantus (glargine) or Levemir. PZI bovine insulin is readily available in the U.S. and many other countries. See http://www .felinediabetes.com/pzi-sources.htm for a useful chart of sources and contact information for providers of this insulin. Your veterinarian can prescribe PZI for your cat from these sources.

Although one small study has shown that Lantus can be used to create remission in new diabetics on low-carb (wet only) cat foods, this study does not really prove that Lantus is superior to PZI, as the method of use of the PZI in the study was not optimal and considering that brand-new diabetics will readily go into remission regardless of the insulin used as long as low-carbohydrate wet foods are fed to these cats. In my experience with this human insulin, the effects of Lantus in the cat are more unpredictable than that of PZI, making regulation and remission more difficult to achieve. Further, Lantus is a human insulin product and at least theoretically more antigenic (allergy producing) in the cat than are the bovine-origin PZI insulins. Bovine insulin has a much closer amino acid structure to the cat's own insulin than does human insulin, a likely explanation for its superior results in managing feline diabetics.

A BLOOD GLUCOSE CONTROL STRATEGY—TIGHT REGULATION

It is conventional wisdom that hypoglycemia in the feline diabetic is to be feared more than any other eventuality. Thus, most traditional protocols perpetuate the patients' diabetes because maintaining a patient's blood glucose in the range above normal (greater than 150 mg/dL) insures that the cat will never recover from its disease. While there is no question that hypoglycemic seizures are to be avoided, it is not necessary to keep a patient's blood glucose above 200 mg/dL, or even above 150, to accomplish this. Through its evolved physiology, the cat *prefers* to function at blood glucose levels below 100! In fact, if we could test our healthy patients without the stress of the hospital environment elevating their blood glucose levels in our clinics, we would realize that most cats are perfectly happy with levels around 60 to 100! In nature, most of the cats' blood glucose is glucose produced by its liver from protein amino acids on an as-needed basis. Large sugar surges from dietary carbohydrate intake, well tolerated by omnivores and herbivores, are essentially unknown to the cat in the wild setting and are clearly unwelcome as well.

Elevated blood glucose is either toxic or suppressive (or both) of the feline pancreas, a fact no doubt related to the almost vestigial nature of this function in a species that evolved with little need to process dietary carbohydrate. Therefore, the objective of managing the feline diabetic is to assist the cat's pancreas to resume some or all of its normal function. This is virtually always possible in the cat that has been diabetic for a short period of time. As a matter of fact, brand-new diabetics often respond to a change of diet alone, and never need insulin because the pancreas has not really gone dormant from chronic hyperglycemia at that point.

Immediate relief from dietary glucose overload can allow immediate reactivation of the cat's own pancreatic capabilities. The cat with acute diabetes, however, like its more chronic colleagues, will *never* be able to consume high-carbohydrate (dry) foods again for its entire life, and its owners must understand this. Such a cat will become diabetic very quickly once again if its pancreas is stressed again by high-sugar foods, or steroid medications, which are toxic in the previously diabetic as well as the dry-food-fed cat.

In the more chronic diabetic, diet alone will often not provide immediate cure. In those cats that have been diabetic a long time, especially those that have been poorly controlled with dry foods and insulin types other than PZI, the road to cure will be longer. This is only logical. The intoxication/suppression of the pancreas in these cats has been prolonged and severe, and in some cases there may be no residual function left at all. However, you will not be able to predict with certainty merely from the duration of the cat's disease process whether a particular cat can be cured.

We have seen cats with relatively long histories respond well, in time (several months), to proper regulatory efforts. Even those that never come completely off insulin due to the duration of their disease and its improper management are much healthier and more clinically normal on a low-carbohydrate diet and PZI insulin at the right dose than they have been previously. *For those cats that do not resume normal pancreatic function with diet alone, the objective of PZI insulin therapy is to bring the cat into a normal range of blood glucose (60 to 130) and keep it there!* I cannot emphasize this enough.

Because continually high blood glucose perpetuates the pancreatic suppression/toxicity that has caused the diabetes in the first place, cure can only happen if insulin is used to effectively bring the diabetic cat into the normal range for glucose in this species. Most normal cats operate when relaxed between 60 and 100. As long as you feed low-carbohydrate wet foods, you will not cause seizures in your pet. In hundreds of cats that I have put through this protocol using low-carbohydrate foods, I have never caused a single one to seizure, despite taking many well below 100 mg/dL. Clearly, the liver in the diabetic cat that is no longer eating dry cat foods becomes capable of producing glucose again, in response to falling blood glucose. This may be because the recovering pancreas can now secrete glucagon to trigger the liver's glucose-releasing capabilities, or because of some other direct effect of diabetic regulation on the liver itself. Whatever the cause, the liver's reawakened capabilities make clinical hypoglycemia a worry of the past, and diabetic cat owners can give up the fear they have been taught about taking a diabetic cat into the normal blood glucose range, where recovery can occur.

The method of managing the feline diabetic that I use has been called "tight regulation." This name describes the fact that this protocol uses proper diet and the correct insulin to bring the cat's blood glucose levels into a tight range around normal for healthy cats. In so doing, it can cause permanent remissions in even chronically ill cats. One of the unique features of this method is the practice of home-testing. I recommend that all owners of diabetic cats purchase a glucometer (the kind human diabetics use to test their own blood sugar levels) at their local pharmacy. Learning to use such a device on a cat is simple and easy; I have never had a client who could not learn to use a glucometer with great skill in a very short time (see www.felinediabetes.com/bg-test.htm). Once you are home-testing, you have all the information you need, at your fingertips, to manage your cat's diabetes—perhaps even managing it right out of existence!

PZI insulin has a peak activity time in most cats at six to eight hours after injection. This means that the blood glucose level in the diabetic cat will be at its lowest point six to eight hours after the last dose of insulin. After this time, it will begin to rise again until another dose of insulin is injected. Because of this, I ask my clients to perform a blood glucose test six to eight hours after each dose of insulin. If the blood glucose is still above the normal range (greater than 150), then another injection of insulin is warranted. In the beginning days of tight regulation, owners typically test three to four times per day and often give insulin, in doses dictated by the blood glucose reading at each test, this frequently as well.

This may seem very time and effort intensive, and compared to the usual once-daily or twice-daily "blind" dosing of insulin that traditional protocols call for, it *is* more work. However, the benefits of tight regulation are huge, and every one of my clients that has tried this method is glad they did. Their cats feel better, are more active and playful, and regain better body condition than they ever experienced using the old methods. Further, over a few days or weeks, many cats require smaller and smaller doses of insulin, less often, and the majority go off insulin altogether over time. The extra time and effort invested in the beginning of tight regulation is repaid manyfold as the patient becomes well again!

The following is a suggested sliding scale for the cat just starting tight regulation. The protocol asks the owner to test at least twice daily, but optimally three or four times daily (every six to eight hours), with doses of insulin given according to the reading at each test:

BLOOD GLUCOSE MG/DL	UNITS OF INSULIN TO INJECT
151–170	0.5
171–185	1.0
186–200	1.5
201–220	2.0
221–250	2.5
251–290	3.0
291–350	3.5
351–410	4.0

Using this protocol, you can expect to start seeing some very "normal" numbers within a few days or weeks of starting. As long as you are feeding your cat ONLY low-carbohydrate foods, you do not need to be fearful of clinical hypoglycemia. In fact, those blood glucose numbers in the 60 to 120 range are the objective of the protocol. Even if the blood glucose drops to 30 to 50, *do not feed sugar syrup or dry food*. A small, high-protein wet-food meal is all you need for a cat at these numbers, and that is more for the owner than the cat. As time passes, smaller doses will achieve the same results than larger ones once did, and you will even start skipping doses as you test and find the blood glucose is still in the normal range many hours or even days after the last dose of insulin. When this happens, you will know your cat's own pancreas is beginning to function on its own. For more information on this method, see www.yourdiabeticcat.com.

A final note: Some veterinarians use a test called a *fructosamine test* (something like the A1c used for diabetic humans) to determine the level of diabetes control in a particular patient on insulin. This test was valuable before the days when owners started home-testing their own cats. The frucosamine test measures a rough "average" of the amount of glucose in the cat's circulation over the three weeks or so preceding the test. If the fructosamine test gives a high value, meaning the cat is not well regulated, a blood glucose curve is then done to determine how to adjust the cat's insulin. Because pet owners who home-test are already doing their own curves at home, yielding more precise information for making these insulin-dosing decisions on a day-to-day basis, the fructosamine test gives no useful additional information in such cases.

INDEX

hair loss, 54, 190, 199
harness, collar v., 44–45
head cold, 58
heart
    diseases of, 100, 118, 120,
        234–36, 241–44, 256
    function of, 242, 244, 256
    problems of, 120, 197, 235,
        242–44
heartworms, 51, 197, 243
heating pad, 104
hepatic lipidosis, 141, 161–64
herpesvirus, 58–61, 71, 73
Heska Corporation, 147
high blood pressure, 226, 230
high-carbohydrate diet, 133,
    137–38, 145–47, 150, 164–65,
    216
high-fiber, diet research into, 145
high-fiber foods, 146, 147, 153, 155,
    216, 271–72
high-sugar foods, 150, 153, 274
homemade meat meals, 136, 139,
    195, 218
hormone, 132, 149, 219, 222,
    230–33, 237
Humane Society of the United
    States, 42
hyperthyroid cat, 230–35
    case study of, 235–38
hyperthyroidism, xii, xviii, 13, 148,
    229–37, 242–43
    appetite and, 230, 235–37
    case study of, 235–38
    heart disease and, 234
    signs of, 230
hypoallergenic diet, 178–79, 187,
    191–92, 194–95, 197–98
hypoglycemia, 146, 149, 155, 273
hyposensitization, 191

IBD. See inflammatory bowel
    disease
IBS. See inflammatory bowel
    syndrome
icterus, 163
indigestible fiber, 22, 137, 145–46,
    169, 216
indoor cats, 44, 65, 92–93, 144, 253
indoor/outdoor habitat, 94

infectious diseases, 57, 68–69, 71,
    245–46, 253, 259
inflammatory bowel disease (IBD),
    xii, xviii, 15, 26, 177–79,
    185–89, 203–4
inflammatory bowel syndrome
    (IBS), 177–78
inhaled allergens, 190, 197
inhalers, 197
injections, 51–52, 191, 194, 233,
    275
injuries, xviii, 12, 43, 101, 212,
    247
insulin, 132–33, 137, 145–56,
    158–59, 272–76
    dosages of, 147, 152–54, 275–76
    injections of, 145, 147, 150–52,
        154, 165, 275
    PZI type of, 154–56, 158–59,
        274–75
interferon, 70, 196
intestines, 49–50, 145, 178, 188, 218

jaundice, 68, 163
joints, 134, 248
junk food, 16, 38, 93, 140

kidney
    dysfunction of, 212, 234–35
    insufficiency of, 217–19, 222,
        224, 234
    problems of, 13, 26, 80, 174, 215,
        234–35
    transplants, 222–23
kidney disease, 38, 208, 211–12,
    214, 220, 234–35
    case study of, 238–39
    chronic type of, 212, 238
kidney function, 221–22, 234, 236
    tests for, 224, 237–39
kittens
    appetite of, 55, 59, 98–99
    foods for, 110, 208, 209
    general behavior of, 33, 59,
        78–80, 106
    litter box for new, 33–35
    litter of, 12, 85, 259
    new, 31, 33, 45, 60, 80, 83–85,
        95
    orphaned, 78, 103–4, 106

lacerations, 101
lack of appetite, 62–63, 68–69,
    162–64, 203, 212
laser scalpel, 196
leash, 44–45
Leukeran, 188
life span, of cats, 207–8
life-stage, concept, 110, 208
lilies, as poisonous plants, 101
Lime sulphur dip, 54
litter box
    failure in use of, 77, 79–81, 171
    materials for, 78–79
    for new kitten, 33–35
    training for, 77–79
litter of kittens, 12, 85, 259
liver
    dry food impact on, 132, 147,
        149–50, 161, 258–59
    dysfunction of, 5, 162, 258–59
    enzyme levels and, 69, 237
    pancreas and, 132, 145–47,
        149–50
    recovery ability of, 274–75
L-lysine, 59
low-carbohydrate diet, 86, 109, 139,
    144, 155, 276
lung disease, 51
lungworms, 197
Lyme disease, 54
lymph system cancers, 202
lymphosarcoma, 202

magnesium, 168–70, 264
males, neutered, 14, 17, 157
mammary/breast cancer, 84, 204
management, of allergies, 191, 197
mange mites, 52–53
Martin, Ann, 21
meat
    baby food type of, 35, 59, 98,
        105, 141
    by-products of, 39, 131, 257, 263
    homemade meals of, 136, 139,
        195, 218
meat baby foods, 35, 59, 98, 105,
    141
meloxicam, 249
Metacam, 249
methimazole, 233

metoclopramide, 226
microchip, 45
milk replacers, commercial, 104
milk thistle, 163
minerals, 13–14, 110, 129, 170–71, 213, 219–20, 255, 263
miracle of birth, 85
mites, 33, 52–53, 193, 197
mosquito, 51, 243
mouth, bacteria in, 123–24, 195
mouth, as acidic, 256

National Research Council, 128, 269
nebulizer, 99
nebulizing, 58, 99
neotenization, domestication v., xix
neutering, xviii, 12, 14, 17, 83, 85, 157
North Africa, 6
nutrient profile, 110, 131, 138, 169
nutrients
    for energy, 6, 13, 111, 129–30, 132, 139
    requirements for, 5, 24, 128

obesity
    in altered cat, 86
    of felines, 136, 138–39, 248–49
    as major feline problem, 128–29, 255
    pet food and, 14, 136, 137
    prevention of, 86, 119, 162
obligatory carnivore
    cat as, 3, 5, 16, 37, 272
    food requirements for, 16, 23, 39, 95, 170, 216
Omas Pride, 268
one-cell parasite, 48
oral health, 119, 123, 124
Orion Foundation, 72
orphaned kitten, 78, 103–4, 106
osteoarthritis, 248
otitis, allergic, 189, 193–94, 199

palpation, 120, 238
pancreas, 156–58, 161, 164–65, 258–59, 274–76
    diabetes and, 132–33, 145
    liver and, 132, 145–47, 149–50
pancreatitis, 161, 164–65

panleukopenia. See feline panleukopenia
parasites, 47–52, 54–55, 106
    allergies and, 186, 191
    external types of, 33, 52
    internal types of, 48–51, 98
parathyroid hormone (PTH), 219
pecking order, 7
pemphigus, 192
perineal urethrostomy, 168
periodontal disease, 118, 123, 256
pesticides, 100
pet food(s). See also cat foods; commercial pet foods; diet; foods
    additives in, 13–14, 21, 170, 255
    by-products in, 39, 257
    inadequate testing of, 25–27
    obesity and, 14, 136, 137
    reading labels on, 261–65
pet food labels, 22, 27, 112, 258, 261–65
Petco, 104
pet-safe toothpaste, 118
Petsmart, 104
phosphate binders, 217, 219, 226
phosphorus, 213, 217, 219–20, 244, 264
    binder, 220, 223, 227
Pitcairn, Richard, 21
plaque, 118
Platinum Performance Feline Wellness, 268
PLI, 164
pneumonia, 61, 100
poisoning, 24, 98, 100, 183, 212
poisonous houseplants, 101
polyps, 194, 199
potassium, 222
potato, 112, 113, 130, 131, 140, 158, 172, 174, 258, 272
pouch foods, 140–41, 173–74, 269, 272
prednisolone, 188, 191
prednisone, 178, 188, 191
prescribed foods, 24, 26, 27
prescription-type food, 170, 181, 244
protein
    deficiency of, 215, 223

requirements for, 5, 213, 215
    restriction of, 213–14, 244
    starvation from lack of, 6, 214
protein-restricted diet, 212–17, 219, 223, 226
protein-rich diet, 109, 137, 155, 159, 164–65, 217–18, 225–27
protocol, for managing diabetes, 271, 276
protozoan, 48
psychological stressors, 174
punishment, corporal type of, 18, 36, 88
PZI insulin, 154–56, 158–59, 274–75

queens, 48, 185

rabies, 65, 74
raw meat, 16, 86, 113, 140, 179–82, 184–86, 258, 269, 272
    contamination of, 181–82, 184, 186
reactions
    injection-site, 74
    polymerase chain, 69
renal disease, 211–12, 214, 223, 234
renal failure, 168, 220
renal insufficiency, 214, 225–26
    case study of, 225–26
renal secondary hyper-parathyroidism., 219
reproductive tract cancers, 84, 204
research
    on cat foods, 5, 13–14, 25–27, 136
    on feeding, 134–35, 184–85, 256–57
resorptive neck lesions, 124, 256
respiratory disease, allergens and, 197
respiratory tract cancers, 197
rhinotracheitis, 58
rice flour, 113, 258
ringworm, 53–54, 193
risk factors, vaccination v., 32, 60, 65, 74–75, 245–46, 259
Rocky Mountain spotted fever, 54–55
roundworms, 48–49